Heimat:
A Critical Theory of the German Idea of Homeland

The idea of *Heimat* (home, homeland, native region) has been as important to German self-perceptions over the last two hundred years as the shifting notion of the German nation. While the idea of Heimat has been long neglected in English studies of German culture — among other reasons because the word Heimat has no exact equivalent in English — this book offers us the first cross-disciplinary and comprehensive analysis, in English or German, of this all-pervasive German idea. Blickle shows how the idea of Heimat interpenetrates German notions of modernity, identity, gender, nature, and innocence, and reminds us of such commonplace expressions of Heimat sentimentality as Biedermeier landscapes of Alpine meadows and castles on the Rhine, but also finds the Heimat preoccupation in Hegel, Nietzsche, and Freud. Always aware of the many literary representations of Heimat (for instance in Schiller, Hölderlin, Heine, Rilke, and Thomas Mann), Blickle does not argue for the fundamental innocence of Heimat. Instead he shows again and again how the idealization of a home ground leads to borders of exclusion.

Peter Blickle is associate professor of German at Western Michigan University.

Studies in German Literature, Linguistics, and Culture

Edited by James Hardin
(*South Carolina*)

Heimat

A Critical Theory of the German Idea of Homeland

Peter Blickle

CAMDEN HOUSE

First published 2002
by Camden House

Camden House is an imprint of Boydell & Brewer Inc.
PO Box 41026, Rochester, NY 14604–4126 USA
and of Boydell & Brewer Limited
PO Box 9, Woodbridge, Suffolk IP12 3DF, UK

ISBN: 1–57113–225–2

Library of Congress Cataloging-in-Publication Data

Blickle, Peter.
    Heimat: a critical theory of the German idea of homeland / Peter
Blickle.
        p. cm. — (Studies in German literature, linguistics, and culture)
    Includes bibliographical references and index.
    ISBN 1–57113–225–2 (alk. paper)
        1. Human territoriality—Germany.   2. Ethnicity—Germany.
3. Group identity—Germany. 4. German literature—History and criticism. 5. Homeland in literature. 6. Nationalism in literature. 7. Nationalism and literature—Germany.   I. Title. II. Studies in German
literature, linguistics, and culture (Unnumbered)

DD61.8 .B55 2002
304.2'3—dc21

                                                            2001043807

A catalogue record for this title is available from the British Library.

This publication is printed on acid-free paper.
Printed in the United States of America.

For Jaimy Gordon,
whose generosity — with her time,
with her ideas,
and with her words —
made this book possible

Contents

Preface

THE GERMAN IDEA OF Heimat [homeland, home, native re-
gion] has lent itself to a wide range of political and cultural
purposes in German-speaking countries since the late eighteenth
century. In recent years German scholars have been interested in
Heimat mainly as one aspect of a *völkisch*, localized nationalism
that eventually became an important element of National Socialism. My study does not attempt to replace these unnerving assessments with exculpatory claims for the fundamental innocence of an
idea that has been so dangerously unstable in meaning from the
beginning, but it does attempt greatly to widen and deepen our
understanding of the idea and its historical uses. It tries to explain
the metaphysical shift in German-speaking cultures after the eighteenth century that resulted in the replacement, literally and meta-
phorically, of the crucifix above the kitchen table with representations of nature. The motifs of such representations are well
known: Alpine meadows; a rushing brook and a field in flower; the
mill and its millwheel — sometimes, in allusion to Schubert's song
cycle, with the miller's beautiful wife standing by; a grazing deer in
the morning sun in a clearing in the woods; the Black Forest
house; boats on Lake Constance; the Rhine with a castle somewhere in the background. My study inquires into the uncanny and
persistent German longing for a space of innocence that Heimat
always implies, for, whatever image of Heimat they invoke, all such
pictures on the wall assure the onlooker that a good soul lives here.

Heimat: A Critical Theory of the German Idea of Homeland
offers the first comprehensive view, in English or German, of the
all-pervasive German idea of Heimat. Working with an eclectic version of a Frankfurt School approach, where elements of culture become the basis for an exegesis of culture as text, the study takes
impulses from the fields of literature, philosophy, psychoanalysis,
sociology, gender studies, and history. As it explores various representations of Heimat at various times and in various social contexts, it approaches the idea of Heimat through philosophically and

sociologically based discussions of modernity and the nation
(chapter 2), through a psychoanalytically informed discussion of
identity (chapter 3), through gender (the feminizing aspects of
Heimat, chapter 4), through German notions of nature and landscape (chapter 5), and through notions of innocence (in childhood, in religion, in language, and, paradoxically, in expressions of
Antiheimat, chapter 6).

Today, just as during any other period since the end of the
eighteenth century, the notion of Heimat is a central and, at the
same time, disturbing part of German-speaking people's attempts
to make sense of the world in which they live. In one of the earliest
uses of the word we find a disconcerting wealth of comforting
metaphors. In 1494 Johannes Geiler von Keisersberg (1445–1510)
writes in a treatise on the pilgrim: "Death guides you to the Heimat [here spelled *heinmut*] of your fatherland, to eternal salvation"
(quoted in Grimm 864). *Fatherland* here stands for the Father's —
that is, the Christian God's — land; in other words, for the Christian religion's paradise; and eternal salvation is reached in the Heimat of that fatherland, which could mean that Heimat is a higher
refuge of that fatherland, or that Heimat and the fatherland are
one and the same. Even in this early manifestation, then, we find
secular and spiritual metaphors intermingling to the point where
they are hardly distinguishable. Also, this fifteenth-century spelling,
heinmut, would seem to suggest etymologically two central symbols of Germanhood, *Heim* [home] and *Hein* [grove], combined
with the warrior attribute of *Mut* [courage]. Although the etymol-
ogy is false, the notion that the courage to fight seems to arise out
of one's home and woods creates an implicitly threatening situation for outsiders.

No doubt, the regressive aspects of the idea — variously translated as "home," "homeland," "hometown," "homestead," "native region" (Lower Bavaria, Frankonia, Upper Swabia, Black
Forest, Appenzell, etc.), or "native country" (Germany, Austria,
Switzerland, or Liechtenstein) — are troubling to us now. Any
concrete interaction with the idea of Heimat in the political realm
has, historically speaking, served sooner or later to further sharp
exclusions of certain groups — usually ethnic minorities, less-
propertied classes, or both. And all too often the idea of Heimat
has assisted in more than mere exclusions.

This book is conceived as an inquiry into an area where geography and modern constitutions of identity intersect in German-speaking contexts. The goal of the study is not to add to the thousands of existing case studies of Heimat (Heimat in Eichendorff, Heimat in twentieth-century German schoolbooks, Heimat in dialect poems of the Erz Mountains, etc.). Instead, it follows the idea on its travels, tracing protean and seemingly omnipresent instances of mental spatialization in German language and thought— and, thus, of mentally created boundaries and exclusions. It wants to make conscious what for the most part has remained unconscious. The study's goal is to reach a historical and critical understanding of the idea of Heimat.

1: Introduction

BEFORE HE TRIES TO APPROACH the idea of Heimat by tracing the history of the word and its meanings from the sixteenth century onward in his essay "Auf dem Weg zu einem neuen, aktiven Heimatverständnis" [On the Way to a New, Active Understanding of Heimat], the German cultural anthropologist Hermann Bausinger tells an anecdote about St. Augustine. "What is time?" the saint wonders out loud, and then answers himself: "I think I know — as long as no one asks me. But as soon as someone asks and I want to explain, I don't know anymore" (11).[1] The same can be said about the idea of Heimat: as long as no one asks what Heimat is, German speakers think they know. But as soon as someone asks, the difficulties begin.

Heimat is an idea that is shared by German-language cultures. To avoid continuous and cumbersome qualifications, and at the risk of certain imprecisions, I have decided throughout this study to allow *German* to refer both to the language and to the political entity Germany. *German,* however, in "the German idea of Heimat" does not mean "German" in contrast to "Swiss" or "Austrian." While local, historical, and social specificities often enter into individual uses of the word, this study is concerned with understanding the idea of Heimat overall rather than with understanding geographically specific instances of it.

This introduction, after pointing out the difficulties one encounters when attempting to translate or define Heimat, provides a preview of key elements in Heimat and an overview of some of Heimat's main characteristics: Heimat is a crucial aspect in German self-perceptions; it represents the fusional anti-Enlightenment thinking in German Romanticism; it is the idealization of the premodern within the modern; it unites geographic and imaginary conceptions of space; it is a provincializing, but disalienating, part of German bourgeois culture; it reflects modern German culture's spatialized interiority; it combines territorial claims with a fundamental ethical reassurance of innocence; and, to achieve this combination, it uses a patriarchal, gendered way of seeing the world. In short, after first showing the challenges the idea of Heimat poses and what is at stake, this introduction, like a row of shop windows, offers readers an opportunity to view — before going in and buying — some of the many different ways in which Heimat is important to German-speaking cultures: how differently it can be shaped and exhibited; how differently it can be looked at, tried on, and tested; how different the fabrics can be; and how different angles, different methods, and different sensitivities participate both in the production and in the consumption of Heimat.

Heimat in Other Languages

Before looking at what Heimat is, I should first qualify a statement scholars often make about Heimat that is, strictly speaking, not true. Heimat is not untranslatable. It is correct that neither English nor French have equivalencies for Heimat, but many Slavic languages do. Slovenians, Croatians, and Serbians call it *dòmovina* and Czechs *domov*.[2] It is probably true, however, that, as the Czech-Brazilian-French-German-Jewish philosopher Vilém Flusser (1920–1991) observes about *domov* in his native Czech, these Heimat equivalents exist "on account of the pressure German exerted for centuries" (16) on these languages.

The Russian word *rodina*, often rendered into English as "motherland" or "Mother Russia," is another term that translates in German into Heimat. Its qualities are close to the German Heimat. It is femininely encoded and invoked for aggressive as well as defensive nationalistic purposes. But there are differences between *rodina* and Heimat. To anticipate some of my observations below: Heimat is much less overtly sexualized than *rodina*. *Rodina* is always based on a mythic mother-son relationship, powerfully eroticized and incestuous. (Ronald Vroon writes, for instance, about Aleksandr Blok's cycle of poems "Rodina" [1907–16]: in "Rodina" one finds a "peculiar, almost perverse juxtaposition of metaphors: Russia becomes a beautiful woman assigned the role of mother, wife and lover, and the poet in turn is transformed into a Christ-like figure ambiguously related as both son and lover to his motherland" [354].) Heimat, to be sure, is frequently sexualized as well, but much less overtly — we will see this phenomenon especially in chapter 4, "Heimat and the Feminine." Whereas *rodina's* sexual qualities (that is, the incestuous longings for the mother) are close to the surface,[3] Heimat's sexual qualities have, for the most part, remained veiled. It takes some effort to find the sexual in Heimat. German speakers will have no difficulty identifying Heimat's gendered nature, but to perceive her erotic qualities it is necessary to accept the fact that innocence in Heimat, as in nature or childhood, might not be as fundamental as German-speakers would usually like to believe. Even then, insofar as Heimat embodies the feminine, the female is sometimes sexualized as the beloved, sometimes longed for as a mother, but hardly ever both together.[4] The beloved is, one could argue, a displaced version of the mother. But it is important that in Heimat this displacement (and suppression) has occurred. A deep cultural horror of the crime of Oedipus seems to have been accommodated in the idea of Heimat from the beginning. Moreover, Heimat is usually presented in contrast to the state, which is a political, public, *vaterländisch* construct. In other words, there is usually a fatherland and a Heimat, even if they both occupy the same geographical space. *Rodina,* on the other hand, is a more all-enveloping, all-embracing metaphor, inside of which the political realm is but a playground, and politicians and their revolutions are but the ephemeral sports and games of boys.[5]

Difficulties in Defining Heimat

Being less overt about its mythic, sexualized qualities, Heimat has been able — unlike *rodina* — to become at times an inconspicuous, almost neutral term in German. Many German speakers use the word Heimat the way they use such words as *tree, house,* or *water*. One might hear any day in my native town a declaration such as "Da ist der Älteste jetzt auf der Heimat," meaning that the oldest son is now running the family farm. Or one might hear a television commentator finish his report about the foreign travels of some head of state, regardless of the country from which the leader comes: "Jetzt ist er in seine Heimat zurückgeflogen" [He has returned to his home country]. There may be some distant potential for religious or spiritual connotation in the word used thus casually; but most German speakers, I daresay, are unaware, until asked, of the curious multiplicity inherent in it.

The difficulties Heimat poses when it comes to describing its referent or referents become clear, however, when one puts the question to educated, self-analytical German speakers. They tend to acknowledge at once that there is more than one Heimat — they know that the word has become a relative term — and yet, somewhat uneasily and without being able to define it exactly, they will admit to reserving a place for Heimat among such terms as *self*, *I, love, need, body,* or *longing*. Helga Königsdorf, for instance, observes that Heimat for her is like a body part "which you can't get rid of even though it isn't quite the way it should be — but which you don't really want to be rid of anyway" (17).

Another aspect of Heimat will, however, remain insistently part of geography, either simply in the form of the house where one was born and grew up, of one's literal native town, of the town or landscape to which one feels native, or, in the largest sense, of the country where one has grown up or at least lived for an extended period.

It is the unconsciously perpetuated omnipresence of the word and its multiplicity of referents that make the idea of Heimat such a challenge for the scholar. If we consider the various translations of Heimat into English, we find such diverse results as "home," "homeland," "fatherland," "nation," "nation-state," "hometown," "paradise," "Germany," "Austria," "Switzerland," "Liechtenstein," "native region," "native landscape," "native soil," "birthplace," and "homestead" — and the list could be continued. The word Heimat to a nonnative speaker often has a peculiar and slippery quality. "Paradise" is not the same as "home" or "homestead" — not usually. But this interesting multiplicity of meanings is in no way unsettling to German speakers. Just the opposite, it seems. The idea of Heimat is everywhere: German *Lieder* [songs] are suffused with the notion of Heimat. German politicians have made Heimat concepts part of war efforts, of discussions of citizen's rights and resettlement, of ethnic exclusions and persecutions, of debates surrounding migrant workers, reunification, the stationing of Pershing II missiles, even of milk production limits within the European Union. The German movie industry of the 1950s capitalized heavily on the Heimat topos. And German literature is so heavily per-

meated with manifestations of Heimat that it is more difficult to
name a writer who has not worked with the idea than to name
those who have.

With such an omnipresent and many-sided word, it is not surprising that scholarly attempts at defining Heimat, in English or in
German, often sound either artificially monolithic or, in their
choice of metaphors, overly broad, otherworldly, and unspecific.
Scholarship on Heimat has been abundant but often limited by its
narrow focus and by division into areas of specialization. Literary
scholars, for instance, tend to reduce Heimat to a literary phenomenon and prefer case studies (Heimat in Hölderlin, etc.). Soci-
ologists often treat Heimat as a functionally defined space with
social, emotional, and institutional elements and neglect its philosophical, gendered, and imaginary aspects.[6] Historians, generally
speaking, see the Heimat topos as a mobile term in the progression
of German provincialism into German nationalism, a development
that they think can be comprehensively studied by careful analyses
of Heimat associations or *Heimatschutz* [Heimat protection associa-
tions].[7] Finally, psychologists, following Sigmund Freud's categories in general and his insights from his essay "Das Unheimliche"
[The Uncanny, 1919], in particular, find Heimat to be a term of
displacement for the female, and especially the mother's, genitals
and womb; and their discussions of Heimat are usually quickly
placed in an Oedipal context.

The idea of Heimat has always been puzzling to those who
have looked at German culture from the outside. Many scholars
channel this puzzlement into a quick negative judgment that
stands in the way of a deeper engagement and inquiry. A statement
by the excellent film critic Anton Kaes is symptomatic of this process. He writes in his essay on Edgar Reitz's fifteen-and-a-half-hour
Heimat (1984), which, to date, is still the most-watched series in
German television history, "Nowhere do kitsch, false consciousness, and real need lie closer together than in the German word
'Heimat'" (1987, 175). The subjectively evaluative "false" in "false
consciousness" creates a distance, based on ostensibly superior
mental awareness, that prevents a more thorough inquiry into the
troubling and generally puzzling paradoxes inherent in the idea of
Heimat.

There is no doubt that Heimat in modern German-speaking situations has played and will continue to play a significant role in constructions of self, identity, and meaning in public, as well as private, spheres. The longing for a specific, differentiated sheltering space is everywhere in German culture, whether it receives in every instance the name of Heimat or not. In Heimat we find, paradoxically, an individualization that is based on a disindividualization, a regression, an idealization of space. The idea of Heimat answers to the longing for a sense of belonging that seems to come without a price. To accept the notion of Heimat for constitutions of one's identity is a willing submission to a cultural construct that is perceived as a natural state of being. It is a joyous discarding of Enlightenment values to lock arms with the man or woman who by chance is sitting next to you in the beer tent or the *Biergarten* and join in the *Schunkeln*, the traditional rocking right and left to the beat of the music with arms locked with whoever happens to be sitting next to you. In the idea of Heimat we find what one could call rudiments of German tribalism that have, historically, proved formative for nationalistic and, often, racist sentiments.[8]

Identity, Geography, the Need for Heimat, and Innocence

Heimat has played a crucial role in many historical moments of German self-perception since the late eighteenth century. The word was deployed as part of the partisan counter-Napoleonic sentiments during the first decade of the nineteenth century, and it is in use again today by those who fear the coming European unification and by at least some of those responsible for xenophobia-driven attacks on foreigners in many German cities. As Celia Applegate writes in the opening pages of her *A Nation of Provincials: The German Idea of Heimat* (1990):

> For almost two centuries, Heimat has been at the center of a German moral — and by extension political — discourse about place, belonging, and identity. Unfortunately, the very ordinariness of the contexts in which the word crops up has obscured the range and richness of what Heimat can tell us about the "peculiarities of German history." (4)

This study aims to provide — through critical reflection on the idea of Heimat — exactly such an inquiry into German-speaking identity and morality, insofar as these are based in a discourse about place and belonging.

Heimat is, as we will see, both a spiritualized province (a mental state turned inside out) and a provincial spirituality (a spatially perceived small world turned outside in). The irrational antihumanism on which the idea of Heimat depends is but a variation of the one that Jürgen Habermas identifies as the true challenge for modern philosophy: the irrational antihumanism of a Friedrich Nietzsche and later of a Martin Heidegger (1985, 93) that puts the nursing of a lost sense of belonging in place of all the emancipatory promises with which the Enlightenment invested reason.

The young Nietzsche, in *Die Geburt der Tragödie* [The Birth of Tragedy, 1872], presents Heimat as that ideal state to which we can return through overcoming the split between the Apollonian and the Dionysian. Heimat is the goal behind the "brotherly bond between the two gods of art [Apollo and Dionysos] in tragedy" (section 22). But the more mature Nietzsche no longer idealizes Heimat. In fact, one of the main characteristics of the pivotal figure of Zarathustra, who represents for Nietzsche a turn to a later stage, is that he leaves Heimat behind him. Hence, the opening sentence of *Also sprach Zarathustra* [Thus Spake Zarathustra, 1883–91]: "When Zarathustra was thirty years old, he left his Heimat and the lake of his Heimat and went into the mountains." And from then on the wise Zarathustra is wise in part because — unlike the people to whom he speaks — he has had the strength to leave his Heimat behind.

Heidegger sees language and the capacity to think as humanity's true Heimat. True Heimatlessness for Heidegger is being without the ability to think — to think, for instance, about Heimatlessness:

> Could it be that the Heimatlessness of man consists in man's inability to think still of his *own, true* trouble in finding a place to live, his inability to think of it *as the* difficulty. As soon as man, however, thinks about his Heimatlessness, it stops being a misery. It is, thought of correctly and well remembered, the only consolation, which *calls* mortals into living. (1954, 162; Heidegger's italics)[9]

Heimat was associated for both Nietzsche and Heidegger with beginnings and endings and with the uniting of the two. One might even go so far as to claim that the idea of Heimat in the German-speaking context was — as I will show in more detail in the chapter "Heimat, Nature, Landscape, and Ground" — a formative element in German philosophy.

Language, identity, geography, politics, and notions of self and reference intermingle in Heimat in a manner that rationally trained thinkers find discomforting. The German idea of Heimat is emotional, irrational, subjective, social, political, and communal. German-Jewish relations are refracted in constitutions of Heimat. Questions of gender, identity, history, and literary genre reflect themselves in various notions of Heimat. Heimat is as much a part of Heidegger's glorification of a sense of belonging as it is to Lukács's *Die Theorie des Romans* [Theory of the Novel] whose most quoted line is "The novel is the form of the idea's transcendental homelessness [*Heimatlosigkeit*]" (107); Heimat is as much a part of Hölderlin's poetry as it is of Adolf Hitler's and Joseph Goebbels's propaganda; Heimat has remained in politicians' vocabularies from Konrad Adenauer to Willy Brandt, Helmut Kohl, and Gerhard Schröder, from Hitler to the new German Right; and Heimat was a central and curious part of the German Left's reaction against — or participation in — the *Sonderweg* debates of the 1980s (the urgent discussions among German intellectuals about whether Germany was already on a *Sonderweg* [special path] toward National Socialism owing to special German, political, economic, and military developments long before Hitler came to power). Interesting and quite telling is the German language's difficulty of finding equivalencies to the English "Home" key on the computer keyboard or the home page on the Internet. Such technological, supermodern devices as computers and the Internet cannot possibly have any truck with the premodern and antimodern connotations of Heimat. Thus, if a German tries to use the German language in this context at all, the "Home" key becomes the "Pos 1" (Position One) key and the home page the "*Einstiegsseite*" — the page where one "climbs in," as into a train or a car, two perfectly modern phenomena.[10]

Whoever studies the countless essays, stories, poems, novels, scholarly books, and films that address or work with Heimat will soon be struck by how many remarkable minds, in trying to come to terms with Heimat, choose to foreground those aporias the Swiss dramatist Max Frisch expressed with his characteristic symmetrical clarity:

> There is no doubt about the need for Heimat; and even though I cannot easily define what I feel is Heimat. . . . I have a Heimat; I am not heimatless; I am delighted to have Heimat. (369)

To have a Heimat and not know what Heimat is has been a dilemma of German thinkers for at least the last two centuries. But Heimat, as mentioned above, is also an idea that makes scholars feel uncomfortable. When dealing with it, intellectually and rationally trained minds have to work with an idea that often seems to defy rational analysis.

Hans Loewald observes in his classical essay "The Waning of the Oedipus Complex" that the "implicit sense of and quest for irrational nondifferentiation of subject and object contains a truth of its own" that "fits badly with our rational world view and quest for objectivity" (1980, 402). Heimat provides German speakers with a topos — in every sense of the word — for such an irrational nondifferentiation between subject and object.

Goals and What Is at Stake

This study is not intended as an exhaustive compilation of manifestations of the German idea of Heimat. Such a compilation would be unmanageably huge. The word-search feature in Directmedia's Digitale Bibliothek, *Deutsche Literatur von Lessing bis Kafka* (1997), can be used to locate instances of Heimat in the writings of the fifty-eight major literary figures included on this CD-ROM. Heimat comes up with a total of 1,168 hits; the word field *heimat** (*Heimat, heimatlich, unheimatlich, beheimatet, heimatberechtigt, Heimatdienst, Heimaterde, Heimatkunde, heimatlos, Heimatsort, Heimatsrecht, Heimatstadt*, etc.) yields 1,536 hits. For the word Heimat there are, to list a few writers (in alphabetical order), 40 hits in Arnim, 39 in Brentano, 86 in Eichendorff, 18 in Goethe, 52 in Heine, 53 in Hölderlin, 133 in Keller, 53 in C. F. Meyer, 125 in Raabe, 39 in Rilke, 28 in Schiller, 76 in Stifter, 47 in Storm, and 90 in Tieck. By itself this list from a highly selective

CD-ROM, which does not include any nonliterary, noncanonical, or post-First World War texts, shows why an exhaustive listing of Heimat manifestations is not possible. There are simply too many.

Similarly, the scholarship on Heimat, usually on Heimat in specific contexts (Heimat in Eichendorff, Heimat in Heine, etc.) is vast. Some useful bibliographical sources for Heimat and anti-Heimat scholarship can be found in Norbert Mecklenburg's two studies of German regionalism, *Erzählte Provinz: Regionalismus und Moderne im Roman* [Narrated Province: Regionalism and Modernity in the Novel, 1982] and *Die grünen Inseln: Zur Kritik des literarischen Heimatkomplexes* [The Green Islands: On the Critique of the Literary Heimat Complex, 1987]. *Die grünen Inseln* also contains a list of what one could argue are the 175 most important novels published in German between 1945 and 1986 that make significant use of the idea of Heimat, many of them as anti-Heimat (293–98), a phenomenon in German letters that I will discuss in chapter 6, "Heimat and Innocence (in Childhood, in Religion, in Language, and in *Antiheimat*)."

Ina-Maria Greverus's *Der territoriale Mensch: Ein literatur-anthropologischer Versuch zum Heimatphänomen* [Territorial Man: An Essay on the Heimat Phenomenon Through an Anthropology of Literature, 1972] can serve as an excellent source of instances of nineteenth- and twentieth-century Heimat praise, as well as of discussions of Heimat in relation to German nationalism during the nineteenth century. Greverus shows in her excellent study how the Heimat idea was "inherent" in all the antagonisms of the nineteenth century and how it "could finally turn into the reservoir of all positively expressed protest values" (284–85).

By far the most extensive list of sources on Heimat can be found in the two-volume, 1,450-page collection *Heimat*— volume 1, *Analysen, Themen, Perspektiven* [Analyses, Topics, Perspectives]; volume 2, *Lehrpläne, Literatur, Filme* [State Assigned Syllabi, Literature, Films] — edited by Will Cremer and Ansgar Klein (1990).[11] It contains a sixty-page bibliography of publications that directly or indirectly deal with the idea of Heimat; the list of books alone is forty pages long. (It includes complete books, as well as articles, essays, and personal accounts on the subject of Heimat published in collections. It does not include articles that were published in periodicals without being reprinted in books.)

Divided into five categories and twenty-six subcategories, with twenty-five to thirty entries on each page, this list of publications to 1990 provides between 1,600 and 1,700 sources addressing the idea of Heimat. Conspicuously, the shortest category is the first one, "Heimat — Conceptual Approaches." Divided into three subcategories ("Philosophical, Sociological, and Cultural Discussions"; "Debates in Relation to the History of Ideas and the Critique of Ideology"; and "Historico-Political References"), this category is only a little over five pages long. Reading, or at least looking in an evaluative way at the 159 entries in this category, one must conclude that the often disappointing findings in case studies of Heimat can be, to some degree, attributed to a lack of theoretical work on the subject.

Yet another source, the American Firstsearch OCLC WorldCat database, lists, under the keyword Heimat, 5,804 entries as of 25 November 2000. A quick look at the first 200 entries shows that about two thirds are fiction or poetry carrying the word Heimat in their titles; some 10 percent are scholarly books dealing with the term in some specific context (in German film, in Eichendorff, in Schubert, in Edgar Reitz's *Heimat,* etc.); the remaining quarter is a mix ranging from *In der Heimat Vincent van Goghs* to collections of Heimat songs and regional celebrations of regions themselves (*Mythos Niederrhein; Heimat Gutenstein,* etc.). The MLA Bibliography lists 211 records under the keyword Heimat (25 November 2000); almost all of them are scholarly publications on Heimat in specific contexts (dialects in pedagogy, Heimat in Maria Beig, *Heimatforschung,* Heimat in the Austrian post-Second World War novel, problems of narrating the Heimat in Christa Wolf, etc.).

Finally, Andrea Bastian's linguistic study *Der Heimat-Begriff: Eine begriffsgeschichtliche Untersuchung in verschiedenen Funktionsbereichen der deutschen Sprache* [The Concept of Heimat: A Study of the History of a Concept in Different Contexts of the German Language, 1995] provides an admirable collection of instances and contexts of Heimat uses (and abuses). Her seventeen-page bibliography, with approximately 500 entries — many of which are not mentioned in other bibliographies on the subject — offers a collection of sources for a linguistic study of the Heimat complex.

Thus, a comprehensive compilation of references to Heimat would be unmanageable; nevertheless, this study would be incomplete without examples that situate the shifts of Heimat in history. The study, therefore, includes selected references to Heimat that illustrate the multivalent qualities of the idea.

The German idea of Heimat, as we will see, lies in interstitial spaces between disciplines and concepts. It enfolds the public with the private, the individual with the social, the self with nature, dream with reality, utopia with landscape; it seeks the preverbal in the verbal, the premodern in the modern, the noble peasant in the burgher, the inside in the outside.

The first surprise that awaits the scholar of the idea of Heimat, though, is that despite the large number of definitions that exist in many fields and forms both in German and in English, there is virtually no overt disagreement between scholars. In other words, even though definitions differ, I have not been able to find anyone who claims that someone else's definition of Heimat would be "problematic" or "limited" or "questionable" or in any other way incomplete or wrong. The reason, I think, is that since Heimat conceptualizations — as we will see — usually come out of a harmonizing and fusional mode of thought that does not recognize an Other, a mode of thought where the dialectics between an I and a Not-I — and, for that matter, dialectics in general ("the consistent sense of nonidentity" [Adorno 1973, 5]) — does not exist, to disagree with someone else's notion of Heimat would be to impose an alien form of reason onto the idea of Heimat (and, thus, to disqualify oneself from the ability to make claims about Heimat from a position of understanding). The tacit assumption is that Heimat can only be understood from within. Therefore, true understanding can come out of only a form of identification, not from a form of analysis.

For instance, Michael Geisler quotes Edgar Reitz in a special issue of the *New German Critique* devoted to Reitz's 1984 *Heimat* series:

> "Heimat," it is said, is part of reality, something within us, the opposite of utopia. Yet if we compare this notion of "Heimat" with empirical reality, it will become utopian, the object of our desires. (48)

This statement is a fascinating example of the polarized inside-outside thinking the idea of Heimat seems to encourage; and yet, it is quoted by Geisler, a scholar of contemporary film and literary theory, as a plausible definition of Heimat. I have observed this lack of critical distance again and again when it comes to definitions of Heimat from usually quite acute commentators. At times it seems — at least to this scholar — as if no one can say anything wrong about Heimat. This discreet silence about anyone else's definition of Heimat, it appears, is part of the highly charged subjectivity of the term. To criticize someone else's Heimat would be more invasively intimate an engagement with the subjectivity of an author than is the culturally acceptable norm among participants in the discourse of Western scholarship.

In light of such difficulties, W. G. Sebald's solution to the problem in the introduction to his *Unheimliche Heimat* [Unhomelike/Eerie/Uncanny Heimat, 1991] becomes an elegant and understandable one. Sebald acknowledges that a systematic study of Heimat "would encounter serious difficulties" — he does not say what they would be. He continues: "All that is possible — and I don't want to attempt any more here — is to look around a little from certain vantage points . . . to see what in each case is called Heimat" (11). Thence he proceeds with his almost 200-page book of essays about Heimat in the work of mostly Austrian authors without any further attempt to make general statements about this strangely pervasive and strangely elusive idea.

A comprehensive critical study of the idea of Heimat that is cross-disciplinary at its base looms as a large void in the scholarship on German culture and thought. Ina-Maria Greverus's *Der territoriale Mensch* goes farthest in this direction. But Greverus acknowledges that, even though her studies of Heimat are much informed by literature, she considers herself mainly an anthropologist (9). And, indeed, in her remarkable and ground-breaking study of the Heimat phenomenon Greverus does not attempt to come to terms with the idea of Heimat in general as it relates to such key areas of culture as, for instance, the history of philosophy, general questions of gender, or the ethical dimensions of the concept of nature, the last of which is an essential element in the perception of Heimat as innocent.

Reasons for the lack of a comprehensive critical study of the idea of Heimat become evident when we consider what is at stake in discussions of the idea: nothing less than the dark underside of German history. Invocations of Heimat — as we will see — always turn up where deep socioeconomic, ontological, psychological, and political shifts, fissures, and insecurities occur. Heimat buries areas of repressed anxiety. It keeps people from being reminded of that of which they do not wish to be reminded. Whenever fearful changes in modern German-speaking societies occur, Heimat is there, as well. Heimat on the surface provides a spatial, relentlessly positive, and secure collective identity, one that is free from private responsibility. Whatever lies underneath Heimat, however, remains for the most part below conscious scrutiny, outside of critical analysis, and hidden by the taboos of modern scholarship.

Such taboos, of course, change over time. Taboos that have at various times blocked scholarly interest in the idea of Heimat include the aversion of nineteenth-century German intellectuals to a true interaction with popular or peasant culture, Wilhelmine Germany's inability to undertake even rudimentarily balanced gender discussions (Heimat at the time being a thoroughly feminized concept), German scholarship's anti-mass culture atmosphere during the 1950s (a hidden anti-Americanism and a not so hidden anti-Marxism), and — in the circle of the Frankfurt School scholars — the post-Second World War taboo against directly investigating anti-Semitism, the idea of Heimat having been clearly instrumental in the Nazi atrocities against Jews and other so-called *Heimatlose* [Heimat-less groups].

My study begins to fill this void in the scholarship on German culture and thought. Although I cannot pretend to deliver an encyclopedic investigation of all uses of the term, my theory provides a grid of fundamental associations and components that the idea of Heimat carries with it at all times, although sometimes it shows more of one face, or undertone, than another. We will see Heimat as a part of modernity and of the discourse of German cultural, as well as political, nationalism (chapter 2); as it contributes to German notions of identity (chapter 3); as it is shaped by gender dichotomizations and by idealizations of the feminine (chapter 4); as part of German philosophy's conspicuous and wide use of grounding metaphors, as well as part of German interactions with nature and landscape (chapter 5); and, finally, as part of German self-perceptions of innocence in childhood, religion, and language (chapter 6). Likewise, all these aspects are part of Heimat.

By treating Heimat variously as a cultural trope, as a container of history, as a symbolic representation, and as an element in the constitution of identity, I hope to provide — through both the lens and mirror of Heimat — an understanding of many German speakers' and writers' ways of negotiating the ontological anxieties with which modernity has confronted us.

Space, Alienation, Provincialism, Nature, Gender, and Self-Healings

Let us again consider the essence of Heimat. Heimat is based in a spatial conception of identity. Heimat constructs are counterphobic conceptualizations expressed in regressive, imagistic terms; they are wish-fulfillments without a price; they provide a world where wars and destruction do not exist or are so far away that they really do not matter; they provide a world where men and women know their roles so perfectly that in due course they come together without strains and crises; and they provide a world where — just by chance, so it seems — since 1935 there have been no Jews and, thus, there can be no question about the Holocaust in present memory or in the past. (These observations refer, of course, to imaginary qualities of Heimat. The reassuring and common memories of Heimat in which no Jews happen to be present stand in striking contrast to the pre-1935 Heimat idylls of Jews themselves. A special issue of the journal *Allmende* [24/25, 1989] devoted to unquestioning identification with the Heimat in German-Jewish writers until the early 1930s is a remarkable and eye-opening document.)

Heimat's relationship to space is a curious one. Modern Heimat conceptions are a kind of popular register of the same kind of spatial self-perceptions that have been fundamental to modern German philosophy from its beginning.

Gottfried Wilhelm Leibniz was among the first modern philosophers who worked on the concept of physical space and its relation to thought and perception. The origins of the theoretization of space in general, of course, trace back much further, to Plato and Aristotle. (Aristotle notes in his *Physics* that "everyone says there is something like 'place' [*topos*], but Plato alone tried to define it as a concept" [209b 16f.; qtd. in Ritter and Gründer 8, 68].

Plato realizes in his *Timaios* that to obtain a concept of space he has to destroy the traditional elements of earth, water, air, and fire. They are not, Plato writes, "letters" [*stoicheia*] in the text of matter; they are syllables that need to be reduced to something general on which they are based. Plato expresses this notion in several images about space — the best known is that space is the "nursemaid of Becoming" [49a; qtd. in Ritter and Gründer 72] — that lead to an essential undefinability of the concept. This process brings Plato to a new concept of space that lies between idea and experience. He calls it the *xóra* [52a], which is sometimes translated into German as the *Ausweichend-Platzmachende* [space that makes space by moving out of the way].)

Leibniz — in contrast to Sir Isaac Newton, for whom space is something quite real — moves the notion of space dramatically in the direction of the ideal and imaginary. But it is Immanuel Kant whose impact on modern perceptions of the concept of space cannot be overestimated. In his *Postmodern Geographies* (1989) Edward Soja summarizes that impact:

> [Space's] most powerful source of philosophical legitimacy and elaboration is Kant, whose system of categorical antinomies assigned an explicit and sustaining ontological place to geography and spatial analysis, a place which has been carefully preserved in a continuing neo-Kantian interpretation of spatiality. The Kantian legacy of transcendental spatial idealism pervades every wing of the modern hermeneutic tradition. . . . (125)

Kant saw the organization of space as a projection of a mental ordering of phenomena. But space never ceases to have a physical side, as well, for Kant. Soja points out, for instance, that Kant lectured on geography for almost forty years at the University of Königsberg, giving the course forty-eight times. The only topics on which he lectured more often were logic and metaphysics (36). Spatiality is so basic to Kant's thought processes that one can almost map his philosophical treatises. He introduces the essential modern dichotomy wherein the I experiences its split into subject and object, a fundamentally spatial conception. The I as subject stands opposite the world, which "constitutes itself as the whole of all objects of possible experience" (Habermas 1985, 308). (Contrary to the common English practice of translating German Idealist philosophy's concept of *Ich* as "ego," I have decided to retain the German distinction between the philosophically informed *Ich* and the *Ego,* which in German is associated with Freudian psychoanalysis. I am, therefore, rendering Idealist philosophy's *Ich* as "I" and the Freudian *Ego* as "ego.")

Habermas points out that Kant expresses the modern world as a *Gedankengebäude* [building of thoughts] (1985, 30). Doubtless thinking of Kant, Habermas sees spatial metaphors in general as a precondition to the philosophy of the subject (360).

The Kantian capacity of the I to be both subject and object has become part of our modern condition of self-consciousness and alienation. The term *alienation* — in German *Entfremdung* — already has a spatial aspect. And in German the opposite of *Fremde* [the alien, the foreign, the strange] is — by no coincidence — Heimat. English, fittingly, does not have an easy translation for either Heimat or *Fremde.*

Thus, Anton Kaes is well justified in interpreting the philosopher Ernst Bloch's understanding of Heimat as the utopian antithesis to the experience of alienation in general (1987, 174).[12] Indeed, the term Heimat in German is a floating signifier used for anything that provides the utopia of a wished-for experience of shelteredness and harmony, an experience of disalienation in a spatially conceived world.

In its premodern longings Heimat stands in (an often only implied) contrast to modern experiences such as alienating city life, the industrial workplace, the technologized mode of existence, the realm of politics, the nation-state, and what Anthony Giddens calls in several of his works the "sequestration of experience."

In other words, if one of the modern condition's most basic qualities is the capacity for detachment and objectivization (even of the subject), and if such detachment and objectivization are experienced as both self-consciousness[13] and alienation, then Heimat answers to the longing for a state where such a distancing, such an alienation that leads to self-consciousness, is reversed. In this context it is easy to understand why Heimat is often associated with innocence and childhood, a state usually linked to a mother figure. Notions of an idealized mother and an idealized feminine are constitutive in expressions of Heimat.

Historically speaking, Heimat constructs have played a significant role in the German-speaking middle classes' civic, conservative, provincial passivity. Thomas Mann described this troubling passive provinciality in the world-traveling German bourgeoisie quite dramatically. In his 1945 speech "Germany and the Germans," delivered in English at the Library of Congress shortly after the end of the war, he declares the "unworldly, provincial, German cosmopolitanism" (1963 [English version], 49) to be an integral part of what he calls "*das deutsche Seelenbild*" (1960 [German version], 1129) — "the German picture," the German "state of the mind" (1963, 49); literally, the image of the German soul.

Again and again in this speech Mann connects seemingly disparate elements in German bourgeois culture under the theme of provincialism versus cosmopolitanism — a theme that we will find to be basic to the idea of Heimat, as well. We see cosmopolitanism and provincialism reflected in the form of a "philistine universalism," says Mann, a "cosmopolitanism in a nightcap" (1963, 49). Mann projects his own image-rich, *seelische* [spiritual] picture of Germany, a Germany full of secretive, uncanny, medieval, wart-nosed, demoniacal elements.

German Romanticism, Mann goes on to say, with its inner sensitivities and its aestheticization of ethics (1960, 1144), with its affinity for the past, death, and beauty, was fundamental to the self-definition of *Deutschland,* which, according to Mann, is Romanticism's "*eigentliches Heimatland*" [true homeland] (1145). But German Romanticism, even though it influenced European thinking "as German spirit, as Romantic counter-revolution" (1963, 64) — that is, counterrevolution against the Enlightenment — refused to accept anything from Europe in return; in particular, it refused to accept the European religion of humanity: European democracy.

Discussions of the idea of Heimat are also relevant to discussions of a German sense of a "*verräumlichte Innerlichkeit*" [spatialized interiority] (Mecklenburg 1987, 247). The German phrase *innere Emigration,* which some intellectuals afterwards used to justify having stayed in Germany during the Nazi years, along with outward passivity in the face of the National Socialist regime, depends on this spatialized interiority. It not only claims that an outward passivity or even collaboration deserves respect (or, at least, sympathetic consideration), since the inner subject can remain un-

affected by an outward passivity or collaboration; it also claims that
it is possible to go abroad inside oneself.

Heimat, the place where one feels at home with oneself and the
world, is primarily, but not only, a spatial concept. To be sure,
there exist no maps of Heimat. Nevertheless, it is safe to assume
that conceptualizations of Heimat play a central role in "shaping
the spatiality of social life" (Soja 121) in German-speaking contexts.[14]

A perfect example is the celebration of Heimat in what is often
referred to as *Alpenheimat* or *Bergheimat*. The statutes of the
Deutsche Alpenverein [German mountain association], established
in 1869, give as their purpose the "promotion of mountain climbing and hiking, especially among youth, the preservation of the
beauty and naturalness [*Ursprünglichkeit*] of the mountain world,
the expansion and dissemination of the knowledge of the high
mountain regions, and through all this, the cultivation and
strengthening of the love of Heimat" (qtd. in Zebhauser and
Körner 11).

Again and again we find the concept of nature basic to German
conceptualizations of Heimat. Seeing nature — or better, the concept of nature — as a created entity is a first step toward a more
theoretical inquiry into the German idea of Heimat. What each
culture and each age think of as being "natural" should not remain
unscrutinized.

The idea of Heimat — like the idea of nature or family — is, as
we will see, class sensitive. In other words, at any time since the last
decade of the eighteenth century we can find different contempo-
raneously existing Heimat conceptualizations in different segments
of German-speaking populations: for instance, the image of the
victimized Heimat in need of defense, which German propaganda
used to mobilize the common man and woman during both world
wars; the contemporary intellectual's frequent equation of Heimat
with any space of unquestioned identity; and provincial Heimat associations' selective memory of a good old Heimat, the preservation of which is their declared goal. Beside all of these, Heimat is
frequently associated with a German middle class's widespread appreciation of nature, landscape, and *das Wandern* [hiking]. In his
Eine Ästhetik der Natur [An Aesthetics of Nature, 1991], especially
in chapter 2, Martin Seel notes the moral dimension of this appre-

ciation of nature: modern Western culture assumes that someone
who is capable of such appreciation is morally good. Thus, through
Heimat's perceived naturalness, to celebrate one's Heimat becomes — among many other things — an act of celebrating one's
own good moral qualities.

Heimat became good and innocent and feminized at the same
time the idea of Heimat became modern. (Heimat was originally a
neuter noun: "*das Heimat.*" In some remote Alemannic and Ba-
varian areas it still is. The feminine form, *die Heimat,* already appears in Middle High German [1050–1350]. But only during the
eighteenth century did Heimat become a predominantly feminine
noun [Bastian 22].) Accordingly, Heimat became one goal of the
subject's inner longing for identification with a supposedly originary nature or landscape. Unlike the idea of the primitive, however, whose beginnings belong to the same era and which, like
Heimat, claims nature for its own, Heimat is constructed not outside of, but around, bourgeois ideals of family, class, gender roles,
history, and politics. In Heimat there exists no inhibition of spon-
taneous impulses; there is no shame and no embarrassment, because such inner self-restrictions are not needed where Heimat is.
The messiness of experience disappears under the steady sun and
the blue sky, dissolves in the vibrant *Feste* and the warm dialect
dialogues.

Heimat is a kind of toothless German critique of modern
Western civilization. It is imagistically structured, close to primary
processes; it is an irrational wish-fulfillment. This consideration explains why Habermas's writings almost consciously shy away from
this area. As Joel Whitebook observes in his *Perversion and Utopia:
A Study in Psychoanalysis and Critical Theory* (1995), because of
Habermas's "uneasiness with regressive phenomena, the workings
of the imaginary and of the relation between the imaginary and the
rational discourse do not enter systematically into his analysis"
(215).

Through critically studying the idea of Heimat it is possible to
come to an understanding of the imaginary in its inner spatiality
and of provinciality as a significant aspect of how social reality is
constituted in a German context, with all its modern discontinuities. Moreover, we see how such imagistically structured represen-

tations of longings lend themselves, in the face of intense ontological anxieties, to Heimat as a mode of self-healing.

It is self-evident for a study such as this one that the closer it moves to the contemporary reshapings of the term Heimat, the more it deals with a situation in flux. Every summer, when I return to Germany, I observe small shifts in the use of the term Heimat. These shifts are in emphasis, in frequency, in the groups that take up the term, and in the urgency of their application of it. Every year there is more that can and should be said about the German idea of Heimat. But with the sharp increase in the use of the term since the mid-1970s, and especially since 1989, with scholarly book upon scholarly book appearing with the word Heimat in its title[15] — many authors exploring but one or two aspects of this highly complex idea — this seems a good moment to interrupt the cataloguing of particular instances and put forth a book that calls attention to its common foundations.

Notes

[1] Translations, if not otherwise noted, are my own.

[2] See also my article "Comparing Longings for a Sense of Belonging: German *Heimat*, Czech *Domov*, Russian *Rodina*," *Germano-Slavica: A Canadian Journal of Germanic and Slavic Comparative and Interdisciplinary Studies* 11 (1999): 39–46.

[3] Cf., for instance, the Russian folk belief that considers it blasphemy for a man to lie face down on the earth.

[4] Gisela Ecker would probably disagree with me here. In her introductory essay to the volume *Kein Land in Sicht: Heimat—weiblich?* [No Land in Sight: Heimat — Feminine?] (Munich: Fink, 1997), edited by Ecker, she writes that since the turn of the century, "mother and beloved or wife in Heimat fantasies melt together into one single imaginary figure" (15). Giving a rather broadly applied Oedipal interpretation to Heimat references in literature and film from about 1880, Ecker does not consider differences — even in her own evidence — between male fantasies that see Heimat as mother and male fantasies that see Heimat as the beloved.

[5] I am indebted to Dasha Nisula and Serguei Oushakine for their helpful comments on my understanding of *rodina*.

[6] A notable exception here is Wolfgang Lipp's 1997 essay "Heimat in der Moderne: Quelle, Kampfplatz und Bühne von Identität" [Heimat in Moder-

nity: Source, Place of Battle, and Stage of Identity] in *Heimat: Konstanten und Wandel im 19./20. Jahrhundert. Vorstellungen und Wirklichkeit* [Heimat: Continuity and Change During the Nineteenth and Twentieth Century. Imagination and Reality], ed. Katharina Weigand (Munich: Deutscher Alpenverein, 1997), 51–72.

[7] Among historical studies on Heimat, *Heimatvereine*, or *Heimatschutz*, Celia Applegate's *A Nation of Provincials: The German Idea of Heimat* (Berkeley: U of California P, 1990) is by far the most aware of the complexities of the term. Her general comments about Heimat are always suggestive. But she, too, studies the idea of Heimat as it manifests itself in Heimat associations [*Heimatvereine*] in one particular region and then extrapolates from these findings.

[8] On European tribalism during the 1980s in general, see the British-educated, Caribbean-born novelist Caryl Phillips's *The European Tribe* (New York: Farrar, Straus & Giroux, 1987). Phillips, born in 1958, relates in this collection of essays his experiences while traveling through Europe for a year. Describing how a customer objected to his presence in a restaurant in Munich; how Parisians express their racism in combination with an admiration for black fashions in music, dance, and food; how an editor in a London publishing house referred to him as a "jungle bunny"; how a customs official at Oslo's Fornebu airport decided to examine only him extra carefully, Phillips shows that tribalism is a vague term that is best observed by transient outsiders.

[9] "Wie, wenn die Heimatlosigkeit des Menschen darin bestünde, daß der Mensch die *eigentliche* Wohnungsnot noch gar nicht *als die* Not bedenkt? Sobald der Mensch jedoch die Heimatlosigkeit *bedenkt,* ist sie bereits kein Elend mehr. Sie ist, recht bedacht und gut behalten, der einzige Zuspruch, der die Sterblichen in das Wohnen *ruft.*"

[10] One can also find the terms *Willkommensseite* (Welcome Page) and *Startseite* (Starting Page) on the German Internet.

[11] This collection is a publication of the Bundeszentrale für politische Bildung, part of the Ministry for Culture and Education, in charge, among other things, of providing political education teachers nationwide with teaching materials. Since *Heimatkunde* [Heimat Studies] is a subject in the elementary schools in several — maybe most — states in the Federal Republic of Germany, this publication has its immediate uses. It also offers much material for teaching Heimat as regional culture in grades 5 through 13 in subjects such as German, Geography, Art, History, Music, Woodworking, and Needlework. Interestingly, the Bundeszentrale für politische Bildung was founded during the Weimar Republic under the name Reichszentrale für Heimatdienst. After the war, it was first renamed Bundeszentrale für Heimatdienst, then given its present name (Gisela Ecker, "'Heimat': Das Elend der unterschlagenen Differenz" [Munich: Fink, 1997], 7–31, here 20).

[12] See, in particular, Bloch's repeated references to Heimat in his 1959 *Das Prinzip Hoffnung* [The Principle of Hope] and in his essay "Entfremdung, Verfremdung" [Alienation, Estrangement] in which he negotiates the tensions between the concept of alienation (as Hegel, Feuerbach, or Marx understands it) and estrangement (*Gesamtausgabe* [Frankfurt am Main: Suhrkamp, 1965], vol. 9, 277–84). Estrangement [*Verfremdung*], a term later central to the aesthetics of Bertolt Brecht, was introduced into German, curiously enough, by Berthold Auerbach, a writer who has the reputation of a Heimat writer, not a pioneer of Marxist aesthetics. Auerbach (=Moses Baruch Auerbacher) first uses the term *Verfremdung* in 1842 in his novel *Neues Leben*. In fact, this German-Jewish writer, the author of the groundbreaking *Schwarzwälder Dorfgeschichten* (beginning in 1843), was the first great Heimat writer and much more, as well.

[13] One does not have to go as far as Martin Buber, who in *Distance and Relation* (1957) turns spatiality — what he calls "the first principle" of human life — into the beginning of human consciousness. For Buber the human capacity for consciousness comes out of this "primal setting at a distance" (summarized in Edward W. Soja, *Postmodern Geographies: The Reassertion of Space in Critical Social Theory* [London: Verso, 1989], 132).

[14] Soja's formulations from his *Postmodern Geographies* do not come out of a discussion of a specifically German situation but out of a discussion of what he calls our contemporary "production" of nature and — by analogy, Soja maintains — of our "production" of mental space. The concept of nature in its relation to Heimat will be addressed in chapter 5, "Heimat, Nature, Landscape, and Ground."

[15] I am thinking here in particular of the following sixteen works that have appeared since 1995 alone, and they are not an exhaustive list:

Heimat — A German Dream: Regional Loyalties and National Identity in German Culture, 1890–1990, by Elizabeth Boa and Rachel Palfreyman (Oxford: Oxford UP, 2000);

Deutsche Heimat Islam, [German Heimat Islam], by Hasan Alacacioglu (Münster: Waxmann, 2000);

Heimat: Leichtigkeit und Last des Herkommens, [Heimat: Lightness and Weight of Where One Comes From], by Thomas E. Schmidt (Berlin: Aufbau, 1999);

Un-heimliche Heimat: Reibungsflächen zwischen Kultur und Nation, [Un-Canny Heimat: Sites of Friction Between Culture and Nation], by Florentine Strzelczyk (Munich: Iudicium, 1999);

Constructing Heimat in Postwar Germany: Longing and Belonging, by Christopher J. Wickham (Lewiston NY: Edwin Mellen Press, 1999);

"Envisioning Empire: Jewishness, Blackness and Gender in German Colonial Discourse from Frieda von Bülow to the Nazi Kolonie and Heimat," by Barbara Ann Shumannfang (Diss., Duke U, 1998);

"— Als hätte die Erde ein wenig die Lippen geöffnet —": Topoi der Heimat und Identität, ["As If the Earth had Opened its Lips a Little—": Topoi of Heimat and Identity], by Peter Plener (Budapest: Druckerei der Loránd-Eötvös-Universität, 1997);

Kein Land in Sicht: Heimat — weiblich? edited by Gisela Ecker (Munich: Fink, 1997);

Heimat: Konstanten und Wandel im 19./20. Jahrhundert. Vorstellungen und Wirklichkeit, edited by Katharina Weigand (Munich: Deutscher Alpenverein, 1997);

The Nation as a Local Metaphor: Württemberg, Imperial Germany, and National Memory, 1871–1918, by Alon Confino (Chapel Hill: U of North Carolina P, 1997);

A Greener Vision of Home: Cultural Politics and Environmental Reform in the German Heimatschutz Movement, 1904–1918, by William Rollins (Ann Arbor: U of Michigan P, 1997);

Heimat, Nation, Fatherland: The German Sense of Belonging, edited by Jost Hermand and John Steakley (New York: Peter Lang, 1996);

Die Heimat heißt Babylon: Zur Literatur ausländischer Autoren in der Bundesrepublik Deutschland, [A Heimat Called Babylon: On Literature by Foreign Authors in the Federal Republic of Germany], by Immacolata Amodeo (Opladen: Westdeutscher Verlag, 1996);

Heimat: Auf der Suche nach der verlorenen Identität [Heimat: In Search of Lost Identity], edited by Joachim Riedl (Vienna: Brandstätter, 1995);

Frauen schaffen sich Heimat in männlicher Welt [Women Make Themselves a Heimat in a Male World], edited by Elisabeth Camenzind and Kathrin Knüsel (Zurich: Kreuz, 1995);

Wem gehört die Heimat? Beiträge der politischen Psychologie zu einem umstrittenen Phänomen [Whose Heimat Is It? Essays on a Controversial Question by Political Psychologists], edited by Wilfried Belschner et al. (Opladen: Leske + Budrich, 1995); and

Der Heimat-Begriff: Eine begriffsgeschichtliche Untersuchung in verschiedenen Funktionsbereichen der deutschen Sprache, by Andrea Bastian (Tübingen: Niemeyer, 1995).

2: Heimat, Modernity, and Nation

A S MODERNITY HAS BECOME ONE OF the key reference points in contemporary critical discussions of any general question in philosophy, literature, sociology, anthropology, or history, each field has tended to shape its own understanding of the concept, an understanding tailored to its own specific lines of inquiry. But common to all definitions is the conviction that the experience of modernity brought Western culture to where it is; that modernity has been a male-centered way of presenting human interaction with the world ("modern man"); that during modernity the belief in God-given religious structures was replaced by man-made (and to a degree negotiable) reflexive processes of structuration; that what is often referred to as the "bourgeois subject" has invested modern categories (identity, the private sphere, reason, the nation-state, family, objectifiable time) with qualities that assumed both interpretive and formative functions. Also, among contemporary scholars who inquire into our current Western situation, it is generally agreed that the mid-1960s can be identified as a period when deep shifts in our modern way of constructing meaning began. Whether we label this new shift a turn toward late modernity, high modernity, postmodernity, or second modernity, it refers to a need for questioning and remodeling our most fundamental constructions of meaning in categories such as place, time, experience, culture, gender ("contemporary men and women"), power, class, and society. *Bourgeois,* with its usually implied antagonisms, began to cease being an almost automatic modifier for the subject and, thus, for subjectivity.

Even though the strong currency of such terms as *myth, paradox, experience, the body,* and the highly amorphous *culture* in our current aesthetics of philosophy show an undeniable antimodern, instead of a truly new, slant, I think that we should not make the mistake of denying that some fundamental shifts are occurring. Habermas's slight repositioning in this respect between 1985 and 1990 confirms this contention. In *Der philosophische Diskurs der*

Moderne [The Philosophical Discourse of Modernity, 1985] he claims that some of those who are considered postmodern philosophers are — by discussing such concepts as truth, theory, and system — still living in the shadow of the last great philosopher, Georg Wilhelm Friedrich Hegel (246). Then, in his 1990 foreword to the republication of the 1962 *Strukturwandel der Öffentlichkeit* [Structural Changes of the Public Sphere], he has become aware of the remarkable contributions feminism has made to contemporary Western thinking and of the formative influence exclusions based on gender had, until recently, on our perception of Western culture. He writes that the transformation of the relationship between the sexes "becomes not only part of the economic system but also part of the private core area of the sheltered space [*Binnenraum*] of the conjugal family" (19).[1] Referring to an essay by Carol Pateman ("The Fraternal Social Contract"), Habermas continues:

> This shows that the exclusion of women has been constitutive for the political public sphere not merely in that it has been dominated by men as a matter of contingency but also in that its structure and relation to the private sphere has been determined in a gender-specific fashion. Unlike the exclusion of underprivileged men, the exclusion of women had structuring significance. (428 [Thomas Burger's translation, slightly modified])

In other words, we can see Habermas (along with many others) becoming aware during the later part of the 1980s — thanks in part to Michel Foucault, whom Habermas discusses extensively on several occasions during this period — that modern Hegelian structures had been significantly shaped by mechanisms of exclusion, and especially by mechanisms of exclusion based on gender.[2]

In this chapter I will look at how the modern idea of Heimat relates to what is often referred to as "modernity." I will show the interplay between modern and antimodern within the modern idea of Heimat. To do so, I will first recapitulate how the two most widely recognized contemporary scholars of Western modernity, Anthony Giddens and Habermas, perceive modernity. In my recapitulations I will focus on their respective areas of strength, rather than on their differences. Giddens and Habermas work, for instance, with somewhat different concepts of identity and of communication. Some of their other differences, though, can be attributed to the different emphases in their studies. Their differences in style, in my opinion, are but surface antagonisms (Giddens is an author of theories through postmodern relativization, Habermas an author of what have been called reconstructive theories). Since a closer analysis of their differences, however, would not bring us closer to a better understanding of the idea of Heimat, I will treat their theories of modernity here as complementary, not as antagonistic.

Giddens takes the more sociological approach of the two, understanding modernity as a posttraditional age wherein the experience of discontinuities in time and space, and the notion of change itself, create a situation that is existentially troubling for philosophers and ordinary individuals alike. Habermas understands modernity more philosophically; for him, the modern age begins quietly around 1500, but more broadly with the Enlightenment, and reaches its maturity after the French Revolution with Hegel. Romantic writers had already noted the sense of *Entzweiung* [separation] from nature in modern consciousness and had perceived it as basic to our modern sense of irony. But Hegel, according to Habermas, first discovered subjectivity (characterized by freedom and reflection), as *the* modern principle. Hegel, looking beyond *Entzweiung,* described how the experience of alienation [*Entfremdung*] plagues the modern conscious subject, which has become subject as well as object to itself.

Not surprisingly, then, in light of Giddens's and Habermas's theories, Heimat in the modern age becomes an antimodern idea. Heimat tends to be invoked when German-speaking cultures are expressing their difficulties in adjusting to modern life. The notion of Heimat requires the existence of an idealized premodern state. It is a longing for a return to a state in which anxieties about reason and the self, essence and appearance, thought and being did not yet exist.

Hegel, in the famous definition of freedom in his *Vorlesungen über die Geschichte der Philosophie* [Lectures on the History of Philosophy], makes Heimat this state of having overcome alienation. "The germ of thinking freedom [*Keim der denkenden Freiheit*]," writes Hegel in the introduction to the "History of Greek Philosophy," where he uses the words *Heimat, heimatlich,* or *Heimatlichkeit* no less than ten times in three pages, "lies in the spirit of the sense of Heimat, in this spirit of the imagined Being-with-oneself,

in this quality of free, beautiful historicity" (vol. 18, 175).[3] Even
though after his early years Hegel, in contrast to the Romantics,
never longed for a return to an originary nature, never longed for a
reunion with nature, in his writing an intermingling of past, spirit,
and present in *Heimatlichkeit* does lead thought to a freedom at
once mental and spatial, in which a "free, beautiful" contact with
history is possible. For Hegel, the Greeks found themselves in this
spirit of freedom and beauty. Thus they not only made their existence *heimatlich* for themselves, but they also honored "their re-
birth in the spirit — which in fact is their true birth" (174).[4]

Heimat heals the rifts underlying the sense of *Entzweiung* from
nature, the experience of alienation; and Heimat is, therefore, a
space free from irony. Inside Heimat interaction with tradition re-
gains its *Naturwüchsigkeit* [sense of being rooted in nature]. Heimat, then, is a selectively idealized memory of the past. In its
premodern longings Heimat stands in (an often only implied)
contrast to familiar modern experiences such as urban alienation,
the industrial workplace, the technologized mode of existence,
mass politics, and the nation-state. The modern notion of Heimat
becomes a bourgeois idyll where all socialization occurs without
repression — no struggle, no violence, just "naturally." In general,
Heimat in its antimodernist stance is part of modernity.

I should say, though, that I agree with Alon Confino, who sees
the question of whether Heimat is modern or antimodern as missing "the essence of the Heimat idea" (241). The details of this
modern versus antimodern contrast are crucial. Taken one by one,
they will lead us into subsequent chapters. Heimat, in an essential
and formative way, contradicts modern developments (urbanization, mobility, abstraction, objectified time, the modern nation-
state, reflexivity, alienation) and, at the same time, by contradicting
them, the idea of Heimat absorbs modern categories and qualities
and joins forces with other modern constructs. In other words, the
idea of Heimat is constituted not in true opposition to, but rather
around, modern bourgeois ideals of family, class, gender roles,
history, and politics. In subsequent chapters I will show the symbiotic relationship of the idea of Heimat with notions of identity
(chapter 3), the feminine (chapter 4), nature (chapter 5), and innocence, as in childhood, religion, and language (chapter 6).

At the end of this chapter, after briefly discussing Heimat as it relates to modern conceptualizations of irony and an objectivized time, I will turn to Heimat and nationalism in the German context of modernity. Beginning with Herder's arguably innocent linguistic and cultural nationalism — his nationalism was based on celebrating individual people's traditions and languages, rather than on states and authority — I show how Heimat, despite all its uses and abuses, has been able to remain in the eyes of most Germans a code word for this innocent, *völkisch* nationalism, that is, for a sort of idealized *Ur*-nationalism that was in place before modern nation-states became the almost exclusive referents of the word *nation*. (Ernest Gellner encapsulates this chronology in his *Nations and Nationalism* [1983]: "It is nationalism which engenders nations, and not the other way round" [55].) Such a nationalism — based in culture and language, predating the modern nations, and today no longer even called "nationalism" — is one of the foundations of the German idea of Heimat.

Anthony Giddens's Modernity and Heimat

The British sociologist Anthony Giddens is probably the most readable source for a comprehensive theory of Western modernity. In the first chapter of his *Consequences of Modernity* (1990) he lists the discontinuities social institutions undergo when moving from traditional to modern social orders: the pace of change accelerates, the scope of change shifts, and the nature of modern institutions (such as cities) is altered (6). These changes profoundly reshape our social life and, with it, our constitutions of identity. As Giddens points out in both *The Consequences of Modernity* and *Modernity and Self-Identity* (1991), the continuing distanciation of time and space, the disembedding of social institutions, and modernity's fundamentally reflexive character create a situation that "is not only disturbing to philosophers but is *existentially troubling* for ordinary individuals" (1991, 21; Giddens's emphasis). All the transformations from a premodern or traditional to a modern society have fundamental effects on our posttraditional Western lives. They alter the way we think about change, as well as about ourselves.

The first major development, the distanciation of time and space, can be, according to Giddens, attributed to the invention of the mechanical clock, which creates "empty" time, and to the separation of space from place, which creates "empty space." Giddens explains the two distanciations in *The Consequences of Modernity*. About the arrival of "empty" modern time, he writes:

> All pre-modern cultures possessed modes of the calculation of time. The calendar, for example, was as distinctive a feature of agrarian states as the invention of writing. But the time reckoning which formed the basis of day-to-day life, certainly for the majority of the population, always linked time with place — and was usually imprecise and variable. No one could tell the time of day without reference to other socio-spatial markers: "when" was almost universally either connected with "where" or identified by regular natural occurrences. The invention of the mechanical clock expressed a uniform dimension of "empty" time, quantified in such a way as to permit the precise designation of "zones" of the day (for instance, the "working day"). (17)

The "emptying of time," Giddens goes on, is a precondition for the "emptying of space," which occurs because place — "the idea of locale" (18) — and space are being torn from each other. The relation between place and space is increasingly determined by relations between "absent" others that are "locationally distant from any given situation of face-to-face interaction" (18). Therefore, Giddens claims, place is becoming more and more "phantasmagoric" as "locales are thoroughly penetrated by and shaped in terms of social influences quite distant from them" (19).

After the continuing distanciation of time and space, Giddens sees "disembedding mechanisms" as the second major modern development. Disembedding mechanisms are expert systems (for instance, hospitals, governments, banks) and abstract systems with their symbolic tokens, such as money, which operate on the basis of "faith in impersonal principles" (114–15).

The third fundamental quality of modernity is its reflexivity. Giddens sees modern reflexivity as distinct from the reflexivity of premodern societies, which was "largely limited to the reinterpretation and clarification of tradition" (37). Modern reflexivity is introduced into the basis of system reproduction: "Thought and action are constantly refracted back upon each other" (38). Doing something one way and not another can no longer be sanctioned with the reason that it has always been done that way:

Combined with the inertia of habit, this means that, even in the most modernised of modern societies, tradition continues to play a role. But this role is generally much less significant than is supposed by authors who focus attention upon the integration of tradition and modernity in the contemporary world. For justified tradition is tradition in sham clothing and receives its identity only from the reflexivity of the modern. (38)

Tradition and the past no longer have intrinsic connections with daily life. Characteristic of modernity is "the presumption of wholesale reflexivity — which of course includes reflection upon the nature of reflection itself" (39). (We may think here of Theodor Adorno's observation in *Negative Dialektik* [1966] that the dialectical principle, or "the consistent sense of nonidentity" [7], that lies at the root of reflexivity also impoverishes experience in the modern world. But the dialectical principle, according to Adorno, is also the appropriate concept for the "abstract monotony" of the modern world. In fact, the agony of dialectics "is the world's agony raised to a concept" [8].)

Giddens's observations about the changes from premodern to modern, from traditional, archaic, and mythic to enlightened, conscious, and reflexive social structures are immediately significant for a study of the idea of Heimat. At least until the mid-1960s, when some aspects of Heimat underwent shifts, the ideals that underlie Heimat are, down to details, a countermodern phenomenon. Heimat in its ideal form is a modern idea that resists modernity. Pace and scope of changes in Heimat are limited; the separation of time and space has not occurred; disembedding is reversed; reflexivity is absent; abstract systems with symbolic tokens (such as money) and expert systems (such as hospitals, governments, and banks) barely exist and are irrelevant for the construction of meaning in everyday life; transformations where work is separate from household, from "leisure time" or "private time," are not an issue.

Formative in Heimat conceptualizations in general is the primacy of place characteristic of premodern settings, which in the modern context has been more and more replaced by disembedding and time-space distanciation. Heimat constructs nullify destabilization and disembedding, returning people to a face-to-face negotiation of time alone. Space is a given in Heimat (or in anti-

Heimat).[5] Thus, in every Heimat conceptualization, time — which is an experienced time, to be sure, rather than an objectified time — is the protagonist, either by shaping bodies, lives, and generations or by working and changing landscapes, houses, cemeteries,[6] farms, and orchards.

In Heimat, small communities live in situations where time and space are, to use a phrase from Giddens's *Modernity and Self-Identity,* "essentially linked through place" (16). A constant temporal and spatial availability of others exists. Communication occurs face-to-face rather than through means that would allow for a spatial or a temporal distance (writing, telephone, fax, e-mail). Where in modern societies, as Giddens observes in several of his books, a faceless trust has become crucial to every interaction with anonymous, abstract systems, in Heimat conceptualizations an impersonal trust in systems and symbols is irrelevant because everything in this locality is known (*bekannt* and *gekannt*). If modernity is "essentially a post-traditional order" (Giddens 1991, 20), then Heimat is a posttraditional reestablishment of an idealized traditional order.

On a more general level one might add that if dialectics is the positive of the negative (Hegel's third form of logic — that is, the logic of speculation or of positive reason [vol. 8, 176–77]), if dialectics through sublimation (or sublation) of the negative is negative and positive at the same time, then Heimat conceptualizations and their effects in history can be seen as the negative of the positive — that is, as the negative, speculative, synthesizing counterdialectics from within modernity and dialectics itself. Heimat is consolation and promise of happiness for those who no longer wish to participate in (the illusion of) the dialectical push forward into the ever new. But by no longer wishing to participate, they *are* part of the new and are participants in the dialectic.

The change from a premodern to a modern society and its fundamental effects on our posttraditional Western lives, as well as on the way we think about change, have been undone in conceptualizations of Heimat. This is one important respect in which the idea of Heimat and the primitive differ. Modern life has supposedly not yet crossed the boundaries that isolate that which it regards as the primitive — the mountain regions in New Guinea, say, or the tribal country in the Upper Amazon region, or Tahiti as Paul

Gauguin painted it. Heimat constructs, by contrast, are usually situated in a locality that is part of, and yet in many ways supposedly untouched by, the modern world. But nature in Heimat is perceived — a characteristic of modernity — as beautiful, not as cruel or as a workplace providing uneasy but authentic survival. Women in Heimat are — again a sign of modernity — feminine and refined, never sexually overt or possessing ambitions, for public office, for example. Childhood — again typically modern — is a time of charming, innocent sunshine. And identity constructs — typically modern — provide, like Heimat, exclusive spaces of harmony and authenticity.

On the other hand, modernity seems in other significant ways not to have reached Heimat conceptualizations. Nothing in Heimat operates on the basis of "faith in impersonal principles." Most important, reflexivity and reason are not an issue. To be sure, the rise of the notion of the individual, the self, the unity of the thinking subject that organizes nature as an object of experience has occurred but, it seems, without causing any rifts that would separate human existence from traditional, mythic life, which exists the same way it has always existed. There is no need for any reconciliation between subject and object or between thought and being or between essence and appearance or between nature and culture. Such a rift has either not occurred or has magically healed in the space of Heimat.

Jürgen Habermas's Modernity and Heimat

Jürgen Habermas's views on modernity are more complex and less readily accessible but just as rewarding as Anthony Giddens's. We find the most comprehensive and explicit statements by Habermas on the concept of modernity in the first lecture of his *Der philosophische Diskurs der Moderne* (1985). There he first recapitulates modernity as Max Weber, Emile Durkheim, and G. H. Mead — the "classic authors of social theory" (10) — saw it: the image of modernity is shaped by Weber's descriptions of the uniquely Western European development of secular reason. For Weber, this development brought about a domination of human institutions by a differentiated, bureaucratically and economically crystallized purposive rationality (that is, by a process of disenchantment). Also,

Durkheim's and Mead's emphases on reflexive interactions with traditions, which have lost their presumed naturalness (their *Naturwüchsigkeit*), helped shape the image of modernity, as did their emphasis on a rationally derived generalization of norms and values; these emphases enlarge the space for choices from previously narrowly defined traditions. Also important are modern patterns of socialization, which strongly encourage abstract ego-identities and individuation.

Modernization as we understand the term today, however, was not introduced until the 1950s, when Weber's critics and supporters alike changed his concept of modernity by bringing about an abstraction of the concept. This abstraction removed modernity from its modern European origins and stylized it "to a pattern of a general developmental process that can be neutralized in terms of space and time" (10). Thus, the inner connections between the concept of modernity and the ascendancy of reason in European history were severed.

After Habermas discusses the effects of the severance between modernization and rationalization and how the term *postmodernism* could become the banner of a neoconservative farewell to modernity, he challenges what are in his hands the rather immobile and passive proponents of postmodernism. Theories of postmodernity, according to Habermas, claim to have left behind the horizons that formed modernity. To see whether they really did so we need to return, Habermas says, to the first philosopher who developed a clear concept of modernity: Hegel. Skillfully he foreshadows his findings; maybe the neoconservatives, the proponents of the concept of postmodernity, are only rebelling against modernity by calling it a farewell: "Maybe, possibly, they are only cloaking their complicity with an old, honorable tradition of counter-enlightenment with [their label of] post-enlightenment" (13).

Hegel uses the concept of modernity as a designation of an era — as in "modern times," which for Hegel circa 1800 meant the three centuries since the discovery of the New World. Habermas points out that the modern world differs from the old one in that its every present continuously renews itself and its relation to the ever new and newly actualized past. As examples he lists the ever new contents and relationships to the past of such terms as *revolution, progress, emancipation, development, crisis,* and *Zeitgeist* [the spirit of the time]. Modernity, in German fittingly referred to as *Neuzeit* — literally, "new time," "new era," or "time of new-ness" — continuously has to create its normativity out of itself anew: "Modernity always sees itself, without an opportunity for escape, referred back to itself" (16). Habermas further observes that "this explains modernity's irritability in its self-perception, explains the dynamics of the restless attempts, continued into our age, to define and 'anchor' itself" (16).[7]

Even though philosophers from late medieval times to Kant had already expressed, in one way or another, the self-perception and self-consciousness of modernity, it is Hegel who turns it into a philosophical problem. In fact, Habermas writes, Hegel perceives the issue of self-perception and self-consciousness "as *the basic problem* of his philosophy" (26, Habermas's emphasis). Hegel first discovers subjectivity, characterized by freedom and reflection, as *the* modern principle. This subjectivity, for Hegel, means, above all, four things: individualism, the right to critique, the autonomy of and responsibility for our actions, and, finally, idealistic philosophy itself. Hegel, according to Habermas, considers it the accomplishment of modernity that "philosophy comes to an understanding of the idea that knows itself" (27).

The key historical events for the success of the principle of subjectivity are the Reformation, the Enlightenment, and the French Revolution. During the Reformation religious belief structures became reflexive, hermeneutic authority became subjective, and religion turned inward, which suddenly made the host dough and the relict bone (28). Furthermore, the proclamation of human rights and the Code Napoleon validated freedom of the will as a foundational right within any political state structure. The principle of subjectivity became formative for modern, objectivizing science (by disenchanting nature and by liberating the perceiving subject), for moral concepts (the Kantian imperative), and for modern art (the absolute inwardness of Romanticism, Schlegel's irony reflecting the self-perceptions of a decentered I).

In modernity, Habermas summarizes, "religious life, the state and society, science, morality, and art, all turn into embodiments of the principle of subjectivity" (29). Both Descartes's *cogito ergo sum* and Kant's absolute self-awareness [*Selbstbewußtsein*] show the reflexive structure wherein the perceiving subject simultaneously conceives of itself as a subject and perceives itself also as an object.[8] Kant uses this reflexive approach as the basis for his three *Critiques* — of pure reason, of practical reason, and of the capacity for judgment. For Kant, reason, reflectively divided into its different aspects, is, according to Habermas, "the highest tribunal in front of which everything that claims validity has to justify itself" (29).

Habermas asks whether this principle of subjectivity can possibly provide modernity with standards, standards that have to come out of the modern world itself and give it a sense of orientation. These standards have to be useful for critiquing a modernity that has fragmented and become distanced from itself.[9] The answer is, of course, that the principle of subjectivity proves to be one-sided. It could be used to undermine the power of religion, which was the only power that could unify [*einigende Macht*], but it is not strong enough "to regenerate the religious power of unification [*Macht der Vereinigung*] within the medium of reason" (31).[10]

The sexual connotations carried by the German *einigende Macht* and *Vereinigung* are lost in their translation into English. But here, in discussing the unifying power of religion, Habermas is subtly pointing to its sexual aspect as well as to its regenerating force, which did not become part of the "proud culture of reflection" (31). (Chapter 4 of this study, "Heimat and the Feminine," will address this point in detail.)

To show the split between belief and knowledge inherent in the disappearance of religion, a split that reason by itself cannot overcome, Hegel uses the term *Entzweiung* [splitting into two]. Philosophy, for Hegel, thus replaces religion as the power to provide harmony and unity (vol. 2, 22–23; qtd. in Habermas 31–32).

But this *Entzweiung,* as Hegel soon realizes, cannot be truly overcome. During his years in Jena (1801 to 1807) Hegel abandons his "mythopoetic version of a reconciliation with modernity" (Habermas 33), which he had shared with his classmates Hölderlin and Schelling. And in *Phänomenologie des Geistes* [Phenomenology of the Spirit, 1806–7] Hegel introduces *Entfremdung* [alienation], as well as Absolute Knowledge, into Western philosophy. In so doing, according to Habermas, he both "steps beyond the products of the Enlightenment (Romantic art, religion of reason, and bourgeois society)" and falls behind the intuition of his younger years: "In the end he has to deny the self-understanding of modernity the possibility of a critique of modernity" (33).[11]

What can we learn from this discussion about Heimat? First, in most uses of the idea of Heimat traditions regain their *Naturwüchsigkeit*. Norms and values exist without the need for options, for identity, or for individualization. When Habermas summarizes that in modernity, "religious life, the state and society, science, morality, and art all turn into embodiments of the principle of subjectivity" (29), his observation that the principle of subjectivity can undermine the power of religion but is not strong enough "to regenerate the religious power of unification within the medium of reason" aims toward places where in German culture we find manifestations of Heimat. Habermas's suggestion that the unifying power of religion did not become part of the "proud culture of reflection" is not entirely correct. Through linked notions of Heimat, childhood, nature, and family a kind of religious union did bring its regenerating forces into the culture of reflection. But it did so by neutralizing almost everything on which the culture of reflection is based. Heimat is childhood in adulthood, the feminine in the masculine, reason without consciousness or alienation (if such an irrational reason can be imagined), nature without death.

Eduard Spranger's extremely influential short book *Der Bildungswert der Heimatkunde* [The Educational Value of Heimat Studies] shows us this perception of Heimat quite dramatically. The book has gone through many editions since it first appeared in 1923, including at least six since the Second World War.[12] Spranger's preface to the second Reclam edition, dated November 27, 1948, quotes his preface to the first edition: "This educational program, born out of the difficulties of the time, would show us a path which leads back to the unity of the people and to the unity in ourselves, that is, it wants to show a program that in both senses leads us back to our true [*eigentlich*] Heimat" (3). The book goes on to argue for the educational value of teaching Heimat, as a German professor of pedagogy such as Spranger perceived it and as German professors of education often still perceive it:

> In our soul, there exists a corner where we are all poets. Whatever stands in connection with our childhood and our Heimat lives in us in such magic colors that not even the greatest painter could depict it; Heimat lives in us with such tender and yearning

feelings, which float and melt into one another, that we would not find satisfaction in this area by even the most sublime lyrical expression. . . . Something deeply religious resonates in the experience of Heimat — even for those who don't want to admit it; and if we say about someone that he has no Heimat then it is as if we said that his deeper existence had no center [*keinen Mittelpunkt*]. In one word: Heimat belongs to the most subjective things in a human life. The content of such emotional values seems to shrink away from any expression.[13] But Heimat is not emotional value alone. The segment of the earth which we call Heimat also has its very specific, objective qualities which can be grasped [*erfasst*] as knowledge. The true and deeper love for one's Heimat is based on the deeper knowledge of this objective essence of Heimat. Therefore we look for Heimat*kunde* [Spranger's italics]. We find in this teaching the natural and spiritual roots of our existence. (5)

This first page of *Der Bildungswert der Heimatkunde* sets out several crucial concepts that contributed to the power of Heimat in the classroom for decades to come (the booklet was written for teachers who were being taught to teach Heimat). All the key words and phrases in this passage point in the direction of the irrational celebration of the rational bourgeois subject: *soul, poet, childhood, lives in us, magic colors, tender and yearning feelings, religious, experience, existence, essence, center,* and *roots*. Clearly, Heimat, for all its antirational qualities, by 1923 has become a principal instrument in the elevation of students to that Humboldtian ideal of bourgeois individuality with its great humanistic goals of reason, self, independence, uniqueness, and the capacity to judge and critique.

(If one thinks of Heimat's close links to nationalist ideas, one might assume from this excerpt that Spranger did well under the National Socialist regime. But despite his writings on Heimat, which were put to propagandistic use by the National Socialists [the first Reclam edition of *Der Bildungswert der Heimatkunde* appeared in 1943], Spranger did not feel any affinity for Hitler's party. In April 1933 Spranger resigned from his post in Berlin but allowed himself to be persuaded to stay on. A decade of increasing tensions and then a year-long guest professorship in Japan followed. After the events of July 20, 1944, Spranger was incarcerated in Moabit Prison in Berlin. The Japanese ambassador intervened, and Spranger was released after ten weeks. This fact did not, how-

ever, keep the National Socialists from sending the author Ernst
Wiechert to Buchenwald for supporting Spranger [Kaes 1983,
679].)

To return to Habermas and his understanding of modernity,
we see that in the modern idea of Heimat modernity's split between belief and knowledge — a split that reason, according to
Habermas, cannot overcome by itself — finally does not have to
confront its failure. Heimat is free "to deny the self-perception of
modernity the possibility of a critique of modernity" (33). Hegel's
notions of *Entfremdung,* the alienation of the self-conscious spirit
from a reality of which the spirit itself is part (vol. 3, 359–92), and
of Absolute Knowledge, an idealized or perfected form of knowledge as "the last form of the spirit" (vol. 3, 585) in which *Entfremdung* would be conciliated, are also not issues in conceptualizations of Heimat. This kind of self-reflection and self-awareness,
this stepping away from and outside of oneself to look at oneself,
either is nullified in conceptualizations of Heimat, or this "primal
setting at a distance," as Martin Buber called it (summarized in
Soja 132), has never occurred. In other words, in the idea of Heimat German culture has retained its "mythopoetic version of a reconciliation with modernity" (Habermas 33). The step Hegel makes
during his years in Jena — away from mythopoetic reconciliation
and toward a system that incorporates alienation while holding out
the almost unattainable hope of Absolute Knowledge — never becomes part of the idea of Heimat.

In Heimat, self-perception [*Selbstverständnis*] does not become
an issue. Those having a Heimat are the lucky ones (or the limited
ones) for whom, as long as they are in their Heimat, neither self
nor perception nor reason can unfold its power for differentiation.
Needless to say, reconciliation as a healing from *Entfremdung* —
from alienation — never becomes an issue, because alienation has
supposedly never happened.

In sum, Habermas's views on modernity that circle around reflexivity and the history of Western reason give us a clear picture of
what Heimat denies and how it effects this denial. But we should
not allow this clarity to tempt us. We could, indeed, see Heimat as
a not overly complex antimodern idea if we test it only against
Habermas's more philosophical concept of modernity. If we re-

member Giddens, though, we need to inquire further into contradictions, or at least tensions, attending the implementation of
Heimat in modernity. In subsequent chapters I will do this for the
idea of Heimat in relation to identity, gender, nature, and childhood. In the conclusion to this chapter I will look at Heimat's relationship to the modern concepts of irony and of time and to the
nation-state, for with regard to time, space, and the imaginary
Heimat maintains a curious balance between specificity and a
mythic generality. There are no literal maps of anyone's Heimat;
and yet, Heimat often gestures toward the specific as far as space
and time are concerned. In Heimat the imaginary and a supposed
reality are not separated; subject and object are reconciled; and
thus Heimat, as we will see, is a space free from irony.

Heimat: A Space Free from Irony

The modern use of the word Heimat — its use as a trope or a concept, rather than in the material sense of "homestead" or as a simple synonym for *paradise* — first occurred during the last decades
of the eighteenth century, a time when the Western world experienced one of its most dramatic reevaluations. As Martin Walser,
still mostly unaware of the options gender studies would add to
Western categories of thinking within a decade and a half, noted in
the first sentence of his 1981 study *Ironie und Selbstbewußtsein*
[Irony and Self-Consciousness]: "The 1790s are probably still the
most interesting decade in the history of those deeds that occur on
paper because reality at that time was still short of one possibility"
(13).[14] The idea of Heimat was very much a part of discovering this
missing possibility of the eighteenth century, which is, of course,
the modern concept of irony. In irony, as Peter Uwe Hohendahl
says in summarizing Lukács, "the attitude of the creative subject
(the writer) toward reality [is described] after he has realized his
own problematic status in this world" (61). Self-consciousness, reflexivity, and irony — "the insight into the discrepancy between
[one's] own desire for a meaningful life and the alienated reality"
(61) — are symptoms of the same developments that produced our
modern notions of Heimat: to long for a Heimat and to perceive
Heimat, we had to become mobile and homeless. Heimat is the
imaginary space where a reconciliation with an alienated, moving

world occurs because the distance between self and self-consciousness is not part of this imaginary real world called Heimat. Therefore, Heimat is a modern haven without irony. (This insight allows us to appreciate fully Friedrich Schlegel's 1797 banner phrase for the theory of irony: "Philosophy is the true Heimat of irony" [152].)

Heimat is related to Schlegel's concept of irony, but it is his concept turned around. Schlegel's irony, which is reflected in the self-experience of a "decentered I" (Habermas 28) for which, as Hegel writes, "all ties have been severed and which wants to live only in the bliss of enjoying itself with its self" (vol. 13, 95),[15] has found its complete cure and denial in Heimat. This finds expression, as well, in a long tradition of German *Heimkehr* literature: literature from Hölderlin to Handke that describes coming home as a self-healing. Reflection, self, experience, center, and ties are all nonissues in Heimat, where unmediated experience occurs in an ideal space (landscape, nature) or in an ideal time (of childhood, of the mother).

Writing probably in 1801, Hölderlin depicts Heimat in his famous poem "Heimkunft"[16] as a place where "everything seems familiar, the 'hello' rushing by / seems from friends, every expression of the faces seems part of oneself."[17] Heimat's first quality here is that it "seems" [*scheint*]. Heimat seems "vertraut" [familiar], "von Freunden" [from friends], and "verwandt" [part of oneself]. One might at first be tempted to look at this Heimat as mostly appearance ("it seems"). But the verb *scheinen* in German signifies not only "to appear" but also "to shine" or "to glow," as with light. Thus, Heimat in this poem, as in many other instances,[18] becomes that which shines, here with familiarity and friends and family. (Heidegger, in his *Einführung in die Metaphysik* [Introduction into Metaphysics], after having just intensively studied Hölderlin, distinguishes at length three ways of *scheinen* that closely resemble the three ways one can understand *scheinen* in this passage by Hölderlin: "Looked at more closely, we find three ways of shining: First, shining as glowing, as bright light; secondly, shining as appearing, as to shine out; thirdly, shining as mere shining, the appearance that something creates. . . . The essence of shining lies in its appearing" [107].[19])

The wanderer who speaks in this Hölderlin poem then exults:
"Of course! It is the birthland, the soil of the Heimat."[20] And the
following lines suggest that Heimat is both goal and origin, is a
return by moving forward. Here it is a return to the womb of the
mother, which is expressed as landscape. Hölderlin connects the
mother and the landscape several times when he talks about
"birthland" ["Geburtsland"], and the wandering man who "stands
like a son at the wave-surrounded / gate and looks and searches
for loving names for you."[21] These already erotic lines ("wave-
surrounded gate," "loving names") are followed by an ecstatic ex-
clamation that lets us know who this "you" is for whom "loving
names" are being sought: "blissfully happy Lindau!" ["glückseliges
Lindau!"]. With this "Lindau" Hölderlin refers to the city on the
shores of Lake Constance. The next stanza completes the union,
fulfills the fusional utopia, relieves existence from anxiety, from
Entzweiung, from that source of irony, the being one and two at
the same time: "There they receive me. O voice of the city, voice
of my mother!"[22]

In Heimat all the ties severed through an ironic gaze have
magically been reconnected: community, youth, a union with nature, landscape, some sheltering feminine side of human existence — all these magically preserved values give the I the chance
to eat its cake and have it, too. In conceptualizations of Heimat
one may live in the bliss of enjoying oneself with one's community-
based self without experiencing the alienation and solitude that are
the usual price for a self-reflexive existence. It is an antidote against
irony, against the alienation of having a self-conscious, reflexive,
and rational self: Heimat is a secular irrationalization of a joyful
self. The differentiated, bureaucratically and economically crystallized purposive rationality has been nullified by a process of reenchantment.

Heimat: A Mythicized Sense of Time

The modern conceptualization of time is, according to Giddens,
one of the main alienating factors in modernity. In *The Nation-
State and Violence* (1985) Giddens describes in interesting detail
the standardization of a world time. Until 1870 there existed as
many as eighty railway times in the United States alone. These

were coordinated in 1883. Not until 1912, after the International Conference on Time in Paris, was there a standard for specifying time and for transmitting time signals around the world (175–76). During roughly the same period — the last decades of the nineteenth century and the first decade of the twentieth — railway, mail, and the telegraph system carved themselves into changing social systems and into the public imagination. At the heart of modern organization, Giddens points out, lies the timetable and its ability to coordinate space and time.

Modern consciousness of time is usually seen in opposition to an earlier, tradition-dependent, more mythic living in and with time. Pierre Bourdieu, writing on the Kabyle people of Algeria, notes in his *Outline of a Theory of Practice* (1972): "The organization of time and the group in accordance with mythical structures leads collective practice to appear as 'realized myth,' in the sense in which for Hegel tradition is 'realized morality' (*Sittlichkeit*)" (159). From our modern perspective, there is the appearance of a prior interaction with time, one where time was perceived as a nonobjectifiable entity inseparable from the social fabric of human interactions. What we perceive as this nonobjectifiable quality also finds expression, as Marianna Torgovnick points out in *Gone Primitive* (1990), in our "fetishistic attention to the dating" of Western art, whereas what is considered primitive lies somewhere outside of this dating and is consequently considered "timeless" (121). (That time has masculine, public connotations, whereas sooner or later the tropes for the primitive become the tropes conventionally used for women [Torgovnick 17] will be addressed in chapter 4, "Heimat and the Feminine.")

"Modern time-consciousness," Habermas writes, "forbids of course every thought of regression, every thought of an unmediated return to mythic origins. Only the future brings the horizon for the awakening of mythic pasts" (108).[23] This view of Habermas's on modern time-consciousness and its relation to regression may be slightly overstated. It is only true if we understand regression literally as a stepping backwards. But regression in our modern time-consciousness can only come out of the future.

From this shift toward the future comes as well our assumption — expressed by Walter Benjamin in his second and third thesis on the concept of history — that all past eras seem to us, the ones presently living, in need of redemption. Every generation before us seems to have waited for its redemption through us. To turn something into Heimat is just such an act of redemption through regression. The springing up of small Heimat museums in every town in Germany, Austria, and Switzerland during the 1970s and 1980s is only one of the latest manifestations of this phenomenon. The early Nietzsche's use of Heimat provides another, quite disturbing, example.

The Nietzsche of *Die Geburt der Tragödie,* as was briefly mentioned in the introduction, sees Heimat where the split between the Apollonian and the Dionysian has been overcome. The return to the *Urheimat* [the original Heimat] is the goal behind the "brotherly bond between the two gods of art [Apollo and Dionysos] in tragedy" (vol. 1, 141).[24] In the next section of *Die Geburt der Tragödie* we read (and we will look at this passage again in chapter 4, "Heimat and the Feminine"):

> What does the enormous historic need of dissatisfied modern culture point to, the collecting of countless other cultures around oneself, the consuming will to know, if not to the loss of myth, to the loss of the mythic Heimat, the mythical womb of the mother? (vol. 1, 146)[25]

Modern, Faustian man who looks for new myths behind his mythless existence finds the beginning of his search exposed quite dramatically here. The mythic womb of the mother had to be abandoned — a loss that can be understood in two ways: the mother's womb itself was mythic, and the time of myth was like a mother's womb.

Nietzsche, who felt that he "came into the fatherhood of this book" somewhat by accident (vol. 1, 11), uses Heimat no fewer than eleven times in the last five sections (twenty-five pages) of *Die Geburt der Tragödie.* Invocations of Heimat are, however, not only numerous but also diverse. Heimat instinct can be "ejaculated": Nietzsche expresses surprise that the Greeks after the Persian Wars are still able to have "such an even, strong ejaculation of the most basic political sensation, of the most natural Heimat instinct, of the original manly lust to fight" (vol. 1, 132–33).[26] In times of strong Dionysian excitement, during which the shackles of Apollonian individuality are loosened, "state [as in nation] and sense of Heimat can nevertheless not live without an approval of the individual personality" (vol. 1, 133).[27] A flight toward one's *Urheimat* can be the highest orgiastic pleasure one can experience through art — here he offers the example of experiencing the music of *Tristan und Isolde* (vol. 1, 135–36). Academics are a limited bunch because they are stuck in their aesthetic terminology and know nothing about the union between the two gods of art — they know nothing about the original pleasure of art, this return to the *Urheimat* (vol. 1, 141–42). Heimat is associated with Germany, which has to excrete the foreign — for instance, the Romanic — elements; this excretion, however, will be impossible without bringing back the German household gods, that is, without the Germans' mythic Heimat (vol. 1, 149). Wagner's music, for instance, can bring back this "long lost Heimat" (vol. 1, 149): "Let no one believe that the German spirit has lost its mythic Heimat forever as long as it still understands so clearly the birds' voices which tell of that Heimat" (vol. 1, 154).[28] The worst "for all of us" Germans, however, "is the long humiliation under which the German genius, alienated from house and Heimat, lived in the service of treacherous dwarfs" (vol. 1, 154).[29]

Heimat in this early work by Nietzsche stands for several things, but exactly what these are remains unclear. The term is always yoked to origins, to a time of myth, and clearly connotes a positive aspect; often it seems the deepest wellspring itself. It is hard to miss the overtly sexual imagery of these references. To Nietzsche, the birth of tragedy is literally a sexual conception. It is progression, regression, and redemption in one. Therefore, Heimat appears variously as sperm, as orgasm, as the radiant energy of the fusion of the Apollonian and the Dionysian. And it is part of the mythic origins of the Germans. Heimat references are inexactly differentiated but are always a surge of energy, like music or orgasm, or a primal source, like the womb.

The early Nietzsche sees Heimat — or, rather, the loss of the mythic Heimat — as standing at the beginning of modernity's quest for knowledge and self-knowledge; and, in the end, Heimat stands, as well, for a way of healing modern culture's immense discontent from having lost myth and the mythic Heimat. He sees true tragedy as providing such a Heimat, a way to overcome the deep cultural rift between the Dionysian and the Apollonian. It is in drama, and in particular in Wagner's operas, that the early Nietzsche sees that "the state and society, in general the rifts between one human being and another, are replaced by an overpowering sense of unity which leads us back to the heart of nature" (vol. 1, 56).[30] This goal of being led "back to the heart of nature," to a mythical experience of time, is what all his conceptualizations of Heimat hope to provide.

When we look at the early Nietzsche, we find that Heimat is wherever he sees a ray of hope in an otherwise bleak world, for thus he depicts modern man's push forward into the sunlit desert of progress — individuality, consciousness, and knowledge. Heimat, for the early Nietzsche, is where present and past, self and nature, reason and will, experience and music are fused. Heimat is where the newly awakened German genius might find itself. (The late Nietzsche will see Heimat as one of those ideas of Judeo-Christian modernity that reveal and support the Western slave-morality by hinging it on some notion of salvation. Heimat is one of the many ideas that the late Nietzsche's *Übermensch* had to stand above. Nietzsche's assessments of Heimat and of Wagner's music follow a perfectly parallel pattern — both are glorified in *Die Geburt der Tragödie,* and both are later presented as having to be left behind in order for the human to reach the *Übermensch* stage.)

We see how Heimat, a locale and a past with transcendental qualities, offers a mythic union, a simplification that we usually associate with tradition. For some, as for the young Nietzsche, this mythic union occurs in art. Past and present, an outer geography (for instance, Germany) and an inner identity naïvely (regressively) expressed outwardly, become one and receive the halo of a redemption in the present that in celebrating what it sees as its tradition celebrates a localized, mythic past.

Heimat, the German Nation-State, and Herder's Cultural Nationalism

The assumption that the regional and local — especially when it is supposedly closer to the traditional and mythical because it is rural — is politically innocent is a basic assumption underlying notions of Heimat. Everything associated with the experience of modernization — the politicization of the everyday, urbanization, alienation in professional and private arenas, alienation in increased mobility, in education, in money, in developments of the nation-state — is negated. In conceptualizations of Heimat the modern nation-state with all its preconditions and by-products simply seems not to exist. Even during the National Socialist period, when Heimat was an important element in propaganda of German superiority, Heimat generally was localized. Where Heimat became synonymous with *Deutschland* during this period, one can observe that the concept of *Deutschland* became at once localized and mythicized: mythic racism, for instance, made *Deutschland* one Heimat (that is to say, like in the early Nietzsche, a locality). In other words, *Deutschland* itself had assumed qualities usually associated with Heimat and not with the modern nation-state.

But, of course, it is not as easy as that. The German idea of Heimat is, strangely, an antinational construct that historically has always served to support a broad and not clearly defined nationalism. German nationalistic sentiment and the German notion of Heimat have always played into each other. Whenever deep shifts in the self-definition of Germany as a nation took place, Heimat was there to counterbalance (in the case of loss of territory and its accompanying phantom pains) and to help integrate (in the case of expansions). Positive Heimat images were conspicuous at such critical junctures in German history as produced Napoleon together with Eichendorff, Bismarck together with Fontane, Hitler and the *Heimatfilm* genre, and the 1950s and the still thriving *Heimatfilm*. The positive Heimat images have also contributed to the success of the Green Party, of the PDS (successor party of the former SED, the single political party of the former East Germany) in the new states, and the continued success of the CSU in Bavaria.

Thus, by celebrating their local beer, their local detergent, their local soccer clubs, their *Trabi*, their tree cakes, their East German *Heimatroman* [Heimat novel] and their *Ostalgie* [nostalgia for the former East German culture], the former East Germans are actually integrating themselves into German Heimat traditions, even though they think that they are defining themselves against Germany as a whole. (In a variation of this process of integration through Heimat sentiments held in common, the boundaries of the new states in 1989 and 1990 at once took account of local identities and, thus, of a past that jumped back to pre-1945. As

Christian Graf von Krockow observes in the afterword to the post-reunification paperback edition of his *Heimat: Erfahrungen mit einem deutschen Thema* [Heimat: Experiences With a German Theme, 1989]: the small Catholic enclave of Eichsfelde, for instance, which had been divided between the two Germanies, celebrated, as soon as the Wall fell, "the 'we' of their sense of Heimat" [159–60].)

The idea of Heimat is both part of the development toward a German nation-state and the expression of an uneasiness with everything that goes along with this development — capitalization, industrialization, politicization. Bismarck, who always knew the limits of possibilities, opposed the exportation of Prussian culture into other regions of Germany — at least overtly. He did not want a centralization as in France or England but preferred to "absorb all German individualities without nullifying them" (qtd. in Hans Schmitt 41). Particularism, often expressed in emphatically localized Heimat sentiments, was and is an essential ingredient of the German nation-state — the nation-state as an administrative and political, as well as an imaginary, entity.

To understand how it was possible for the particularizing idea of Heimat to become part of the German movement toward a nation-state we first have to take a step back and look at the curious and puzzling interrelations between nationalism, "Germandom," the modern German nation-state, and Heimat: in other words, we must survey German geocultural conceptualization in a wider historical context.

Norbert Elias's analysis of German peculiarities can assist us here (whether we subscribe completely to Elias's terminology and categories or not). Elias, in his *Studien über die Deutschen: Machtkämpfe und Habitusentwicklung im 19. und 20. Jahrhundert* [The Germans: Power Struggles and the Development of Habitus in the Nineteenth and Twentieth Centuries, 1989], emphasizes four special aspects of German development toward the modern nation-state. He begins by pointing out that Germanic and then German-speaking tribes were never protected by natural boundaries. The geographical situation of German speakers, between peoples who spoke Latin-derived languages on their western and southern borders and Slavic-speaking peoples on their eastern border, was special in that the edges of the German territory east-, south-, and westward constantly moved. Every side ruthlessly took advantage of the others' weaknesses. Today's tensions in Belgium between Flemish and Walloon are, according to Elias, as much a part of this struggle between Latin-derived language groups and Germanic language groups as were the historic territorial disputes in Alsace-Lorraine (8–9).

Elias sees the second Germanic peculiarity as closely linked to the first: the uncertainty about its borders finds an equivalence in the inner identity constitutions of German-speakers. "They suffer," he writes, "from a physical uncertainty, doubt their self-worth, feel themselves debased and humiliated, and they have a tendency toward wishful dreams [*Wunschträume*] about the revenge they want to take on those who have brought their situation upon them" (13). "The structural weakness of the German state" and related traumatic experiences — for instance, during the Thirty Years' War or in defeat at the hands of Napoleon — bring with them, as Elias's summary shows, "a much idealized emphasis on military attitudes and warlike actions" (13–14) on the social level, as well as on the level of personal identity structures.

The third special aspect in Germany's achievement of modern statehood Elias sees in the many breaks and discontinuities of the process. He looks at the capitals of France, England, and Germany over the last 1,000 years as symbolic illustrations. London and Paris were consistently the capitals of England and France, while Berlin is a young city. Vienna and Prague were other capitals for German *Kaiser* [emperor] and *König* [king]. But no one remembers that when Walther von der Vogelweide was in Vienna in the late twelfth century, long before it became the capital of the Habsburg Empire, he was there as a member of the court of the Frankonian-Bavarian Babenberger. The German kaisers of the time, Frederick I Barbarossa and Henry VI — I might add to illustrate Elias's point — came from the Staufer dynasty and held court in any number of *Pfalzen* [palaces]; their ancestral castle (of which only vestiges now remain) was located on the Hohenstaufen, which today, compared to London and Paris, represents a not very famous hill northeast of the not very famous Swabian town of Göppingen.

Germany is full of sharp stops and radically new beginnings: 1918 and 1945 are just two recent extreme ones, and 1933 is another. In another discontinuity, eighteenth-century court culture hardly became part of what Elias calls throughout his book *der deutsche Habitus* [the German *habitus*], a never explicitly defined national character based in language, traditions, customs, and history. Yet another break can be seen in the fact that, despite Wagner's *Die Meistersinger,* the culture of the German medieval city plays a rather negligible role in the image Germans have of themselves today (16–17).

The fourth special aspect is that in German history the Classical period in literature and philosophy was characterized by a sharp antagonism between bourgeois culture and the nobility at court. German bourgeois culture was virtually cut off from access to political and military power. Goethe was an exception; but Weimar was a relatively small state with little influence. All of these factors resulted in a clear distance between military nobility and the ideals set forth by the German Classical period. Thus, much of German bourgeois culture during the nineteenth century adopted military ideals instead of those of German Idealism (21–23).

Elias's review of the special aspects of Germany's achieving modern statehood allows us to see several things, not the least of which is how German Idealism's ideals could remain so painfully and longingly distant — like K. in Franz Kafka's *Das Schloss* [The Castle] — from access to true power in the political and military spheres. The German educated middle class — in comparison to those of France and England — was left out of the political decision making process. K. never gains access to the castle.

This review of Elias's studies on the Germans leads us to the links between Germany, Germanhood, Heimat, and nationalism. We find the idea of Heimat in every one of Elias's special aspects of German development toward the modern nation-state. Heimat identifies German territory, with or without natural boundaries. Heimat reassures German speakers of their self-worth, their identity, and their uniqueness. Heimat is part of German speakers' "tendency toward wishful dreams [*Wunschträume*]"; in this case, however, the wishful dreams are not so much "about the revenge they want to take on those who have brought their situation upon them" as they are about how the world would be if only everything evil and foreign did not continually invade it. In this case, the violated Heimat is what lies at the beginning of the desire for revenge.

Also, Heimat is a way for German bourgeois culture to have ideals without having to — or being able to — prove and implement them in the political everyday.

All of this shows us Heimat as an aspect of German speakers' dealing with the many breaks and discontinuities in their modern history. Even if everything else changed, Heimat was still there and could still be relied on.

From this disempowered but ideal-ridden German bourgeoisie there arises, as well, the discrepancy between various forms of nationalism. German-speaking countries historically show — except during the National Socialist period, when such differences were to a large degree forcibly eliminated — a remarkable distance between political nationalism, expressed as the nation-state, and cultural-linguistic nationalism, expressed in cultural artifacts and in celebratory invocations of tradition.

The geographies where German is primarily spoken never coincide fully with Germany as a nation-state. The incongruency between linguistic-cultural nationalism and political nationalism in modern German history always creates a tension between "German" and "Germany." An answer to the question "What is Germany?" is usually possible; an answer to the question "What is German?" remains ever elusive. The very title of Hermann Bausinger's book on this subject, *Typisch deutsch: Wie deutsch sind die Deutschen?* [Typically German: How German Are the Germans? 2000] points to this incongruency.

A man who greatly helped to shape this difference between cultural-linguistic nationalism and political nationalism was Johann Gottfried Herder (1744–1803), a Lutheran minister whose writings, especially his early and most influential ones, represent a fascinating and highly formative combination for the future of European thought; he fashions a religious humanism enriched by a radical individualism that was probably derived in part from his Pietistic background but that he transfers to whole peoples, or what he calls "nations." He was a proponent of an experience- and tradition-based particularism, of communal identities, and of linguistic nationalism (the right to which he afforded to every nation). Thus, Herder was one of the first to be thrilled by Ossian and the original, authentic voices of each "*Volk*" [people] or "*Nation*."

Herder made abundant use of the term *nation* as well as of composites such as "*Nationalgeist*" [spirit of a nation], "*Genius der Nation*" [genius of a nation], and "*Nationalcharakter*" [character of a nation]. *Nation* was a key term that prompted eighteenth-century German philosophers to think about how people moved from traditional life in communities into modern societies. But nations were not the complex nation-states of the future. *Nation* was used synonymously with *Volk*. *Nationaltheater* at the time referred to the people's theater and stood in contrast to *Hoftheater,* the theater of the court. Nations were associated with origins, with life in communities. They were defined by a common tradition, a common past, and especially by a common language (which was, after all, the symbolic embodiment of this common tradition and past). In other words, during the time of most of Herder's writings there were no modern nation-states, and nationalism, a term Herder probably coined (Berlin 181), had quite different connotations from those it has now. (Isaiah Berlin writes that unlike Johann Gottlieb Fichte's or Friedrich von Schlegel's, "Herder's form of nationalism remained unaltered throughout his life" [156–57]. But then, Fichte died in 1814, Schlegel in 1829. Herder died in 1804, before Napoleon had inflicted his humiliation on German tradition and culture — that is, on what Herder would have thought of as the German *Volk* or the German nation.)[31]

Berlin, in his *Vico and Herder: Two Studies in the History of Ideas* (1976), discusses Herder as standing at the beginning of what Berlin calls Populism (a pluralistic *Völkisch*ness), Expressionism (not the period in art but the method of understanding through empathy [*Einfühlen*]), and Pluralism (human history for Herder was not a linear progression based on a commonly shared universal rational truth, because each culture and each period in each culture had its own truth). Herder's profound influence on European culture — often anonymously absorbed, as in the case of Hegel, rather than acknowledged — has not, however, exhausted itself with these three already immense contributions. Herder was also, as Berlin writes, "the father of the related notions of nationalism, historicism, and the *Volksgeist,* one of the leaders of the romantic revolt against classicism, rationalism, and faith in the omnipotence of scientific method" (145). In addition, he was a "dominant influence on . . . existentialism, and, above all, on social psychology, which he all but founded" (147).

Herder absorbed Jean-Jacques Rousseau into the tradition of German thought. (The idea of Heimat in the modern sense and the works of Rousseau begin to appear at about the same time in German intellectual life. As early as 1762 the first German translation, by Johann Jakob Schwabe, of Rousseau's *Émile* offers an instance in which "*son pays*" is rendered into German as "Heimat." "The Heimat of the rich man," we read there, "is every place where money can do everything" [250].[32] Later translators of Rousseau's oeuvre, including *Émile,* use the term Heimat much more frequently.) Like Rousseau, Herder saw culture as something natural and the organized state as "the coldest of all cold monsters" (Berlin 162). Nations — in contrast to states — were organisms that grew and changed through some inexplicably present *Kräfte* [strengths]. He attributed the different developments of culture (differences in languages, customs, histories, traditions, etc.) to a large degree to physical and geographical factors, to which he referred under the general term (absorbed from Montesquieu) of "climate." No nation, however, was superior to another. "To brag about one's country," Herder writes in his 1794 *Briefe zur Beförderung der Humanität* [Letters in Promotion of Humanity] "is the stupidest form of boastfulness" (vol. 17, 211, Berlin's translation [157]).[33] Twenty years earlier he had written in *Auch eine Philosophie der Geschichte zur Bildung der Menschheit* [Yet Another Philosophy of History for the Education of Humanity]: "Each nation has it own center of bliss [*Mittelpunkt der Glückseligkeit*] in itself just as each ball has its own center of gravity [*Schwerpunkt*]" (vol. 5, 509).

What lies, however, "at the heart of all of Herder's ideas" according to Berlin is "the notion of belonging" (195). Herder "conceived and cast light upon the crucially important social function of 'belonging' — on what it is to belong to a group, a culture, a movement, a form of life" (194).

This central notion of "belonging" would, within a few years, become a central theme in German Romanticism. Thus, Herder can be seen as the one who intellectually prepared the scene for the German idea of Heimat to become what it has become since the late eighteenth century. Herder wrote that one needs to "feel at home." "Whoever does not feel at home," summarizes Berlin, "cannot create naturally, freely, generously, unself-consciously, in the manner Schiller called 'naïve,' and that Herder, whether he admits it or not, most admires and believes in" (196).

Berlin then presents his conclusion that all of Herder's talk about national character, *Volksgeist*, etc. "comes to this alone":

> His notion of what it is to belong to a family, a sect, a place, a period, a style, is the foundation of his populism, and of all the later conscious programmes for self-integration or re-integration among men who felt scattered, exiled, or alienated. (196–97)

To cut men off from their *Klima*, from their "living centre — from the texture to which they naturally belong . . . is to degrade, de-humanize, destroy them" (197). (Berlin expresses his suspicion here that "Hegel's famous definition of freedom as *bey sich selbst seyn* [to be at home with oneself, within oneself, and to be con-scious of oneself], as well as his doctrine of *Anerkennung* — recip-rocal recognition among men — . . . owe much to Herder's teaching" [199]. Where humans feel at home, they participate in what Berlin refers to as "collective individuality" [200, 212].) This concept of Herder's becomes, as Berlin points out, a precursor to the notion of alienation (202).

All of this reads like a definition of the idea of Heimat, except that Herder never uses the term. But what he presents as a basic precondition for feeling human and alive — the "notion of being at home," the sense of "feeling at home" — are what Heimat is all about: one's own language, one's own memory, one's own "cli-mate" of existence.

Berlin also points out a utopian aspect in Herder's thought, one of which Herder himself took no notice. It is a formative, as well as a characteristic, element in the idea of Heimat and is ac-companied here, as usual, by a striking unawareness. Berlin shows that Herder did not share Kant's and Hegel's opinion that the in-dividual must suffer for the improvement of the species. In fact, va-riety of any sort (of climates, nations, or languages) did not entail conflict (163). All peoples lived peacefully next to each other, each one in its own space and climate, which, as if by magic, never en-croach on anybody else's space and climate. This, again, is a basic quality of Heimat: it is free of conflict. The contemporary Austrian author Reinhard P. Gruber puts it as follows: "Even though the beauty of everyone's Heimat cannot be compared with the beauty of someone else's Heimat, because Heimat is incomparably beautiful, everyone (as well as every other one) would resist the idea that his Heimat should border on an un-Heimat" (322–23).[34]

Heimat can, to be sure, be victimized; but Heimat is where one feels at home, where one's language is spoken, where one has absorbed the climate so much that it is part of oneself without one's being aware of it. One becomes aware of it only after one has lost part of it through moving, education, a change in the fortunes of that geographical region one calls Heimat, or some other form of distanciation.

There is, to be sure, much discussion surrounding how truly innocent Herder was in his use of the term *nation*. He certainly celebrated every people's (that is, "nation's") language and tradition. No one nation had more rights than another, according to Herder, and he truly appreciated difference and pluralism. He fought the notions of universal truth and of one kind of reason. And he was truly shocked when the French Revolution turned ruthlessly violent — not without extensive use of the term *nation*. In 1794 he warned in *Briefe zur Beförderung der Humanität* of the dangers that "*Nationalwahn*" (vol. 17, 230) — national insanity, or, more to the point, insanity about one's nation — could bring about.

But Herder, in his many celebrations of the German nation, made much use of comparisons. He saw German and Germany in danger of losing themselves, especially in French culture, language, and reason. In his eyes the German nation needed to be rescued. This idea made for some rather violent turns of phrase in his writings — more violent than his own belief in a conflictless pluralism should have allowed. It is hard, if not impossible, to reconcile innocence with such lines as "Spew out . . . the Seine's ugly slime! // Germans, speak German!" (vol. 27, 129)[35] or "The philosophy of the French language hinders the philosophy of thoughts" (vol. 4, 427).[36]

Still, even if the innocence was not untroubled, and even if Herder's name became severely implicated in later bloody implementations of a German nationalism, his divisions and his celebrations of a prepolitical, or an apolitical, Germanness have endured as the basis of the notion that in the division between culture and politics, as in that between language and power, culture and language are fundamentally innocent, whereas politics and power are altogether capable of not being innocent. In that sense, even though he did not use the word Heimat in any of his major texts, Johann Gottfried Herder is the intellectual father of the modern German idea of Heimat as it relates to nationalism.[37]

Notes

[1] Thomas Burger's translation into English, which was consulted but not quoted here, omits the spatial metaphor "Binnenraum" ("Further Reflections on the Public Sphere," rpt. in *Habermas and the Public Sphere*, ed. Craig Calhoun [Cambridge: MIT Press, 1992], 421–61, here 428).

[2] Cf. also Carol Pateman, *The Sexual Contract* (Stanford CA: Stanford UP, 1988); Joan Landes, *Women and the Public Sphere in the Age of the French Revolution* (Ithaca NY: Cornell UP, 1988); and Geoff Eley, "Nations, Publics, and Political Cultures: Placing Habermas in the Nineteenth Century" in *Habermas and the Public Sphere*, 289–339, esp. 307–19.

[3] "In dieser existierenden Heimatlichkeit selbst, aber dann dem Geiste der Heimatlichkeit, in diesem Geiste des vorgestellten Beisichselbstseins, des Beisichselbstseins in seiner physikalischen, bürgerlichen, rechtlichen, sittlichen, politischen Existenz, in diesem Charakter der freien, schönen Geschichtlichkeit . . . liegt auch der Keim der denkenden Freiheit. . . ."

[4] "ihre geistige Wiedergeburt — was ihre eigentliche Geburt ist. . . ."

[5] During the 1970s and 1980s, as will be discussed in chapter 6, "Heimat and Innocence (in Childhood, in Religion, in Language, and in *Antiheimat*)," Germany saw an anti-Heimat trend in literature and film. Novelists, playwrights, and movie directors made it a point to show how brutal and full of bad smells the German Heimat truly was, if you dared to notice. This Heimat exposed how much the traditional Heimat is based on an abuse of women, on cruelly enforced hierarchies, and on an unquestioned legitimacy of propertied interests. But these anti-Heimat authors and directors, as well, had to privilege space and turn locale into a given entity in their works. See also the chapter "'Heimatliteratur' or 'Antiheimatliteratur'" in my *Maria Beig und die Kunst der scheinbaren Kunstlosigkeit* [Maria Beig and the Art of Appearing Primitive] (Eggingen: Edition Isele, 1997).

[6] Cf. Mikhail Bakhtin's discussion of the cemetery topos in his *Formen der Zeit im Roman* [Forms of Time in the Novel] (Frankfurt am Main: Suhrkamp, 1989), 174–77; and Michel Foucault's discussion of the cemetery as heterochronic heterotopia in "Of Other Spaces," trans. Jay Miskowiec, *Diacritics* 16 (Spring 1986): 22–27, here 26.

[7] "Das erklärt die Irritierbarkeit ihres Selbstverständnisses, die Dynamik der ruhelos bis in unsere Zeit fortgesetzten Versuche, sich selbst 'festzustellen.'"

[8] "Es handelt sich um die Struktur der Selbstbeziehung des erkennenden Subjekts, das sich auf sich als Objekt zurückbeugt, um sich wie in einem Spiegelbild — eben 'spekulativ' — zu ergreifen" (29).

[9] "Die Frage ist jetzt, ob sich aus Subjektivität und Selbstbewußtsein Maßstäbe gewinnen lassen, die der modernen Welt entnommen sind und gleichzeitig zur Orientierung in ihr, das heißt aber auch: zur Kritik einer mit sich selbst zerfallenen Moderne taugen" (31).

[10] "Aber dasselbe Prinzip [das Prinzip der Subjektivität] ist nicht mächtig genug, um die religiöse Macht der Vereinigung im Medium der Vernunft zu regenerieren. Die stolze Reflexionskultur der Aufklärung hat sich mit der Religion 'entzweit und sie *neben* sich oder sich *neben* sie gesetzt'" (31, quoting Hegel's *Differenzschrift* [vol. 2, 23]).

[11] "Daraus ergibt sich das Dilemma, daß er dem Selbstverständnis der Moderne am Ende die Möglichkeit einer Kritik an der Moderne bestreiten muß."

[12] The third edition was printed in 1952, the seventh in 1967.

[13] This notion that the content of such emotional values seems to shrink away from any expression is represented in traditional Heimat novels by a glorification of non-verbal communication that is much more capable and perfect than any words could ever be. Andrea Kunne in her *Heimat im Roman: Last oder Lust?* [Heimat in the Novel: Burden or Pleasure?] (Amsterdam: Rodopi, 1991) remarks on the motif of silence in the Heimat novel genre that it is always positively encoded, the best known instance being the title of Ludwig Ganghofer's famous 1906 novel *Das Schweigen im Walde* [The Silence in the Woods] (107).

[14] "Die Neunzigerjahre des 18. Jahrhunderts sind vielleicht doch das interessanteste Jahrzehnt in der Geschichte der Taten, die auf dem Papier stattfinden, weil die Wirklichkeit noch eine Möglichkeit zu wenig enthält."

[15] "Dies ist die allgemeine Bedeutung der genialen göttlichen Ironie, als dieser Konzentration des Ich in sich, für welches alle Bande gebrochen sind und das nur in der Seligkeit des Selbstgenusses leben mag."

[16] Hölderlin poems in which Heimat — in most cases a return to one's Heimat — play an important role (their approximate dates, if known, in parentheses): "An den Aether" (1797–98), "Der Wanderer" (first version 1797–98, second version 1800–1801), "Die Heimat" (first version, second version 1800–1801), "Mein Eigentum" (1799–1800), "Rousseau," "Diotima" (second version, third version 1800–1801), "Rückkehr in die Heimat" (1800), "Stuttgart" (first version 1800–1801, second version), "Heimkunft" (first version 1800–1801, second version [second version discussed here]), and "Patmos" (first, second, third, and fourth version, all 1803–1806).

[17] "Alles scheint vertraut, der verübereilende Gruß auch / Scheint von Freunden, es scheint jegliche Miene verwandt."

[18] Cf. Hölderlin's terms *heimatliche Sonne* [sun of the Heimat] and *heimatliches Licht* [light of the Heimat] in his *Der Tod des Empedokles;* Eichendorff in his poem "Treue" talks of the *lichte Heimat* [the bright Heimat] and in *Ahnung und Gegenwart* of a "deeper Heimat of which the one in this world shines as but [or: seems but] a pleasant reflection" ("tiefere Heimat, von welcher jene nur ein lieblicher Widerschein zu sein scheint"); Robert Walser starts his musings "An die Heimat" (*Der Samstag* [Basel] May 1905; rpt. in *Das Gesamtwerk,* vol. 1, ed. Jochen Greven [Geneva: Helmut Kossodo, 1972], 233–34) — we will look at this short piece in more detail in chapter 4, "Heimat and the Feminine" — with "The sun is shining. . . . It is Sunday, and in the Sunday it is morning"; and Ernst Bloch, as we will see in chapter 6, "Heimat and Innocence (in Childhood, in Religion, in Language, and in *Antiheimat*)," states that "Heimat is that which shines everyone into his or her childhood, but it is a place where no one has ever been" (*Gesamtausgabe* vol. 5, 1628).

[19] "Genauer betrachtet finden wir drei Weisen des Scheines: 1. den Schein als Glanz und Leuchten; 2. den Schein und das Scheinen als Erscheinen, den Vor-schein, zu dem etwas kommt; 3. den Schein als bloßen Schein, den Anschein, den etwas macht. . . . Das Wesen den Scheines liegt im Erscheinen."

[20] "Freilich wohl! das Geburtsland ist's, der Boden der Heimat."

[21] "steht wie ein Sohn am wellenumrauschten / Tor und siehet und sucht liebende Namen für dich. . . ."

[22] "Dort empfangen sie mich. O Stimme der Stadt, der Mutter!" Interestingly, the first version differs in this line. It reads: "Dort empfangen sie mich, o süße Stimme der Meinen!" — There, they receive me, o sweet voice of my people. It is quite possible that "mother" here stands not only for mother and mother tongue, but as a metonymy for Swabia. Cf. the early ode "Keppler" (1789), in which the nineteen-year-old wrote the line "Mutter der Redlichen! Suevia!" [Mother of honest men! Swabia!] and the first line of "Die Wanderung," written some twelve years later (1801–1802), where we read, "Glückselig Suevien, meine Mutter" [Blissfully happy Swabia, my mother].

[23] "Das moderne Zeitbewußtsein verbietet freilich jeden Gedanken an Regression, an die unvermittelte Rückkehr zu den mythischen Ursprüngen. Allein die Zukunft bildet den Horizont für die Erweckung mythischer Vergangenheiten."

[24] "Bruderbunde der beiden Kunstgottheiten in der Tragödie."

[25] "Worauf weist das ungeheure historische Bedürfniss der unbefriedeten modernen Cultur, das Umsichsammeln zahlloser anderer Culturen, das verzeh-

rende Erkennenwollen, wenn nicht auf den Verlust des Mythus, auf den Verlust der mythischen Heimat, des mythischen Mutterschoosses?"

[26] "Wer würde gerade bei diesem Volke . . . noch einen so gleichmässig kräftigen Erguss des einfachsten politischen Gefühls, der natürlichsten Heimatinstincte, der ursprünglichen männlichen Kampflust vermuthen?"

[27] "Staat und Heimatssinn [können] nicht ohne Bejahung der individuellen Persönlichkeit leben."

[28] "Glaube Niemand, dass der deutsche Geist seine mythische Heimat auf ewig verloren habe, wenn er so deutlich noch die Vogelstimmen versteht, die von jener Heimat erzählen."

[29] "Das Schmerzlichste aber ist für uns alle — die lange Entwürdigung, unter der der deutsche Genius, entfremdet von Haus und Heimat, im Dienst tückischer Zwerge lebte."

[30] "dass der Staat und die Gesellschaft, überhaupt die Klüfte zwischen Mensch und Mensch einem übermächtigen Einheitsgefühl weichen, welches an das Herz der Natur zurückführt."

[31] Cf. the English term *nation* as it was, until quite recently, used in the context of Native American cultures. And Native Americans continue to refer to themselves as nations (the Cherokee nation, the Navajo nation, etc.). Here *nation* is defined exactly in the Herderian sense of a common or closely related language and common traditions rather than by passports or borders or political governments. Cf. also the designation for whatever Germany stood for during Herder's lifetime: *Sacrum Imperium Romanum Nationis Germanicae*, The Holy Roman Empire of the German Nation.

[32] "[Des Reichen] Heimath sind die Orte, wo das Geld alles vermag."

[33] "Unter allen Stolzen halte ich den Nationalstolzen . . . für den größesten Narren."

[34] "Zwar ist die Schönheit der Heimat eines jeden einzelnen nicht mit der Schönheit der Heimat jedes anderen einzelnen vergleichbar, weil die Heimat unvergleichlich schön ist, doch würde sich jeder einzelne (und auch jeder andere einzelne) dagegen wehren, daß seine Heimat an eine Unheimat grenzen sollte."

[35] "O spei aus, vor der Hausthür spei der Seine / Häßlichen Schlamm aus. // Rede Deutsch, o du Deutscher."

[36] "Die Philosophie der Französischen Sprache hindert also die Philosophie der Gedanken."

[37] I am indebted to Lonnie R. Johnson for his help in the research of this link between Herder, nationalism, and the idea of Heimat.

3: Heimat and Concepts of Identity

SEVERAL YEARS AGO, WHEN I WAS ABOUT TO begin work on my master's thesis at an American university, I wrote my parents in Germany that I was going to spend the foreseeable future researching the idea of Heimat in contemporary German literature and culture. My father, now retired, was at the time the principal of a school for multiply handicapped children. He quickly wrote back:

> Heimat? I believe that, for all the attempts at definition that resonate in this word, with all its individual and emotional aspects, Heimat cannot be grasped in general terms. One's entire past experience — childhood, family ties, relationships with friends, landscape, city or town — hardly allow a bundling into a general, abstract concept. And still, this word is so often in use. In our children in the Haslachmühle [his school] we find that their ties to their parents' home and to their familiar surroundings are the same as with mentally highly developed children. We only observe in children who show no emotional responses — for instance children with strong autistic tendencies — that they don't care where they are. They want their own, small world into which they are spun or in which they are imprisoned. Every change unsettles them. They often show tic-like behavior and persist in it at home and at school. Children who react with strong emotion when they come to the Haslachmühle because they have to let go of or loosen ties to their parents' homes are often homesick and suffer from the separation until they feel more at ease with us. With time, they develop in the Haslachmühle a sense of shelteredness, of security, and they form new ties. They like to go home during vacations but also like to return afterwards. Recently a mother from our parent-teacher-liaison group said that our children simply have two Heimaten. Very rare this plural form. A number of years ago I told parents who were afraid that their child would grow homesick after her arrival: "Let's hope she does grow homesick." They were surprised: Why would I say something so cruel? "If your child does not grow homesick," I said, "then I know that she doesn't have a Heimat," that is, I know that she doesn't have any emotional ties to her parents' home.

This letter from my father makes several relevant observations on the idea of Heimat: we find Heimat's highly "individual and emotional aspects." Whether they preclude a generalization or, indeed, theoretization ("cannot be grasped in general terms" because of "all the different backgrounds of experience") may, however, be doubted. (In intimate communication between family members it is still assumed that there is some difference between what is "individual" and what is "general." The common Frankfurt School insight that the notion of the individual is to an important degree culturally determined — and, thus, can be generalized — is missing from the family dinner table.) The reference to "one's entire past experience — childhood, family ties, and relationships with friends, landscape, city or town" is doubly relevant, first because it introduces the concept of experience — so important to German culture since German Idealism[1] — and second because it intuitively puts into parallel structure intimate human relationships and relationships with landscapes, houses, and places. In other words, the spatial aspect of experience is treated like the concretization of the emotional attachment to friends. Locale stands for friends and family. Parents and personal ties are expressed in terms of space.

In another observation, we read that autistic children may not have a sense of Heimat because they are incapable of an emotional, subjective interaction with other human beings. At best, other people represent to them something like infrastructure for the autistic personality.

Most important about the letter from my father — and this leads to this chapter's point of inquiry — is the observation that children with strong autistic tendencies do not experience a loss of their Heimat because they do not care where they are as long as their own, small world remains intact. What autistic personality structures are commonly understood to be missing — we need only think of Bruno Bettelheim's title *The Empty Fortress* (1976) — is a sense of self with an ability to have healthy interactions with the world that surrounds it. The interrelationship between a sense of self and the perception of one's world is a central aspect in the formation of a sense of Heimat.

This chapter investigates the close correlation between historical shifts in the understanding of Heimat and parallel shifts in the notion of the self. I apply the psychoanalytic concept of sublimation to show how the social phenomenon of Heimat is energized by transformative processes in which the qualities that each historical period deems most desirable are projected onto an idealized geography. As I have said earlier, Heimat constructs are counterphobic conceptualizations expressed in regressive, imagistic terms. They are wish-fulfillments without a price; they provide a world where wars and destruction do not exist or are so far away that they do not matter; they provide a world where men and women know their roles so perfectly that they come together in due course without strains and crises; and they provide a world where the experiences of alienation are magically healed in this feminine and feminizing construct. We see Heimat — like concepts of nature, nation, or family — as an attempt at unity and centeredness in the face of disjunction and fragmentation.

Such an attempt at unity can be seen as one result of what Joel Whitebook describes as the ego's impulse "to impose its own artificial and rigid unity on the world" (Whitebook 1995, 109). This manner of interacting with the world is speculative in the etymological sense of the word — a mirror image of the longed-for oneness of the ego (Samuel Weber 13). Heimat is a fusional, utopian concept capable of providing a socially acceptable, modern expression of unity, of the masculine coming together with the feminine in a world drawn up by men alone. This way of thinking about the seemingly irrational and contradictory qualities of Heimat helps resolve some of the deep tensions inherent in the concept and also introduces some of the categories of the next chapter, "Heimat and the Feminine."

One could say that until the mid-1960s Heimat helped a male world to sublimate a longing for union with what it perceived as the feminine. Heimat was a man's world's socially acceptable way of participating in a group act where everyone was part of the celebration and shared in an imaginary, supposedly individualized, highly feminized partner. Since the late 1960s a change has begun to occur, though, one that — in generally more intellectual, less rural circles — questions this old notion of Heimat and attempts to expose its underlying assumptions. Such attempts at realism were categorized in the late seventies and eighties as representations of an anti-Heimat — a Heimat where brutality and ugliness flourished — just as (and we will look at this aspect, as well) many traditional theoreticians of identity might consider recent developments in psychoanalytic theories to be anti-identity theories.

One last point in my father's remarkable letter on the idea of Heimat is his observation that the word is rarely used in the plural, Heimaten. Fittingly, the pluralized "Heimaten" is most often heard in the context of guest workers and other immigrants and their children in Germany.[2] But usually, German speakers still assume Heimat to be unique by definition: one can have only one true Heimat. This uniqueness is implied when people speak of someone having found a "new Heimat" or a "second Heimat." Either the first and original Heimat remains the Heimat, or the stress is on the idea of a successive, forever singular Heimat. But for German speakers the notion of Heimaten, two contemporaneous Heimaten, used to (and still often does) quickly bring up associations of painful outsiderdom, split personalities, and schizophrenia. Such associations, even if they are slowly beginning to wane (the philosopher Vilém Flusser, for instance, writes proudly, "I am heimatless because too many Heimaten are stored inside of me" [15]), point to a close interrelation between traditional, hermetic notions of identity and their reflection in traditional conceptualizations of Heimat. The questions this chapter asks, therefore, are: Can one consider conceptualizations of Heimat as outward representations of an inner sense of self? And can one see notions of an inner self as unacknowledged inward projections of conceptualizations of Heimat? It is my contention that Heimat, as Whitebook says of sublimation in a somewhat different context, is a "frontier entity . . . between the mental and the physical" (1995, 260–61). As such, it is like the "addendum" [*das Hinzutretende*] with which Adorno augments Kant's impulse of the will. It is an impulse that drives the "intramental and somatic into one, beyond the sphere of consciousness" (1966, 288), and it represents "the rudiment of a phase in which the dualism of extramental and intramental had not yet thoroughly solidified" (227).[3] The binary distinctions between inner and outer, between self and world, and between reason and irrationality already presuppose differentiations that the idea of Heimat usually does not accept.

Heimat and the Self

The question of where a self begins can, of course, be looked at and theorized from many points of view. Historically, the philosophies of René Descartes, Gottfried Wilhelm Leibniz, and Immanuel Kant are often considered the beginning of notions of modern selfhood and individuality. Yet, it is easy to see that their theories as to what constitutes a self vary fundamentally. Descartes's concept of the self as *res cogitans,* a thinking thing, a substance of the soul that is the basis for all consciousness (ca. 1640), shifts in fundamental ways in Leibniz's monadology (ca. 1715) and in Kant's differentiations between an empirical and a transcendental I (ca. 1780). Bettelheim, in his studies of autistic children (many of them published in *The Empty Fortress,* which appeared in 1983 in German under the title *Die Geburt des Selbst* [Birth of the Self]), sees the beginning of a sense of self in autistic children as occurring at the point at which an Other, a Not-I, is found in language. But whether we see the beginning of a self in some sort of separation-individuation process — as is usually the case in psychoanalytically based theories (for instance, in Bettelheim, Freud, Cornelius Castoriadis, and Margaret Mahler and Fred Pine) — or whether we look at the self, as Giddens does with his somewhat more sociological-philosophical approach (besides Erik Erikson and D. W. Winnicott, he cites Ernst Bloch and Paul Tillich), as essentially connected to "a sense of ontological security," to hope, courage, and a "basic trust" (Giddens 1991, esp. 38), we cannot help but realize that, in the end, we are cursed and blessed with the troublesome self that is the source of both much modern anxiety and creativity. We know we have to have some sort of self to be able to live a functional life in human society; but at the same time we do not know for sure where this self comes from, what it is, or how exactly it permeates every moment of our existence.

It is certainly no coincidence that first representations of the modern idea of Heimat, as well as first philosophies of identity, appear at about the same time in German cultural history. And it is no coincidence that since the end of the eighteenth century shifts of notions of identity and of Heimat have occurred in close parallel to one another. For if modernity's legacy of dialectics is, as Adorno maintains, the world's agony of an impoverished life raised to a concept (1973, 6), then the concept of Heimat is, as a social imaginary, the answer to a Not-I, to a hermeneutic split between the subject as an object and the subject as a subject. (Fittingly, Martin Heidegger carefully connects language and Heimat through a suggestive use of the Greek verb *dialégein* — to converse with each other. For Heidegger, *dialégein* is the etymological source for both dialect — that is, the language of Heimat — and dialectics [1964, 100].) Heimat is the outwardly projected consolation of an identity's suppressed awareness of an inner anxiety that is conceived in the act of reflexivity itself.

And as it is possible to tell from children's play with toys and dolls what is on their minds without them ever becoming fully conscious of it, we can infer from German social negotiations of Heimat what psychic anxieties are crucially present yet only indirectly expressed.

We do not have to enter into the debates among Emile Durkheim, Claude Lévi-Strauss, and Pierre Bourdieu as to whether psychic and symbolic representations reflect social structures or the other way around. Nicholas Dirks, Geoff Eley, and Sherry Ortner provide a quick summary in the Introduction to *Culture / Power / History* (1994): whereas Durkheim "had argued that 'mental' and symbolic representations reflected social structure, Lévi-Strauss turned Durkheim on his head" (15). Bourdieu tries to turn Durkheim right side up, but with a political twist. He argues that "the structures to be found in cultural forms were 'transformed, misrecognizable form[s] of the real divisions of the social order'" (15, Dirks et al.'s brackets). Bourdieu's theory of practice, written in part against Lévi-Strauss's structuralism, "assumed certain objective mental structures in human beings" (15). Bourdieu wanted to show how "real divisions" become masked in naturalization and how this process seeps "into people's heads, bodies, and selves" (16).

Arguing for the primacy of the social or psychic imaginary is, for our purposes, not helpful. It suffices — in fact, it is necessary — for us to assume a close and symbiotic interrelationship between an individual and a collective. My notion of identity here loosely combines the early Erik Erikson's sociologically oriented idea of I-identity development between collective and psychosocial crises, G. H. Mead's self through social action, and the Lacanian-Freudian Marxist Cornelius Castoriadis's notion of the social imaginary. I am leaving aside here the obvious contradictions to which complete subscription to the identity theories of these three psychoanalysts would lead. Castoriadis's notion of the originary monadic magma of the soul and Erikson's formative notion of the collective stand, for instance, in complete contrast to each other. But Erikson, Mead, and Castoriadis have in common — and I will work with — indirect, highly socially sensitive appropriations of Freud. They also all see a healthy self as developing in some sort of reflexive balance between complete merger and complete monadic isolation.[4] As Margaret Mahler and Fred Pine observe in *The Psychological Birth of the Human Infant: Symbiosis and Individuation* (1975), normal functional identity is constituted somewhere between complete merger and total isolation.

It would be misleading to look at expressions of Heimat as simply symbols of a shared identity. Heimat *is* shared identity. Ina-Maria Greverus notes that "Heimat resembles identity" (1987, 9). But in the multitudes of discussions that one can have about the interrelation between the individual and society and the many thinkers whom one can quote in such a discussion (Freud, Durkheim, Lévi-Strauss, Bourdieu, Parsons, Mead, etc.), the claim for similarity between social structures and constitutions of identity is the weakest. Heimat is not only like identity, it *is* identity. Heimat is more than a trope of identity. It is a way of organizing space and time and a communally defined self in order to shape meaning. Heimat is identity manifested in a social, imagistic way.

It is here that we find one aspect of what seems to make Heimat so typically German. Heimat — like *Stammtisch* [regulars' table at a local inn] or *Verein* [club] on a popular level or Kant's concept of *Innerlichkeit* [interiority], Fichte's and Schelling's *Ich* [I], or Hegel's concept of *Sittlichkeit* [virtue] on a philosophical level — is a concept that hovers somewhere in the negotiable space between the private and the public. A rather rigid division between private and public in many American social theories (or in the American appropriation of European social theories) limits their usefulness (or their reuse) in a European — or, at least, in a German — context. The American emphasis on individuality is reflected, as well, in American psychoanalysis's foregrounding of ego psychology — something toward which at least the French psychoanalytic tradition shows, according to Whitebook, a "general hostility" (1995, 178).

From this perspective we see that the German tradition of self-reflection is less truly self-reflexive than it may seem to those of us steeped in notions of American individualism. We see this resistance to self-reflexivity manifested in the limited German acceptance of a general psychoanalysis — which was always small, so small that psychoanalysis is still closely linked with pathology. We see it also in the German attitude toward certain stress-related illnesses or persistent forms of milder depression. Instead of counseling — the American method that presupposes the curing effect of an increased degree of self-expression and self-knowledge — Germans go to a *Kur*, a stay in a spa, where the body is taken care of. The mind, the self, and reflexivity are usually left out of all of that. Even the term for self-awareness, *Selbstbewußtsein*, introduced and used in the late eighteenth and early nineteenth centuries as that for which it literally stood, an awareness of the self (that is, the result of a self-analytic process), at some point — probably not until the second third of the twentieth century[5] — in German non-academic circles turned into what is known in English as self-confidence. The concept of *Selbstbewußtsein* shifted in the process of being transferred from a culture of positive interiority to a culture of narcissistically conceived identity structures, so that in contemporary German *Selbstbewußtsein* refers almost exclusively to the knowledge of one's positive abilities and one's manner of displaying them.

Heimat, Loss, and *Heimweh*

This shift leads us to an existing, almost accidental kind of research into the qualities and effects of Heimat. As is often the case in research, a detected lack helps to establish first effects and then existence. Indirectly, there are studies on Heimat dating back as far as the seventeenth century. The effect of the loss of one's Heimat — *Heimweh* [homesickness] — was considered a disease as early as 1688,[6] when a medical student, Johannes Hofer, presented in Basel, Switzerland, a dissertation titled "De Nostalgia, Oder Heimwehe." Until the second half of the eighteenth century *Heimweh* was so much associated with Swiss mercenaries, who

were sent all over Europe to fight, that it was often referred to as
die Schweizer Krankheit [the Swiss Disease].

If we understand *Heimweh* as a longing to return home not
only to one's house — which is usually not all that is missed — but
also to the social situation left behind, then *Heimweh* becomes
Heimatweh, and the analysis of those who fell ill with this disease
and were treated with varying success over the centuries can give us
an idea of what Heimat was for those who no longer had it.

Thus, Greverus, in her anthropological study of the Heimat
phenomenon, is well justified in using *Heimweh* to point out certain qualities of Heimat. She aptly summarizes the results of three
centuries of research into homesickness when she notes that the
empirical case studies show especially "egotistical people with immobile minds incapable of adjustments" (1972, 117) as suffering
from *Heimweh.* If we combine this finding with the definition of
Heimweh in the *Neue Herder* encyclopedia of 1949, where homesickness is described as a "painful longing for one's Heimat," as the
opposite of *Fernweh* [the longing for faraway places], and as "a
uniquely German word, soaked with sentiment," then we have arrived at a crucial point. Homesickness, continues the *Neue Herder,*
"in younger people who have a disposition toward psychopathology can become intense enough to cause morbid depression with a
loss of appetite and strength" (vol. 1, 1632).[7]

Overstating the case, one could say that if *Heimweh* is only an
intensification of the experience of loss of something possessed in
common by most German speakers (that is, a sense of Heimat),
then we can make a first attempt at a theory of Heimat. Heimat
provides "egotistical people with immobile minds incapable of adjustments" with a means of avoiding their potential "disposition
toward psychopathology," which might lead to depression, a loss
of strength, and — a catastrophe for any German — a loss of appetite. By having Heimat, one has everything the loss of Heimat
might take away: one lives sane in a sane world, is strong, and has
an appetite.

Humor aside, it is noteworthy — and reinforces an important
point about the idea of Heimat — that *Heimweh,* through the loss
of one's Heimat, is a forced process of individualization, whereas
having a Heimat is the permission to remain asleep in a disindi-
vidualizing world. Thus, Greverus is not entirely correct when she

describes the securing of one's sense of Heimat as "an ego-centered process," "an irrational behavior aimed at the satisfaction of the ego" (388). More precisely, one would have to say that the concept of the ego in Heimat is one of an unconscious or preconscious, group-dependent, social and geographical ego, which is not exactly an ego in the traditional Freudian sense. In other words, securing one's sense of Heimat is a way for the ego to have a sense of self without needing to be aware of it, and so the solitude of the individual in the world is nullified. Understood in this way, one's sense of Heimat is indeed an ego-centered process, an irrational behavior aimed at the satisfaction of the ego; but now that satisfaction consists of being unaware and unselfconscious, of one person's being able to lose himself or herself in the cheerful monotony of *Blasmusik* [brass music], another's ability to feel good about himself or herself in nature on well-marked hiking trails, and yet another's ability to seek the secure enclosure of the *Männergesangverein* [men's singing circles] or the *Fussballverein* [soccer club] ("Elf Freunde müsst ihr sein" — the commonplace slogan for amateur soccer teams, "You have to be eleven friends [in order to play soccer]") or the *gemütliche Beisammensein* [cheerful togetherness] of *Kaffeetrinken* [drinking coffee] with the family in the garden on a Sunday afternoon.

Vilém Flusser observes that "Heimat lies beyond waking consciousness" (17); and that "Prejudices are part of all Heimaten" (21). Heimat is given by birth. What makes this local and national patriotism so *verheerend* [disastrous] is "That it places family relations above chosen relations, places . . . biological-ideological relations above friendship and love" (24). Helpful terms for approaching the German idea of Heimat and identity come from Werner Blessing, who identifies Heimat as belonging to the sociological categories of "*Kollektivsingular*" [collective singular] and "*Subjektobjektivität*" [subjectobjectivity] (179). Gisela Ecker defines Heimat as a "symbol of the collective" (29). Probably the most helpful term can be found in Isaiah Berlin's discussions of Herder. Never using the term Heimat specifically, Berlin is discussing Herder's notion of people's identities as based in language and social contexts (what Herder calls "climate"). Berlin speaks of a "collective individuality" — putting the phrase in quotation marks, probably to express its paradoxical nature. But the term "collective individuality" is perfectly appropriate for the idea of Heimat.

Jean Améry calls homesickness a self-alienation (19). In such a conception the self is always at least partially one that perceives itself as in need of a home and grounding. A self away from its grounding is perceived as reduced or damaged. Relief comes from the return to a symbiotic relationship with this space. The Swiss playwright Max Frisch expresses this idea with the line "this landscape knows you" (366), which turns landscape and nature into that which Neville Symington, in his *Narcissism: A New Theory* (1993), calls a "lifegiver," someone who (or, in this case, some-*thing that*), by providing the confines of a symbiotic atmosphere, is sensed as giving life. Some pathologically dependent people express this notion as feeling alive only as long as they are "in the bubble" together with the lifegiver.

Flusser writes: "The mysterious sensation of Heimat ties human beings to things. Both are bathed in this mystery. . . . This confusion between things and people, this ontological error that takes an "it" for a "you," is exactly what prophets called heathenism and what philosophers think of as magical thinking and what they are trying to overcome" (19). The modern German notion of Heimat provides to some exactly such a bubble in which they feel alive. Just as the autistic shell provides protection against an appallingly painful outside world, the lifegiver and his or her bubble protect against a "black hole" of despair (Frances Tustin; qtd. in Symington 81 and 104).

Heimweh — homesickness — is the expression of the sensation of a partial death. To defend against feelings of intense abandonment, writes James Masterson in *Psychotherapy of the Borderline Adult: A Developmental Approach* (1976), "the borderline patient clings to the maternal figure, and thus fails to progress through the normal developmental stages of separation-individuation to autonomy" (29). I do not suggest that every German-speaking person who has some form of response to the idea of Heimat is a borderline adult suffering from developmental arrest. Nonetheless, a borderline disorder is but an extreme case of a narcissistic personality structure, a personality structure that has become increasingly relevant to our contemporary Western world. A narcissistic personality suffers from a sense of its own unreality until it sees itself reflected in the eyes of another. Narcissistic self-satisfaction is a way of defending against the usual contemporary ontological pains and anxieties. By finding its own image only in the gaze of the other — an exterior framework that is, in a way, as much a protective shell as the shell of autism — the narcissistic personality is protected from references to its own emptiness, against that "black hole of despair." It is protected against feelings of isolation, futility, and annihilation, against "pre-Oedipal rage," and against fear of fragmentation (Whitebook 1985, 150).

Heimat and Regression

If we look at representations of Heimat through history from a slightly different angle, one with a sensitivity to power and gender, we notice that Heimat conceptualizations at any given time are closely linked to the class and gender interests of a narcissistically conceived masculinized self, a male subject, a male ego. Heimat usually represents an idealized loser in gender or class questions (women or peasants), but always from the point of view of the winner (the bourgeois male). Heimat, one could say, brings back that which ascendancy claimed as a sacrifice from the victor.

We can also view this phenomenon from a Freudian perspective. Freud ends *Die Traumdeutung* (1900; translated as *The Interpretation of Dreams*, 1955) by addressing how dreams effect a dreamer's future. He restates his well-known conviction that dreams are expressions of the dreamer's wishes and goes on to describe two paths through which a wish, in being expressed, actually affects the dreamer's future. The first path, the path of the pleasure principle, is — to use Whitebook's summary — "short, regressive, and autistic" (1995, 208); it is the path of the person who establishes a "perceptual identity" (Standard Edition, vol. 5, 566 and 602) in a hallucinatory manner. The second path, the path of the reality principle (567 [footnote added in 1914]), requires a person to have a strong and conscious ego that does not allow regression to proceed too far but, instead, translates the wish into a forward-directed pursuit. (I am not completely at ease with the terms *pleasure principle* and *reality principle*. Marcuse, in *Eros and Civilization: A Philosophical Inquiry into Freud* [1955], introduced *performance principle* to designate "the prevailing historical form of the *reality principle*" [35, Marcuse's italics] — for the 1950s. None of these terms is uncontroversial or perfectly suited for our discussions here. Since, however, I am unaware of any other terms that are equally comprehensive and in comparably wide circulation, I will use *pleasure principle* and *reality principle* as imperfect but functional tools with which to discuss the regressive aspect of the idea of Heimat and its relationship to questions of gender, identity, and class.)

Clearly, maturity is associated with the second path, the conscious ego that does not allow the psyche to move too far "backward." The idea of Heimat, on the other hand, is closely linked to the first, in that it is short, regressive, and autistic. It is the path of no resistance, the path of what Freud calls the pleasure principle. It establishes a "perceptual identity" — maybe not in a hallucinatory manner, but certainly in a manner that precludes (to continue the Freudian diction) a nonselective reality testing. Representations of Heimat usually show an ego that longs to have a place where, in its weakness, it can exist in a preconscious sheltered state of ego-dedifferentiation. These representations come out of a process where the "backward motion" of the psyche (and the backward motion away from the pains associated with modernity) is allowed to proceed — in the eyes of many, proceed too far. Notions of Heimat do not translate wishes into forward-directed impulses. Instead, they become part of the strangely passive, disempowered, helpless social resignation of a bourgeois and petit-bourgeois male who senses himself in a hierarchical system to be a winner (over nature, over women) but one who, in winning, has lost his keys to happiness and now tries to find them again in Heimat. (If we remember from the last chapter the metaphors Eduard Spranger invoked in his *Der Bildungswert der Heimatkunde* — "a corner of our soul," "painter or poet cannot express our shining uniqueness," "the floating in us," "the melting together in us" — we realize that this is the bourgeois subject's language of love, devotion, wooing, and sexual experience. In other words, we can see the representation of Heimat in schools as the socially prescribed sublimation of a sexuality bound to be frustrated in adult life. Fusional utopias are replacing human partners.)

Freud's pragmatic statements in *Das Ich und das Es* (1923; translated as *The Ego and the Id*, 1962) about the essentially weak ego's possible resources for strength and for an individual identity show a close and, in fact, symbiotic interaction between an outside world and the constitution of a self. Freud describes three possible sources of strength for an ego: it may obtain strength through mediation between perceptions and reality (what I think of — in a literary scholar's analogy — as the power of the translator); it can also achieve strength through interposing "the process of thinking" (to continue the literary analogy, through interpretation); and finally, it can appropriate some of the id's energy for its own purposes by transforming id into ego (in literary terms, by making a text a part of oneself). *Identification* is a commonly used term for this last process; *merger* or *symbiosis* are the psychoanalytic terms. In all three cases Freud sees the ego as making use of "borrowed forces" (Standard Edition, vol. 19, 25). And he gives us his famous image of the ego being in relation to the id "like a man on horseback, who has to hold in check the superior strength of the horse" (25).

The last source of strength, the appropriation of id into ego, is especially useful for looking at representations of Heimat, for a close interrelationship (and a transfer of identity) always exists between Heimat as "the social imaginary" (a term coined by Castoriadis in his *The Imaginary Institution of Society,* 1987) and the constitution of an individualized identity of — paradoxically — ego-dedifferentiation. In other words, through Heimat one's ego receives strength, and one obtains an identity by not having one. One's ego — despite often giving the illusion of being individualized — becomes a geographically situated group ego in which the individual melts into one with space, nature, landscape, and the imagined, selectively remembered tradition of a certain region. (Think of the ease with which Heimat images turn into clichés. Clichés are an expression of a loss of an earlier uniqueness — one may also say, of an earlier true individuality. The educated person's aversion to clichés is, in part, an expression of a fear of falling into a form of disindividualization. This proximity to commonplaces [*common places* in the literal, as well as the metaphoric, sense] also helps to explain scholars' unease in dealing with Heimat.)

In Heimat the separation between a perceiving subject and a perceived object is erased. Nature becomes culture; the subject becomes nature; the inherently male subject becomes one with some feminized entity: with nature [*die Natur*], landscape [*die Land-schaft*], childhood [*die Kindheit*], language [*die Sprache*], or, in Ernst Bloch's writing, even with true democracy [*die Demokratie*].

If we accept (in the tradition of Horkheimer) a close interrelation between human notions of the individual self and the forms that cultural symbols and institutions assume,[8] we find that one often stands for the other, one emphasizing a subjective-anthropological, the other a more (to use Horkheimer's short-hand) "objectivistic approach" (Horkheimer 142). Such an assumption necessarily reads the regressive, irrational tendencies of institutions as another form of the reactionary desires of the self — a generally discomforting notion, especially in the German context.

We should not, however, forget that regression can assume progressive functions as well, that it can become "the vehicle of future liberation" (Whitebook 1995, 33). Even though fantasy, if looked at from the standpoint of an assumed mature reality principle, is inherently unrealistic, regressive, and in some ways even false (evaluated as "utopian" in the negative sense); even though fantasy is part of the products of the mind that live outside or in contrast to the mature reality principle; fantasy still contains a truth value of its own (33). And this truth value inherent in the regressive and utopian fantasies of one generation often significantly helps shape the realities of the next.

D. W. Winnicott's essays "Transitional Objects and Transitional Phenomena" (1953) and "The Location of Cultural Experience" (1967) make several claims about the experience of art and childhood that have been disputed. I do not dispute their validity here but only wish to inquire into Winnicott's categories. He describes cultural experience in terms identical to those with which constitutions of Heimat can be described. Winnicott states that for the infant the division of inner and outer is not yet formulated, and this description is true for Heimat representations, as well. Winnicott writes that the sort of satisfaction that we assume that the infant experiences when lost in play "is retained in the intense experiencing that belongs to the arts and to religion and to imaginative living" (1953, 242). The same holds for representations of Heimat. All these kinds of experience have, according to Winnicott, "no climax" (1967, 98). Again, I am not arguing that Winnicott's claims hold for the experience of art in general. What we can clearly see, however, is the congruency of the fields of signification. What Winnicott projects into the experience of art is the experience of memories of childhood, which is at least one sort of experience associated with Heimat — through Heimat the subject becomes one with some aspect of life that has been removed through an experience of growing up (which is always, to some degree, an experience of distanciation and alienation). And, remarkably enough, it is an experience of union that — I think this idea is what Winnicott expresses, among other things, when he points to the climaxless qualities of infant experiences — remains innocent, sexually and otherwise.

The psychoanalytic concept of sublimation is ever relevant in this context. In fact, Heimat is, to a degree, a form of sublimation. It does not matter whether we see sublimation, with Freud, as probably taking place "through the mediation of the ego, which begins by changing sexual object libido into narcissistic libido and then perhaps goes on to give it another aim" (Standard Edition, vol. 19, 30) or whether we see it, with Whitebook, as narrowing the gulf between object world and self and thus as "a kind of reconciliation of the subject-object dichotomy," of the mother-infant dyad (252) or see it, with Hans Loewald as belonging in the area of ego development in general as an internalized "reconciliation" (33).

In all these respects Heimat is a form of sublimation. But Heimat is sublimation with a twist, because it has the added dimension of being geographically grounded. It belongs to a region. Therefore, it has boundaries, even though these are more tangible in the minds of insiders and outsiders than they are as dividing lines on a map. Still, this group-individuality, this shared sublimation called Heimat, can also suddenly turn, when the time is right, into a political concept and take on exclusionary (for instance, anti-Semitic) colors. Despite such occasional turns, though, Heimat retains — as we will see in more detail in chapter 6 — an unshakable, basic innocence.

For average German speakers Heimat is the basis and the result of their daydreams. It is promise and actualization rolled into one. But Heimat can also become — like dreams, which are equally regressive and imagistic in their representations — the source of new categories of the thinkable and, therefore, an instrument for emancipation. This transformation is currently happening in minority circles (be they Turkish-Germans, homosexuals, farmers, citizens of the former GDR, or members of the political Right and far Right). These developments are a variation on those that occurred in the early nineteenth century when the notion of Heimat was a tool of resistance against Napoleon's occupation of the German states. Between 1800 and 1813 Heimat became a code word for intellectual partisans.

Friedrich Schiller's *Wilhelm Tell,* written between 1802 and 1804, represents a perfect instance of this phenomenon. Heimat appears five times in the play, whose central question is whether murder is a justified option for freeing oneself from a tyrant. Even without the surrounding context, the statements about Heimat are clear in their antityrant position: "Sadly, your Heimat became a foreign land to you!" (166); "And when I came into the valley of my Heimat, when I found my father, blind and robbed, I didn't cry" (176); "Whether the lake or the mountains separate us, we still are one people of one blood, and it is *one* Heimat out of which we came" (181); "I will find my happiness in my Heimat" (203); "I will sit myself on this stone bench, put out here to afford the wanderer a brief rest, here is no Heimat" (245).[9]

This Heimat became a subversive one because it was defined in opposition to Napoleon and his occupying forces. In this context Carl Schmitt, in his *Theorie des Partisanen: Zwischenbemerkung zum Begriff des Politischen* [Theory of the Partisan: An Interjection on the Concept of the Political], considers Heinrich von Kleist's play *Hermannsschlacht* [Arminius's Battle, 1808, first printed 1821], "the greatest partisan literature of all times" (15). It is not until Hermann has ordered the dismembered body of a raped woman, Hally (killed by her father to spare her shame), to be sent with fifteen messengers to the fifteen tribes of the Germans (act 4, scene 6) that Hermann's uprising becomes unified and successful. To galvanize the Heimat protectors into action, there has to be a woman to defend — even if she is in fifteen pieces. In one passage of Kleist's play the Roman *legat* [ambassador] Ventidius promises to bring the Roman empress Livia a lock of Thusnelda's (Hermann's wife's) golden hair as soon as the Germans are conquered. Germany is referred to by the feminine name "Cheruska" and as "the Heimat of those locks" (act 4, scene 9). The sexual symbolism of "Heimat of those locks," which can also stand for Thusnelda's sexual organ, is hard to miss. Whoever has the land possesses the Heimat of the locks.

Heimat fulfills different functions in different contexts. It is not a stable signifier. The changing notions of Heimat in history parallel, as may be expected, the changing notions of identity in history. The sense of humiliation and violation that Germany experienced under Napoleon, for instance, reflected itself in a notion of Heimat as victim. In contrast, the overly harmonistic, autonomy-privileging Western ego theories dominating the 1950s occur at a time when representations of Heimat champion an unquestioned center, an artificial and rigid unity of life within the sheltered, sunny space called Heimat. More recently, posttraditional identity theories have presented us with different versions of a decentered subject (the fragmented self, the "subjective splinters" [Negt and Kluge 395]), and here identity often includes a somatic dimension. These representations of Heimat become anti-Heimat (just as identity becomes anti-identity) if looked at from the point of view of traditional notions of Heimat (or of traditional theories of identity).

Heimat provides on a social level that which a self at ease with itself is supposed to provide on a personal level. Giddens combines the two notions when he speaks in several of his works about the human need for ontological security. Although he does not work with (maybe is unaware of) the idea of Heimat, one of Giddens's commentators, in allusion to Hegel's famous definition of freedom (*bey sich selbst seyn*), summarized this sense of an ontological security to which Giddens repeatedly refers as "a psychological state that is equivalent to feeling 'at home' with oneself and the world" (Cassell 14).

What was called Heimat in German premodern society structures — primarily one's own homestead (fields, house, livestock, extended family with hierarchical role and labor divisions) — provided, for that time at least, a low ontological level of anxiety. It provided means for survival and knowledge of one's place in a society where survival was basic. Heimat belonged to those who could share in this structure through property relations (marriage, inheritance). But most people (in total numbers) did not have a Heimat in that sense. Maids and farmhands, day laborers, traveling journeymen, craftsmen and craftswomen, *das fahrende Volk* [storytellers; actors, often in troupes; poets, bear tamers, musicians, magicians, physicians, or jokers — traveling people who would offer their services for entertainment at courts and in marketplaces] usually had more transitory lifestyles. To be able to call a place one's Heimat was a privilege, whereas mobility, as ever in German-speaking contexts, was treated with suspicion and associated with uncertainty, poverty, dishonesty, or worse.

As my father's letter exemplifies, since the second half of the eighteenth century Heimat has become increasingly associated with an inner emotional capacity to attach oneself with personalized memories of experiences to a place, a family, a specific landscape. What the Heimat that was one's own farmstead once provided, the more subjective, individualized idea of Heimat now provides: a low ontological level of anxiety, which is to say, identity, a sense of belonging — and all of this without the pain of having to come to terms with modernity's *Entzweiungen* [splits and fragmentations].

This is to express it positively. Expressing it negatively, one might say that wanting to have one's own Heimat is the beginning of that small, autistic, windowless world in which those who feel the need for the defensive structure of a Heimat begin to spin or imprison themselves. In either case, though, the defensive structures of a self and of a Heimat fulfill the same purpose: they provide a sense of ontological security at the expense of those who are not given access because they might threaten this small world — women, Jews, transient workers, those who do not speak the local dialect.

Notes

[1] Cf. Shierry Weber's essay "Aesthetic Experience and Self-Reflection as Emancipatory Processes: Two Complementary Aspects of Critical Theory" in *On Critical Theory,* ed. John O'Neill (Lanham MD: UP of America, 1989), 78–103.

[2] Cf. the following publications with Heimaten in their title: Pierre Kembo Mayamba's *Verlorene Gefühle: Leben zwischen zwei Heimaten* [Lost Feelings: Life Between Two Heimaten] (Frankfurt am Main: Haag + Herchen, 1995); Artur Kalnins's *Kapverdeaner zwischen Hamburg und Kap Verde: Emigration, Heimaten, Identität und soziale Wirklichkeit* [Cape Verdeans Between Ham-

burg and Cape Verde: Emigration, Heimaten, Identity, and Social Reality]
(Frankfurt am Main: Peter Lang, 1991); Kemal Kurt's *Was ist die Mehrzahl
von Heimat? Bilder eines türkisch-deutschen Doppellebens* [What is the Plural of
Heimat? Pictures of a Turkish-German Double-Life] (Reinbek bei Hamburg:
Rowohlt, 1995); Tommaso Morone's *Migrantenschicksal: Sizilianische Fami-
lien in Reutlingen. Heimat(en) und Zwischenwelt. Eine empirische Untersuchung* [The Fate of Migrants: Sicilian Families in Reutlingen. Heimat(en) and
the World Inbetween. An Empirical Survey] (Bonn: Holos, 1993); and *Neue
Heimaten, neue Fremden: Beiträge zur kontinentalen Spannungslage* [New
Heimaten, New Worlds Abroad: Contributions to the Tensions on the Con-
tinent], ed. Wolfgang Müller-Funk (Vienna: Picus, 1992).

[3] "Das Hinzutretende ist Impuls, Rudiment einer Phase, in der der Dualismus
des Extra- und Intramentalen noch nicht durchaus verfestig war."

[4] Cf. Erik Erikson, *Identität und Lebenszyklus* (Frankfurt am Main: Suhrkamp,
1970) and Cornelius Castoriadis, *The Imaginary Institution of Society*, trans.
Kathleen Blamey (Cambridge MA: MIT Press, 1987).

[5] The *Deutsche Wörterbuch von Jacob und Wilhelm Grimm* (Leipzig: S. Hirzel,
1905 [for the letter "S"]) and the 1910 *Muret-Sanders Dictionary* do not yet
contain "self-confidence" as one of the meanings of *Selbstbewußtsein*. By the
1970s the *Muret-Sanders Dictionary* (1974), as well as the major German en-
cyclopedias (the 1973 Brockhaus and the 1977 Meyers), contain "self-
confidence" as either the first or the second definition of *Selbstbewußtsein*.

[6] *Heimweh* as a word is first documented in 1569, when a Swiss soldier is re-
ported to have died of homesickness: "der Sunnenberg gestorben von heim-
we" — Sunnenberg died of homesickness (qtd. in Greverus, *Der territoriale
Mensch* [Frankfurt am Main: Athenäum, 1972], 112).

[7] The word, originally Swiss, was introduced, according to the *Neue Herder*
(Freiburg im Breisgau: Herder, 1949) into written German during the Ro-
mantic period: "Heimweh: schmerzende Sehnsucht nach der Heimat; Ggs.
Fernweh; dem Deutschen eigentümlich, gemütsgetränktes Wort, aus der
Schweiz von den Romantikern in die Schriftsprache übernommen. — Das
Heimweh kann sich bei Jugendlichen, besonders bei psychopathisch veran-
lagten, zu krankhafter Niedergeschlagenheit mit Appetitlosigkeit und Kräfte-
verfall steigern."

[8] In his essay "Traditionelle und kritische Theorie" (1937) Horkheimer observes that society can appear (and is judged) as an individual (*Traditionelle
und kritische Theorie* [Frankfurt am Main: Fischer, 1992], 205–59, here 245–
46).

[9] "Leider ist die Heimat / Zur Fremde dir geworden!" (166); "Und als ich
kam in's heimatliche Thal, /. . . / Als ich den Vater fand, beraubt und blind,
/ . . . / Da weint' ich nicht!" (176); "Ob uns der See, ob uns die Berge
scheiden, / . . . / So sind wir Eines Stammes doch und Bluts, / Und Eine

Heimat ist's, aus der wir zogen" (181); "Ich soll das Glück in meiner Heimat finden" (203); "Auf dieser Bank von Stein will ich mich setzen, / Dem Wanderer zur kurzen Ruh' bereitet — / Denn hier ist keine Heimat" (245).

4: Heimat and the Feminine

THE FRANKFURT SCHOOL WAS WELL AWARE of some of the costs the implementation of German Idealism extorted from the German intellectual tradition. One such cost was (and is) a curious ambivalence pertaining to questions of gender. Discussing Adorno, Joel Whitebook points out in his *Perversion and Utopia* that in Western intellectual history "the sexual impulse . . . is excised by Kant's philosophy in order to achieve the transcendental purity of its argument and the autonomy of the moral law" (259). Kant's division of what he considered "culture" into three sexless categories of reason (science, morality, and art) became formative for German philosophy, according either to future scholars' acceptance of it or resistance to it. (This triple-pronged rationality can be observed in — to name but two of the most influential figures — Max Weber, who was influenced by the neo-Kantians Emil Lask and Heinrich Rickert, and Jürgen Habermas, above all, probably, in his *Theorie des kommunikativen Handelns*. Both men work with differentiations among three "value spheres," each with its own sphere of logic.[1]) As Horkheimer notes, the Kantian exclusion of sexuality led during the eighteenth and nineteenth centuries to strict divisions between idealistic love and sexual desire in bourgeois norms and values (197). The patriarchal taboo against using one's wife for sex subjected the woman by casting her as a higher creature (294). Furthermore, because of an ever-increasing split between subject and object, between ego and id, and between idealist devotion and sexual desire, the individual failed to perceive the mother as a social and sexual person. This failure created within culture, according to Horkheimer, "the inhibited inclination toward the mother which returns in the gushing, sentimental receptivity for all symbols of dark, preserving, motherly forces" (197–98).[2]

Indeed, the late eighteenth century began to display within culture a "gushing, sentimental receptivity for all symbols of dark, preserving, motherly forces." We need only think of German Early Romanticism and its many darkly feminine symbols, such as night, darkness, wells, brooks, mermaids, shady gardens and dark woods, and the beautifully singing bird of twilight, the nightingale [*Nachtigall*], whose very name might explain in part why she became the proverbial Romantic bird. One could argue that dreams themselves, in early German Romantic writers, are often treated as messages from this darkly feminine night.

If we look at the historical context out of which this observation arises, we realize that the darkness Horkheimer associates with preserving, motherly forces is not only the nightly darkness of German Romanticism but also — since for the Frankfurt School in exile National Socialism was the phenomenon that needed to be understood — the long, not very differentiated, dark motherly shadows of National Socialist mythology. (Horkheimer and Adorno offer a complex, maybe even confused, understanding of Heimat. In their *Dialektik der Aufklärung* [Dialectics of Enlightenment, 1947] they write, for instance: "That the idea of Heimat stands in contrast to myth — which the fascists are attempting to turn into Heimat with lies — is the innermost hidden paradox of the epic" [85].[3] In other words, whereas Heimat for most observers is an essential part of the myths embedded in the German language — and the National Socialists made use of it to further German nationalism — Horkheimer and Adorno see myth and Heimat as, paradoxically, opposite entities. It is the National Socialists, according to Horkheimer and Adorno, who try to twist myth into Heimat.)

Moreover, German Romanticism has not only dark, preserving, motherly forces but also, as if in contrast, shining, innocent, feminine forces. It has the mother, and it has the bride. And the idealization of both has become transubstantiated into symbols ranging from wells to flowers, from the fertile earth and her loyal farmer to shining landscapes in which one thing nestles against [*sich anschmiegt*] another.

Heimat is such a symbol of preserving, motherly, or at least feminine, forces. But Heimat, although it contains nightingales and twilights, is not part of the darkness. One of its main qualities is that it shines brightly. Heimat is the shining bride or shining motherhood. But as such, Heimat is strongly implicated in two centuries of bourgeois subjection (that is, subjugation and subjectification) of women.

Clearly, the idea of Heimat participates in the historical idealization of the feminine and maternal and, thus, in the limitation of
opportunities for self-realization in women. In this chapter I will
document the feminization of rural space in literature and philol-
ogy and then trace the social implementation of this process of idealization and limitation of woman. To illustrate how Heimat is at
once charged with the feminine and complicitous in the denial of
actual power to women I borrow Elisabeth Bütfering's example of
the way German family farmsteads (also called Heimat) were
passed from father to son. Women can never fully identify with
Heimat, says Bütfering, just as women were passively included in
such transactions — the widowed mother or unmarried sister
would usually stay on the farm as cook and farmhand — yet were
excluded from the line of ownership and control. In the last part of
the chapter I summarize and discuss how, since the mid-1960s,
women such as Bütfering, Helga Königsdorf, Annegret Pelz, and
Gisela Ecker have begun critically to engage this feminization of
space as part of challenging the limited and limiting options for
identity handed down to them.

Heimat as the Ideal Woman (Imagined by Men)

During the second half of the eighteenth century gender, especially
the feminine as an all-pervasive but rarely openly stated Other, became formative in many social arenas, public and private. Heimat
conceptualizations — not despite but with and through the ideally
projected healed rift between subject and object, thought and being, essence and appearance, nature and culture — helped to implement a gendered view of the world. Heimat became a locus
where "fusional utopias" between male and female could be
lived — at least from a male perspective. In other words, from the
male point of view the modern split between male and female is
healed in the great feminized and originary space of Heimat, where
authenticity and disindividualization go hand in hand, and where
the one who lives at home may remain unaware of any tensions or
incongruities between the two.

Looking at Heimat representations of the last 200 years we
come to understand that conceptualizations of Heimat and the
feminine are closely related. One could even go so far as to say that

Heimat is so much like the ideal woman that it is a trope for each specific period's idealization of femininity. And in one case, which in its sexual directness is highly unusual, Heimat is a woman. The Swiss author Robert Walser writes in 1905 in a short prose piece titled "An die Heimat" [To My Heimat]:

> At one time I cried. I was so far from my Heimat; so many mountains, lakes, woods, rivers, meadows, and valleys lay between me and her, the beloved, the admired, the adored. This morning she embraces me, and I forget myself in her voluptuous embrace. No woman has such soft, such commanding arms; no woman, not even the most beautiful, such sensitive lips, no woman, not even the most sensitive, kisses with such infinite ardor the way my Heimat kisses me. (233)[4]

Walser is probably best known among Germanists for his brilliantly bitter-ironic portrayals of stuffy, sunny bourgeois pleasures. Here, as well, he is not quite as celebratory of his Heimat as might first appear. Typically, Walser reiterates bourgeois values, inflating them into such exaggerated praise that affirmation turns into irony and loving subversion. Thus, Walser points at some of the essential qualities of the turn-of-the-twentieth-century idea of Heimat: Heimat has all the qualities — seen from this male perspective — of a perfect woman in bed, only she is better than any woman could ever be.

The idea of Heimat — like notions of the ideal woman — changes with historical and social contexts. In premodern peasant cultures Heimat had the simple material meaning of one's own farmstead. The perfect woman in that societal structure was a *Bäuerin* [farmer's wife], not a *Magd* [farm girl] or *Näherin* [seamstress] or *Milchmädchen* [dairy maid]. She was a workhorse who, besides bearing children, provided her share of labor, immense practical knowledge, and resourcefulness to a common operation, the farm. (Oskar Maria Graf's autobiographical *Das Leben meiner Mutter* [The Life of My Mother, 1946] is an astonishingly sensitive and detailed portrait of such a woman's life.) She was healthy and had a firm character. An inner, subjective, emotional dimension was not only not expected of her but was seen as a negative quality — a useless, wasteful luxury and a potential source of weakness and disease. The *Bäuerin* [peasant woman] was quite like the Heimat of that world, of that reality. She typically married onto her husband's farm or Heimat, leaving the Heimat where she grew up; and there she was — besides giving birth to offspring — the material provider and preparer of bread, butter, meat, and eggs. This Heimat does not wish for outer or inner beauty. Inner beauty was not an issue (no one dreamed that such a thing as "inner beauty" could be anything but a first sign of mental disorientation). And outer beauty was suspect because it could enthrall men and divert much-needed resources. Thus, beautiful women in this premodern peasant world were suspect, associated with traveling groups or the city or the world of superstition.[5]

The modern idea of Heimat came into usage during the last third of the eighteenth century, at a time when a general secularization of religious forms of thinking started to shape the realm of the social imaginary as well as of the newly found psychic imaginary. We find an early instance of how changes in the idea of Heimat participated in this general secularization of religious forms of thinking in 1767 with Moses Mendelssohn's use of Heimat in his *Phaedon oder über die Unsterblichkeit der Seele* [Phaedon, or On the Immortality of the Soul]. This Enlightenment philosopher perceives Heimat as a place where the *Geist* [spirit, mind] feels at home because it is surrounded by the community of thought. "Reason and reflection," he writes, "lead our spirit from the sensual impressions of the physical world back into its Heimat, into the realm of thinking beings" (101).[6]

Heimat participates in this secularization of religious forms of thinking along with other key cultural concepts of German self-perception such as the self, the individual, reason, democracy, childhood, nature, and country (as in countryside). A common feature of all these concepts that entered German cultural self-perception during this period is an underlying binary structure. For every concept we can easily provide another to complete the antinomal binary pairings: For Heimat, it is *Fremde;* for the self, it is the Other; for the individual, society; for democracy, absolutism; for childhood, adulthood; for nature, culture; and for the country, the city.

Another common characteristic of these pairings is that gender associations impose the category of male and female on each: the self, the individual, absolutism, adulthood, culture, and the city are encoded masculine; the Other, democracy, childhood, nature, the country are encoded feminine. Heimat is associated with the feminine, with staying at home, *Fremde* with the masculine, with going out into the world. Usually the longed-for aspect — the one that was missing or not immediately present, at least from the male perspective — became the idealized, feminized one. This holds true for the exotic or beautiful Other, democracy, childhood, nature, and the country, as well as for Heimat.

Over the last two decades this binary gender pairing has been shown to be constitutive of many aspects of Western life and culture. And the various implementations of it in the social domain reflect back into the dynamics of gender and allow for a rich panoply of images. As Eduard Fuchs observed in 1909, descriptions and images of women during the seventeenth, eighteenth, and nineteenth centuries are a "composite of each period's most desired attractive qualities" (139).

Woman, as the supposedly natural creature, is, according to Horkheimer and Adorno, "the product of history which denaturizes her" (119).[7] Jürgen Habermas observes in 1990 that the cultural exclusion of women since the eighteenth century has been responsible for structural formations far beyond the small space of the primary family (1990, 19).

Hans Peter Herrmann shows in his introduction to *Machtphantasie Deutschland: Nationalismus, Männlichkeit und Fremdenhaß im Vaterlandsdiskurs deutscher Schriftsteller des 18. Jahrhunderts* [Power Fantasy Germany: Nationalism, Masculinity, and Xenophobia in Eighteenth-Century German Literary Discourse about Fatherland, 1996] and in the three essays he contributed to the volume — on the formation of modern patriotism, on masculinity, and on the topos of Germany as the fatherland during the eighteenth century — that the "national project" was one of simultaneously gaining a masculine identity and mastering women (25). Goethe's Götz, Werther, and Wilhelm Meister, Schiller's Karl Moor, and Arminius in the various Arminius plays are all part of the eighteenth century's increasing emphasis on "the inner unity of the male psyche and the man's delimitation toward the outside" (163). Needless to say, this development promoted a binary, gendered view of more than just the human.[8] One of the main qualities with which masculinity became associated was Germanness. Between 1740 and 1769, Herrmann points out, the image of the female figures shifted. In Johann Elias Schlegel's Arminius play of 1740 Thusnelda is able to defend herself when needed; she walks upright and goes to the battlefield, and Arminius consults with her as an equal before going into battle. In Klopstock's Arminius play of 1769 women need protection. Thusnelda stays out of the range of danger during the battle and is reduced "to being fearful for Arminius" or "to being thankful that he returns in good health" (175).

Lynn Hunt's *The Family Romance of the French Revolution* shows similar significant shifts in gender roles occurring in French novels around 1750 and again during the 1780s and 1790s. A tyrannical father figure is replaced by a good father who, in turn, is replaced by a "band of brothers." Hunt observes that by 1790 the murder of the tyrannical father had been accomplished in the novels before the king himself was killed (chapter 2). The surviving band of brothers was, however, now confronted with liberated women who had previously been controlled by the father. With regard to women Hunt shows — using the publicity surrounding the trial of Marie Antoinette — how extensive the fear of a "loss of sexual differentiation" (115) and gender reversal was during the Revolution. The band of brothers, therefore, had to exclude women, for instance, from the public sphere. "Women acting in the public sphere . . . were likened to beasts," writes Hunt. "They lost their femininity and with it their very humanity" (116). Hans Peter Herrmann's scholarship shows likewise how women's exclusion from the public sphere had occurred in the German Arminius plays by 1769.

In 1770, though, we can still also observe a remarkable double gendering in the idea of Mother Germany and Germany the Fatherland. Johann Gottfried Herder's "Vaterländische Gedichte" [Fatherland Poems] contains the 136-line-long "An den Genius von Deutschland" [To the Genius of Germany] about Germania, the mother figure who leads and guides and brings forth Germany. The ambiguous male-female engendering of Germany between fatherland and mother could be demonstrated no more clearly than in this poem. No fewer than five times we find the fatherland described as either an attribute of the mother or as the mother herself. A strange gender tension runs through the poem. Herder writes, for instance, about the noble sons whom he implores "to

defend the mother, fatherland, as a wall, which the fathers were"
(the original German is as ambiguous and unclear as the English
translation: ". . . zu beschützen / die Mutter, Vaterland, // als
Mauer, die die Väter waren"). A few lines later Herder writes quite
clearly: "Only the servant did not recognize you, you noble god-
dess fatherland!" ["Knecht nur hat dich nicht erkannt, / du Adel-
göttin Vaterland!"] And this fatherland even has a womb:
"Fatherland! o far from your womb, the desert was the lot of my
youth" ("Vaterland! o ferne deinem Schoos, / war Wüstenei mein
Jugendloos"] (vol. 29, 329–31).

By 1780 this motherly element of the German fatherland is
also expressed through the term Heimat. In Schiller's *Die Räuber*
(The Robbers), written in 1779/1780 and first printed in 1781,
we read three times of Heimat. (Both Ina-Maria Greverus and
Hans-Georg Pott claim that Johann Heinrich Voss's 1781 translation of *The Odyssey* offers the earliest instances of Heimat, in the
modern sense, in literature. Leaving aside Mendelssohn's 1767 use
of Heimat in his *Phaedon* and the Johann Jakob Schwabe 1762
translation of Rousseau's "son pays" in *Émile* as Heimat — one
could argue that these two usages were not yet altogether modern — Schiller's use in *Die Räuber* is still slightly earlier than
Voss's.)

The barely twenty-year-old Schiller uses Heimat each time with
a different emphasis, and these emphases presciently represent most
of the formative elements in the modern idea of Heimat. The
opening scene closes with a long soliloquy by Franz von Moor, the
Iago-like younger brother of Karl von Moor. Angry to despair at
his fate of being second-born and ugly, Franz cries out:

> That is your brother! Which means: He was shot out of the same
> oven that shot you out into the world — therefore, may he be
> holy unto you! — What an indeed complex consequence, this
> funny conclusion reached from the neighborhood of bodies and
> extended unto the harmony of the spirits, from the same Heimat
> to the same sensations, from the same food to the same inclina-
> tions. (19)[9]

Here we see the superimposing of Heimat and the mother's
womb.

The second time Schiller uses Heimat in *Die Räuber* is in act 4,
scene 1, where Karl, the older brother who, through a malicious

scheme by the younger Franz, has been forced to live in exile, returns incognito to his home country. Ecstatically, he greets the
land and landscape he calls Heimat:

> I greet you, soil of my fatherland! (*He kisses the earth.*) Sky of my
> fatherland! Sun of my fatherland! — and open fields and hills and
> streams and woods! I greet you all! — how delicious the breeze
> in the air from my Heimat mountains! how balmy the joy that
> flows from you toward the poor refugee! (87)[10]

Here Heimat combines nature, fatherland, and a feminized landscape all at once. Heimat and *fatherland* are used synonymously.

The third time Schiller works with the word Heimat in *Die
Räuber* is when Karl encounters what he thinks to be the ghost of
his father. Franz has taken advantage of a fainting spell of his father's to bury the latter alive, but the old man escapes the grave.
Karl, in this scene reminiscent of *King Lear,* comes upon the wandering ghost of his father and says sadly: "I will have masses read
so that this lost spirit may be sent into his Heimat" (112).[11] Here
Heimat is used in the older sense of paradise, as in the line from
the 1666 German Protestant hymn "Ich bin ein Gast auf Erden"
(I'm but a Guest on Earth), by Paul Gerhardt: "Mein Heimat ist
dort droben" [My Heimat is up there] (147). In short, the Heimat
of this traveler is in heaven.

So, in this play by Schiller from around 1780 we find three of
the crucial areas of reference for the idea of Heimat, two of them
what I would call modern — Heimat as an originary mother's
womb and a native landscape — and one a continuation of a much
older tradition of seeing Heimat as the paradise of eternal salvation.

We find the beginning of these formative processes for the
modern idea of Heimat in the second half of the eighteenth century. But they did not receive their almost universal institution
within the German-speaking world until the second half of the
nineteenth century (Herrmann 191; Dörner 212). Ina-Maria
Greverus reports in her chapter on popular adoration of the Rhine
that a large number of *Germania* songs of the Wilhelmine era replace the fatherland complex with a motherland complex, giving
the *Germania* cult a new component: "Germania, the 'beautiful,
noble, proud, strong woman' in her union with father Rhine: this
is no longer the almighty father, the strong man, but the flight of

'tired heroes' to a giving mother-woman-figure, the heroes able nevertheless to hold on to their own self-esteem-preserving image of protectors 'ready to defend'" (295).

Johann Jakob Bachofen's 1861 study of matriarchal cultures, *Das Mutterrecht* [The Mother Right], claims that an originary matriarchal society structure preceded the patriarchal one — a thesis that was quite influential in social anthropology during the second half of the nineteenth century and the first third of the twentieth. Even if a nineteenth-century writer did not speak of matriarchy, he might acknowledge the centrality of the myth of the female. For the young Nietzsche of *Die Geburt der Tragödie* of 1872, as mentioned earlier, Heimat is that which can be returned to through the synthesis of the Apollonian and the Dionysian. "What does the enormous historic need of dissatisfied modern culture point to," asks Nietzsche, "if not to the loss of myth, to the loss of the mythic Heimat, the mythical womb of the mother" (vol. 1, 146)?[12]

Ferdinand Tönnies, in his sociological classic *Gemeinschaft und Gesellschaft* [Community and Society, 1887], divided Western existence within modern societal structures into a system in which every individual human quality and awareness, every social form imaginable, is part of either a masculinized, conscious, progressive society or a feminized, intuitive, reactionary sense of community.

From Tönnies's divisions into universal male and female categories it is not far to Freud's findings on the sexuality of the mind and to Otto Weininger's infamous *Geschlecht und Charakter* [Sex and Character, 1903], in which the baptized Jew Weininger tries to stem, in what he considered measured, masculine, scientific German prose, the uncontrolled irrationality flowing into German-speaking culture through Jews and women. Even though Weininger maintained that he was thinking about ideal types, for him men provided structures for meaning, whereas women and Jews, both incapable of reason, provided the *un-Sinn*, the senselessness of impersonal procreation. Thus, male individuality, in Weininger, has to subdue women and Jews and must rise above collective and familial chains.

It is no surprise that this period also nurtures the idea of Heimat. Feminization of space and of an idealized premodern world find expression at this time in village and Heimat literature by Ludwig Anzengruber, Peter Rosegger, Ludwig Thoma, and

Ludwig Ganghofer, as well as in the institutionalization of *Biergär-ten* in Munich and other German-speaking cities (beer gardens glorify the outdoors and provide, in the form of a fenced-in natural space, a locale for drinking one's *Schoppen* [half-liter of beer, but in southern Germany also "baby bottle"]). Meanwhile in operetta and *Singspiel* [musical-comedy] halls, people, often newly arrived in the city, were presented with popular, often invented, traditions of the rural Heimat.

An internalized male-female dichotomy that shapes every aspect of life and meaning is one of the constitutive elements — maybe even *the* central element — of this modern period's consciousness. (I use *modern* here in the narrower sense, as in "modern art.") The period's most recognized images, be they literary, musical, or from the visual arts, all thematize this dichotomy from a male perspective with a great sense of urgency. In literature we think of such iconographic works as Theodor Fontane's *Effi Briest* (1894), Charles Baudelaire's *Les Fleurs du Mal* in Stefan George's 1891 translation,[13] Arthur Schnitzler's *Reigen* (1896–97)[14] and Hugo von Hofmannsthal's libretto for Richard Strauss's *Der Rosenkavalier* (written 1909/1910); in architecture we think of the feminized roundings of the *Jugendstil* with its stylized flowers and hostility to sharp edges; in music, such gender-polarized and yet gender-fusing works as Strauss's *Salome* (1905) and Claude Debussy's *Prélude à l'après-midi d'un faune* (1894), or Gustav Mahler's symphonies with voice that all make use of predominantly upper registers (1887–1908).[15] About modern art Marianna Torgovnick writes that "if we had to choose a single painting that exemplifies modernism in art, it would probably be Picasso's *Les demoiselles d'Avignon* (1907)" (119) — Pablo Picasso's cubist rendering of a brothel. "Its only rival as a modern icon," Torgovnick goes on, "(chosen by certain cognoscenti) would be Manet's *Olympia*" (1863).

The fusional utopian fantasies of the period permeate even the bourgeois tradition of mountain climbing. Consider, for instance, the fulminations of Ernest Bovet, president of the Swiss *Heimatschutz* [Association for the Protection of the Heimat], in 1912 against the construction of a cable car [*Drahtseilbahn*] to a mountaintop: "The white mountaintop is to the mountain climber a proud virgin whom one conquers slowly through devotion and endless love. She has an elevating effect on the soul for the rest of one's life. To the hero of the cable car, she is a waitress with whom one fools around for half an hour" (qtd. in Burckhardt-Seebass 310–11).[16]

The thematization of the woman is everywhere. The Oedipus complex has much to recommend it as a symbol (or a symptom) of the period between about 1880 and 1910, at least within a bourgeois context. Heimat during this period is an imagistically processed Oedipus complex in which the son's incestuous longings to reenter the mother (as in nature) become a socially shared and accepted state "of fusional perfection" (Whitebook 1995, 49).

The period between 1880 and 1910 is the source of those gendered images of Heimat that still saturate the idea. As the German theologian Helmut Gollwitzer put it bluntly in the early 1980s: We all come out of a mother's womb. Heimat is the extension of the mother's womb [*der weitere Mutterleib*] in which one grows up. "We all have to leave our Heimat, just as we have to leave childhood," observes Gollwitzer: "'Man has to go out into hostile life,' writes Schiller in his 'Glocke'" (124).

But at the same time, and probably most importantly, the idea of Heimat with its feminizing aspects sedimented itself in thought and language beyond conscious awareness of its sexual significations. Heimat became a word closely associated with both innocence and gender. The deep structure of its formative gender dichotomy was there; sexual innuendoes could be felt, but for the most part — the quotations from Nietzsche, Walser, and Bovet are exceptions — they were not expressed at the time.

Heimat, Freud, and the Uncanny

Nietzsche's allusion to Heimat as the mythical womb of the mother was an aside, hidden behind a larger argument about the Apollonian and Dyonisian in art; and Walser's short prose fragment, originally published in the small Basel newspaper *Der Samstag* in May 1905, did not reach a larger audience until Walser's rediscovery in the 1960s and 1970s. It was not Nietzsche or Walser but Freud, in his essay "Das Unheimliche," who was first widely heard on the subject and eventually taken seriously for his insight that the ideas of Heimat and of the feminine were essential parts of one another. Every line in "Das Unheimliche" gravitates toward the central paragraph of the essay in which the *Heimliche* — not in the sense of that which is secret but in its more literal sense of the homelike, the Heimat-like, the familiar — and the *Unheimliche,* the uncanny, are presented as but variations of the same thing. (My English translation, which uses "homelike" for *heimlich* and "uncanny" for *unheimlich,* cannot duplicate the closeness between the German *heimlich* and *unheimlich.*) Freud states:

> It sometimes happens that neurotic men declare the female genital to be something uncanny to them. But this uncanny thing is the entrance to the old Heimat of humankind, to the location in which everyone of us has lived first. "Love is to be homesick," says a jocular expression; and when a dreamer dreams of a location or a landscape and then still thinks in his dream, "That looks familiar; I've been here before," then the interpretation[17] may replace the location or the landscape with the mother's genital or body. Therefore the uncanny in this case as well is that which was formerly home, that which has been known from the beginning. The prefix *"un"* in this word, however, is a marker of displacement. (258–59)[18]

The sexual charge in the idea of Heimat continues to affect discussions of Heimat, as well as the use of the term Heimat, today. W. G. Sebald, for instance, discusses in his *Unheimliche Heimat* examples of literary representations of Heimat as "perfect examples of longing-filled, idyllic writing" (24) without any sign that he has noted the sexual tones in the Austrian writer Charles Sealsfield (Karl Anton Postl, 1793–1864), who describes in his *Österreich, wie es ist* (*Austria as It Is*)[19] a "landscape that nestles against the lightly undulating country" and orchards and wheat fields that "lie bedded in the deeper depressions (of this landscape)" (24).[20] In his 1986 essay (reprinted in *Unheimliche Heimat*) on Hermann Broch's *Bergroman* [Mountain Novel] Sebald refers to the "equation nature-mother-Heimat" (124) as he would to a cliché. And one does not object to such an assessment, especially for the period between 1933 and 1945. (Broch began work on *Bergroman* in 1934 and had not finished revising it when he died in 1951.) This surely was the epoch when, with the assistance of National Socialist propaganda, the ideal woman was a mother, nature, and Heimat. In fact, the tropes of femininity were being mythicized to such a degree that latent eroticization turned into crude ideology. But Sebald refrains from looking closely at femininity and Heimat. And yet, he approaches the subject repeatedly. In a 1989 essay on Peter Altenberg (reprinted in *Unheimliche Heimat*) Sebald observes that one assumes "natural Heimat" — according to the societal structures in which it [*sie* (the feminine form)] is supposedly *für immer aufgehoben* [lifted up forever[21]] — "to be in the natural essence of woman" (69). The original German reads "im natürlichen Wesen der Frau." But he stops there.

Two other opportunities to inquire more closely into the connections between Heimat and male constructs of an ideal woman or mother occur in this essay when Sebald mentions without comment a lake whose color Altenberg describes as "milchblau" [milk blue] (66) and when he observes that Altenberg spent exactly twenty-three summers in Traunsee, the place the Austrian novelist associates with a sense of Heimat. Again without further comment Sebald writes: "Curiously, he [Altenberg] was also twenty-three years old when there occurred a deep and irreparable rift between him and his mother" (67). From our later perspective, much German Heimat scholarship until the late 1980s looks like a willful repression of a more general awareness that male notions of the feminine are formative in the idea of Heimat.

Friedrich Kittler, to name an exception, discussing in a 1986 essay nostalgia in Kleist's *Hermannsschlacht* and Schiller's *Wilhelm Tell,* notes that in both plays a woman who can become a symbol for Heimat has to be introduced (159) because to perform the miracle of teaching Heimat anew to people who have lost their Heimat one needs more than a physician. The only ones capable of performing such miracles are poets and women (155). Kittler goes on to discuss the connections between woman, mother, and Heimat — not in general, however, but only in Kleist's *Hermannsschlacht.* He finds that for warriors there is no "tellurian Heimat without a mother idol" (160).

Whether it is a mother idol or a feminized myth, we can almost always observe gender as a formative element of Heimat, whereas it is quite the exception when we find it, as in Kittler, to be an overt element in a discussion of the idea of Heimat. Scholarship that tiptoes around the awareness of the formative feminine in the idea of Heimat was, and to a large degree still is, the norm. For instance, Alon Confino, in his *The Nation as a Local Metaphor* (1997), half of which is devoted to studying Heimat in late nineteenth- and early twentieth-century Heimat associations, does not engage gender as a formative element in Heimat at all. Consider the following passage:

> Heimat was often addressed in the second person singular: "O you [*Du*] my Heimat, you my native land / How my heart has turned to you full of love!" Anthropomorphizing Heimat was seen as neither ridiculous nor preposterous, but elicited instead an intimate relationship with it. Thus a reader of a Heimat book was not an outside observer to an unfolding of facts, but always an integral part of the narrative, the landscape, and the history. "It is a bright May morning," opens a Heimat book for Kirchheim unter Teck, "I would like to take you by the hand, dear reader, and to lead you into the quiet splendor of the valley's spring." (102–3)

It is hard to miss the overtly sexual quality in these sentences. And it is even harder to understand how gender as a formative quality in Heimat can so often be conspicuously left out of discussions of Heimat. Only since the 1970s do we find some still rare cases that restate, sometimes quite bluntly, what Freud saw in 1919 in his essay "Das Unheimliche."

Until the late 1960s this unabashed superimposition of nature, landscape, and the feminine remained the unchallenged norm; it was not taken up by scholars until the 1970s and 1980s. At the risk of overstating matters slightly, one could say that until the mid-1960s German scholarship on this issue did not move beyond the Freud of "Das Unheimliche." Then, in the Heimat scholarship of the 1970s and 1980s we finally, albeit still rarely, read these implied recapitulations of Freud: that Heimat is simply the extension of the mother's womb (Gollwitzer 124), or that all homesickness is "an unconscious wish to return to one's intrauterine past" (Johannes Lindner on homesickness in 1951, but cited for Heimat in general in 1972 by Greverus 117), or that "the *männerbündnisch*-oriented *Eidgenossen's* regression toward a yearningly serenaded Heimat is a compensation for the neglected feminine parts [of one's individual identity]" (Hans Marti, qtd. in Greverus 1972, 338). But a sentence by Lothar Baier about the countryside ("das Land") could be extended to woman and then used as a caption for the entire period between German Idealism and the late 1960s: "We want to know so little in detail about the country [or, we might add, about woman], so it seems to me, in order that it [she] remains an uninscribed surface onto which we can project, without hindrance, images of our wishes and of our manias" (49).[22] True, some lyrical rephrasings of the same insights enrich the picture. Ernst Bloch, for instance, remarks in his 1959 *Das Prinzip Hoffnung* [The Principle of Hope] in the chapter "Reiz der Reise" [The Charm of Traveling] — especially in the subchapter "Fernwunsch und historisierendes Zimmer im neunzehnten Jahrhundert" [The Longing for Faraway Places and the Historicizing Room in the Nineteenth Century] — that "a harem's canopy hung over almost all the *intérieurs* of the nineteenth century" (vol. 5, 441).[23] Bloch, realizing that travelers look in the exotic of faraway places for a *"genaues Widerspiel zur Heimat"* [precise counterimage to one's Heimat] (vol. 5, 437) — sees the exotic in nineteenth-century *intérieurs* as the return of an exotically reversed Heimat into one's own home. But in all of this we are looking with a man's eyes into a feminine, imprisoning space — the harem's canopy as a precise counterimage to one's unique Heimat, the harem's many women for one man as a precise counterimage to one Heimat for many men.

Women's Voices on Heimat

Since the 1970s women's voices have taught us to rethink some basic assumptions that had remained virtually unquestioned since Kant and Hegel. Not until women themselves began critically to challenge both the identities handed down (or up) to them and their roles in modern Western language and tradition did we begin to see the shift that we are currently experiencing, a shift no less revolutionary than eighteenth-century Enlightenment and Idealism in those moments when the idea of the bourgeois self began to unsettle the imaginary and political world order. Not only has recent scholarship shown that many previously unquestioned assumptions about gender were much more constitutive of our social and psychic identity, imaginary and otherwise, than we had previously been able to think; it has also begun to democratize literature, the arts, and, to a degree, scholarship. (In the wake of Gilles Deleuze and Felix Guattari's *Kafka: Toward a Minor Literature,* translated into English in 1986 — especially the influential chapter "What is a Minor Literature?" — much scholarship has reflected a turn toward an awareness that for the scholars of culture there are, in a sense, only minor literatures.)

Crucial is the inquiry now underway into the gendered way of constructing home, space, and territory. Caren Kaplan's 1987 article "Deterritorializations: The Rewriting of Home and Exile in Western Feminist Discourse" does exactly that. After recapitulating some of the then-recent feminist writing on centers and margins, dominated by issues of power (still very Foucaultian), she presents a study, based on two texts,[24] of issues of "home," feminist theory, location, identity, and positionality in personal narratives. In the end Kaplan celebrates "a new terrain, a new location, in feminist poetics" that she has found in the two writers whom she considered. She sees a "space in the imagination which allows for the inside, the outside, and the liminal elements of inbetween" (197). Overall, this essay on ideas of home, territorialization, and exile is, for the mid-1980s, a not untypical mix between a politically engaged style and an enthusiastic if uncritical celebration of a newly discovered feminine self. (It should be noted that since publishing this essay Kaplan has gone on to write highly refined, theoretical scholarship. Her latest book, *Questions of Travel: Postmodern Discourses of Displacement* [1996], shows her as an outstanding scholar on issues of negotiable space — for instance, in travel, tourism, exile, and metaphors of feminism. As such, however, she no longer pays much attention to the idea of "home." Except for a short passage on Adorno's notion of "writing as 'home'" [118–19], the notion of "home" in *Questions of Travel* has been reduced to an ideal construct that is frequently mentioned but is useful only in its capacity to provide contrast to different forms of displacement.)

Equally relevant for us — despite a slightly different aim — is Annegret Pelz's "Karten als Lesefiguren literarischer Räume" [Maps as Figures for Reading Literary Spaces, 1995], in which she discusses a 1588 map that shows Europe in the shape of a woman in a long dress. Italy represents the right arm, Spain the head, Portugal the crown, England a scarflike piece of clothing, Denmark the left forearm and hand, France (Gallia) the chest above the décolletée, etc.[25] Above this queen's (or princess's) crowned head (that is, above the organ commonly associated with thinking), the map reads "Occidens." Close to the woman's right breast the Danube begins and, flowing by her reproductive organs, runs all the way past the bottom of her dress to the Black Sea at the right edge of the map. There, directly opposite the "Occidens" by the head, we read "Oriens." The Orient is linked by the Danube to an origin in Europe — to Europe's reproductive organs and the breast.

Pelz shows through the allegory of this map the close interrelations between gender, notions of space, and European geography from the sixteenth century to the present.[26] The title of the map, "*Europa prima pars terrae in forma virginis*" [Europe, the first place of the earth in the form of a virgin], combines a mythical relationship with space (Europa, daughter of Phoenix) and a feminization of space in early modern cartography. Pelz observes that, fittingly, in 1588 this female figure does not have any feet. The dress supposedly covers them, but Pelz is certainly right in pointing out that these hidden "signs of self-ownership [*Selbstbesitz*]" (118) also indicate that virgin Europa cannot participate in arranging her own relationships in space. Pelz goes on to discuss how eighteenth-century travel literature by women worked to detach mythical images of the world from the female body.[27]

At the end of her essay Pelz looks at a few texts in which *intérieurs* in women authors — Charlotte Perkins-Gilman's 1891 *The Yellow Wall-Paper*, Virginia Woolf's 1929 *A Room of One's Own*, and Unica Zürn's 1958 *Das Haus der Krankheiten* [The House of Illnesses] — indicate how their own bodies become strangers to them. In the end Zürn's text — just like Kaplan's — is allowed to stand for a new way of mapping the female body, one that is no longer a handbook for male hegemony over the individual female body space. Now, just as in Kaplan's observations, "the hierarchical spaces of the old allegorical map are so intertwisted that one can no longer differentiate between orient and occident, between body and space, between inner and outer, between space and time" (124).

Among women who joined the philosophical and theoretical discourse on the idea of Heimat since the late 1980s, Helga Königsdorf, Elisabeth Bütfering, and Gisela Ecker are remarkable. Königsdorf, born in 1938 and a physicist by training, began publishing her creative work in the mid-1970s in the former GDR. In a journal-like inner voice Königsdorf writes in her autobiographical *1989 oder Ein Moment Schönheit: Eine Collage aus Briefen, Gedichten, Texten* [1989 or a Moment of Beauty: A Collage of Letters, Poems, Texts] about the reunification year 1989. The book includes the text of a talk she gave in Marburg (then still in West Germany) on January 22, 1989, with the title "Dichtung und Heimat." Clearly alluding to *Dichtung und Wahrheit* (Poetry and Truth, 1811–13), the curious autobiography in which Goethe shapes the factual truth of his life according to higher (that is, aesthetic) rules, Königsdorf mixes in a refreshingly unsystematic, impressionistic way various approaches to the idea of Heimat. For one thing, she connects her own feelings about the term — and this is missing from most other writers on Heimat — with her feelings about the word *deutsch* [German]. Heimat for her is no apolitical entity. Instead, Königsdorf tries to understand her own ambiguous feelings about both Germany and Heimat. She tries to analyze her experience of longing for a new Heimat after she has lost her old one.

Königsdorf begins her speech with a simile: "Some words are like freshly fried, sugared *Krapfen* [doughnuts]. When you put them into your mouth, they first taste sweet, and afterwards the tongue develops blisters from the burns." She goes on to explain why, at first unconsciously, she stopped using the word Heimat. "To give up one's Heimat," she writes, "can be like surgery necessary for survival." In giving up the word Heimat, she gained and lost at the same time. She lost "that valley where the horizon was so close." She lost "an outer identity." But at the same time she gained, because an "inner identity became necessary." For Königsdorf, Heimat is "dangerous like a drug." She knows that she is addicted to Heimat, and Heimat would mean losing her self in a need to belong ["meine Sehnsucht nach Zugehörigkeit"].

And suddenly, in a perfectly foreshadowed associative jump, Königsdorf moves from the Heimat where she is in danger of losing her sense of self to the word *deutsch*. *Deutsch* becomes one of the possible words offering a sense of *Zugehörigkeit* [belonging]. At first, *deutsch* seems as neutral as a subject in school — as in *Sport, Musik und Deutsch*. (In her own biography this period must have occurred around the age of nine or ten.) But when she looks deeper, she finds behind that seemingly neutral word an alarming discomfort. She remembers being an object, an object that was supposed to become part of the "Final Solution." (Königsdorf has a Jewish grandmother.) "Ich war ein für die Endlösung vorgesehenes Objekt" [I was an object designated for the Final Solution]. "I," "object," and "German" have become one; and, fittingly, in 1989 Königsdorf is also reminded of her pious school-essay topics, such as "die Einheit Deutschlands" [the Unity of Germany], for which she had received good grades. But during her first trips abroad (she was, I infer from the text, thirteen or fourteen), even though she had no personal guilt, she felt shame for the word *deutsch* in her passport. Thus, her essay "Dichtung und Heimat" begins with her reflections on words that first taste sweet and then burn blisters on the tongue; passes through that Heimat that makes the subject, the self, disappear; and ends with shame for the word *deutsch* in her passport, her *Ausweis*, which, itself a dangerous word, carries in it not only identification, as in *sich ausweisen*, but also *ausweisen* [to expel or deport].

In Königsdorf's terms, Heimat is an ungendered concept. Instead, it has physical qualities or is felt through physical sensations: it burns and so creates blisters like a too-hot, sweet dessert. But its absence creates pain, as well. Heimat for her is like a body part "which you can't get rid of even though it isn't quite the way it should be — but which you don't really want to be rid of anyway" (15–17).

Elisabeth Bütfering, an almost unknown German historian and political scientist who since 1991 has made her living outside of academia, approaches the idea of Heimat from a new and thoughtfully conceived, theoretical yet personal, angle. She was invited in 1990 to contribute an article to the collection of Heimat materials edited by Will Cremer and Ansgar Klein for the Bundeszentrale für politische Bildung. Bütfering asks probing questions in this essay (and fought hard for them to remain in the text[28]). Having been asked to write on "Heimat aus Frauensicht" [Heimat from the Woman's Point of View], she asks in an early footnote: "May I conclude from the proposed description of my subject that all other contributions approach Heimat from the point of view of men?" (417).

At the beginning of her article, published under the title "Frauenheimat Männerwelt: Die Heimatlosigkeit ist weiblich,"

[Woman's Heimat, a Man's World: Living Without a Heimat is Feminine], she notes that as far as she can see (and the present author has to concur), even though it seems obvious that Heimat signifies different things for men and women, gender difference has never been among the paradigms for discussion of the idea of Heimat. Thus, looking at Heimat could serve, she thinks, as a good example of how an obvious male-centeredness at once determines and severely truncates one model of our common world: so far "all historical, social, cultural, and psychic implications of Heimat" (417) betray their male origin.

After offering examples of how in scholarship the idea of Heimat is associated, conventionally but without reflection, with such subjects as homestead, mother, and *Mutterboden* [mother soil], she makes the way homesteads were passed on from one generation to the next stand paradigmatically for discussions of Heimat up to 1990 (417). Farmstead and property in German peasant society were for centuries passed on from father to son. The *Bauer* [farmer] on a specific day *übergab* [handed over] *die Heimat* [the farm along with all its property] to his oldest son, or, if he did not have a son, maybe his son-in-law. From then on he was the *Altbauer* [old farmer], who helped on the farm. But he was no longer the one making decisions. His son, now the *Bauer,* was responsible for the operation of the Heimat. Women had no say in the matter. They were included in the transaction, becoming maids and farmhands to their son, their husband, their older brother, or their nephew. The only other decent option women could decide on for themselves was, for centuries, the convent. (The Swabian expression for the day when the eldest son gets married and, often the same day, takes over the family farm, is that on this day the younger brothers and sisters go "to their Heimat's funeral" [*Schwäbisches Wörterbuch,* qtd. in Bausinger 1984, 12–13].[29] This expression did not mean that the Heimat was dead to everyone — only to them.)

It is easy to see how women were likely to have at best an ambiguous relationship to this Heimat that included them, that made use of them, without giving them any real choice. Bütfering shows that the same can be said for women's relationship to the modern idea of Heimat. Reviewing the most widely circulating scholarship on Heimat, Bütfering comes to the conclusion that even though both Ina-Maria Greverus and Hermann Bausinger see the strong interrelation between the feminine and spatial qualities of Heimat, they never thematize how this supposedly feminine world came about for either the men whose perspective was formative in it or for the women who were its models and captives; nor did they thematize women's experiences of feeling like a stranger in this man's world or begin to visualize the inner worlds of Heimat — the insides of houses and the Heimat emotions of women themselves. (While this characterization is certainly true of Greverus and Bausinger, a few fictional examples show eloquently this experience of living as a stranger in a man's world. Maria Beig and Anna Wimschneider are probably the two best-known portrayers of country women living in men's worlds. Beig's five books of the 1980s and her 1997 *Annas Arbeit* [Anna's Work] and Wimschneider's 1984 *Herbstmilch* [Autumn Milk] are about women's painful self-alienation in a masculine peasant world. One of the most memorable examples, however, of a woman waking up away from her Heimat the morning after she has married a farmer and moved from her family farm to his can be found in Oskar Maria Graf's 1946 *Das Leben meiner Mutter*.)

Bütfering, herself feeling like a stranger in this 900-page collection of essays, finds that in the space allotted to her (some twenty printed pages, or approximately 10,000 words) she can provide but a first step and, defining Heimat broadly, cursorily show many possible directions in which future scholarship might go. She says in another footnote: "In general it seems altogether unrealistic to me to let the woman's (women's) perspective(s) on such a topic be represented by one female contributor while numerous men present theirs" (419). The collection of essays contains pieces by thirty-eight male and seven female contributors. But the other contributions by women are on such applied aspects of Heimat as workers' migrations, sites of childhood, local radio stations, tourism, personal memorials, and family names and have in common a lack of interest in questions of gender. Bütfering is, therefore, not unjustified in feeling alone in presenting Heimat from a consciously female perspective.

Again noting the lack of gender-sensitive scholarship on Heimat, this time in the field of the sociology of literature, Bütfering proceeds to outline twelve approaches reconceiving the idea of

Heimat with a sensitivity to gender. In discussing some of the approaches she gives "subjective and associative" (419) hints of possible results.

The suggested approaches fall into three categories. The first proposes to interview women about what Heimat means to them as women. Bütfering's own unsystematic poll among her friends suggests a highly complex situation, with Heimat provoking a wide range of associations. Often, Heimat is that which a woman needs to get away from in order to have a chance to exist. Alternative idylls to Heimat, then, are independently created homes or apartments, a social network of friends, a partner, or a job. In some cases such alternative idylls are again called Heimat. Cities or towns are considered Heimat only in the rarest cases. But most important, far fewer women formulate answers to the question about their thoughts about Heimat than simply refuse to answer the question. The majority of women react with incomprehension and irritation. Bütfering summarizes:

> Obviously Heimat for most women is not a category which they are accustomed to using to describe their emotions and their life situations. At the same time their associations show a deep insecurity and defensiveness against roles assigned to them early in life and against traditional rankings. (421)

The second category of approaches, according to Bütfering, should look into outside definitions and roles assigned to women when Heimat is at issue. Bütfering suggests an analysis of women's roles in *Heimatliteratur,* Heimat films, songs, etc., as well as of historical sources. She makes preliminary attempts to gather seemingly ahistorical traditional images that aim at equating Heimat and femininity. In local songs of praise, for instance, towns, regions, or cities often become one with an object that is to be conquered. Tübingen is described in the *Tübingen-Lied,* a nineteenth-century student song in praise of the city, as "lying beautifully like a bride" (421; citing Greverus 1972, 325).

In part, Bütfering says, this work has already been begun — but only begun — by Ina-Maria Greverus's analysis of nineteenth-century repertoires of *Männergesangsvereine* (Greverus 1972, 303–24) and by Klaus Theweleit in his *Männerphantasien* [Male Fantasies, 1977], especially the first volume, subtitled *Frauen, Fluten, Körper, Geschichte* [Women, Floods, Bodies, History]. She suggests that similar work might be undertaken by analyzing the gendered polarities inherent in such binaries as *Vater Staat* [father state] and *Muttersprache* [mother tongue] or by analyzing the close correlation between constructs of identity and constructs of femininity.

The third category of approaches should inquire into women's perceptions of and reactions against these "outside definitions" and role assignments and, as a variation of this, should look further into social expressions of accommodation or reaction to the patriarchal idea of Heimat. Here much is happening already as far as women's social roles in general are concerned. But a focus on the idea of Heimat, in particular, is missing. Bütfering cites a well-known quotation from Karoline von Günderode, not only, as is usually the case, for its expression of the imprisoned female self but also for its reference to Heimat. Günderode (1780–1806) wrote around 1800: "And Heimat turns into prison. Therefore away, away into the open space, out of the tight, dull life" (428). Bütfering notes with resignation that Günderode knew perfectly well that the open space was not available to her, a woman. But she observes that it is time to wonder why Günderode saw Heimat — and not home, house, family, marriage, motherhood, or the kitchen — as turning into prison.

In cataloguing women's perceptions of and reactions against outside definitions and role assignments, Bütfering suggests that it will be important to look at recent women's autobiographical writings as a new women's history of Heimat — a history, that is, of women's occupation (or nonoccupation) of space, public and private. Overall, Bütfering's article points to many rich frontiers for further study of Heimat.

When one is looking for it, the feminized quality of the idea of Heimat appears in almost every representation of it since 1780. It is striking. Beatrice von Matt in her essay "'Wer Heimat sagt, nimmt mehr auf sich': Max Frischs Auseinandersetzung mit der Schweiz" ["Whoever Says Heimat Takes on More Than That." Max Frisch's Encounters with Switzerland] looks, for instance, at various of Frisch's protagonists — all of whom are male — and their attitudes toward Switzerland (that is, toward what, according to Matt, Frisch perceived as his Heimat). She finds that all of Frisch's protagonists have troubled and tense love relationships, both with women and with Switzerland. And, indeed, Frisch's oeuvre is the record of lifelong parallel agonies of afflicted attachment and addictive detachment. But Matt remains focused on Frisch and his works and does not try to make statements about qualities of Heimat in general.

One has to remain curious about the results of a gender-sensitive engagement with Heimat in the contemporary German context. None of the studies Bütfering called for in her 1990 article have — as far as she knows[30] — been carried out in Germany.

On the other hand, there are signs that Heimat is beginning to be investigated from gender-sensitive angles. In the United States, for instance, the session "Heimat and the Topographies of Memory" at the German Studies Association Conference in 1997 showed that work of this kind is in progress. Brigitte Rossbacher, Friederike Emonds, and Anna Kuhn spoke on how German women writers of various periods have appealed for a redefinition of the idea of Heimat, lest Heimat continue to exclude women and, at the same time, use them. (Emonds's essay appeared in print as "Contested Memories: Heimat and *Vaterland* in Ilse Langner's *Frau Emma kämpft im Hinterland*.")

Despite its promising title, the 1995 essay collection *Frauen schaffen sich Heimat in männlicher Welt* [Women Create a Heimat for Themselves in a Male World] (eds. Elisabeth Camenzind and Kathrin Knüsel) does not provide a serious inquiry into the idea of Heimat. Rather, it demonstrates the confusion feminist psychologists and psychoanalysts experience when trying to feel at home either in the world in general or in the field of psychoanalysis in particular. Still, the book shows — implicitly rather than explicitly — that Heimat could potentially be a crucial element in gender-sensitive negotiations of psychoanalytical categories.

Indications of gender-sensitive new work on Heimat can, however, be found in the 1997 essay collection *Kein Land in Sicht: Heimat — weiblich?* [No Land in Sight: Heimat — Feminine?] Most of the contributions go back to a symposium that was held in Paderborn in 1994. The twelve essays and the introduction, all by women, show that the topic was seen as an important area of inquiry.

Ecker's two contributions to the volume best advance scholarship on gender and Heimat; the other contributions, although they make for fascinating reading, are, in the main, case studies of aspects of gender in German culture that are linked, as if in hind-sight, through introductions or conclusions to the Heimat idea.

Ecker's introduction to the volume, "'Heimat':[31] Das Elend der unterschlagenen Differenz" ["Heimat": The Misery of the Neglected Difference] presents a valuable review of what has and has not been done so far in the area of gender-sensitive research into the idea of Heimat. Curiously, Ecker is quite ungenerous toward Bütfering, reading her crudely and incorrectly as "complaining about there not being enough 'Heimat' for women" (10). But overall her review, despite a rather unwaveringly Oedipal interpretation of Heimat, shows that the idea has a long tradition of being femininely encoded and that users of Heimat remain by and large "unconscious" (30) of this feminine quality. She shows that the attributes of Heimat have to remain veiled in the unconscious in order for the concept to retain its powers. Ecker demonstrates further that female characters often have the undeclared function of representing the Heimat. Male figures desire the Heimat, but they are capable of moving away from it and returning (130). A gender-sensitive perspective, she writes — disregarding Bütfering, but otherwise correctly — has, "so far, amazingly, not been explicitly adopted in discussions of Heimat" (10). Thus, her stated goal is to introduce aspects of gender into Heimat research (10), to counter the suppression of "the neglected difference." In her essay on Clara Viebig and Maria Beig (the former active from the turn of the century until the end of the Weimar Republic, the latter from the early 1980s through the present), Ecker shows these women writers as representing Heimat for their audience both in what they write and in their persons (130–31).

In the introduction, in a memorable spatialization of her findings on an 1895 novel — which remain valid when applied more generally — Ecker observes that "while the male figures of the 'Heimat' . . . are given differentiated features, the center and the outside are statically embodied by the motherly-feminine figure and the figure of the Jew respectively." Both motherly-feminine figure and Jew "are being defined by the metaphoric aspect of 'Heimat' and exhaust themselves with this function" (16).[32]

This multiple image of Heimat from Ecker's introduction — the feminine and motherly figure in the immobile center, the male figures in the negotiable and changing spheres about this center, and, on the outside, the highly mobile Jewish figure who stereo-typically represents everything that arises from a new time and a new social order and that is endangering of the Heimat (16) — leads well into the first essay in the book, Silke Wenke's study of the reshapings of the *Neue Wache* memorial [new vigil monument] in Berlin. "Die Mutter in der Mitte Berlins: Strategien der Rekon-struktion eines Hauptstadtzentrums" [The Mother in the Middle of Berlin: Strategies of Reconstructing the Center of a Capital] ad-dresses the new installation of a Käthe Kollwitz mother figure holding her dead son in Germany's "Zentrale Gedenkstätte für die Opfer von Krieg und Gewaltherrschaft" [Central Memorial for the Victims of War and the Rule of Violence]. ("War" and "the Rule of Violence" [*Gewaltherrschaft*] are, indeed, impersonal formula-tions in this naming of the Neue Wache.) Again, the motherly is in the immobile center.

It is clear that research on the formative aspects of gender in Heimat is just beginning. But despite the early stage of the work, we can see that many new insights into German self-perceptions regarding innocence, nature, geography, utopias, sexual fantasies, and national identities, as they are based in assumptions about gender, are waiting to be discovered. In the process much defen-siveness and uneasiness will have to be overcome. Gisela Ecker found that out quickly — not surprisingly, if we consider how deeply implicated Heimat has been in assumptions of German in-nocence and in the centuries-long domination of women. She ob-serves in a footnote that looking "critically at the cultural circulation" of the Heimat concept during work on her book *Kein Land in Sicht: Heimat — weiblich?* had some surprising conse-quences:

> While working on this topic, it was an unexpected surprise for me that people smelled behind every critical statement about "Hei-mat" the intention to destroy their individual sentiments about the place of their childhood — as if it were not possible to respect these highly concrete ties and to criticize at the same time the cultural circulation of an idea. (12)

The defensiveness about one's idealized space (or time) of child-hood as represented in the term Heimat is but one of the many defenses that will need to be breached to introduce gender into discussions of Heimat. Other areas where taboos seem likely to spring up are of an ethical ("no one of good moral qualities gives Heimat a bad name") and a sexual ("there is nothing dirty about what is natural") quality. We can also expect self-protectiveness from local, as well as national, patriotisms, especially where they intersect with individual constitutions of identity ("someone who thinks critically about Heimat cannot possibly be part of it"). Nevertheless, there is no doubt that such discomfiting work needs to be, and is in the process of being, done.

Notes

[1] For a discussion of this topic, see Thomas McCarthy's "Reflections on Rationalization in the *Theory of Communicative Action*" and Habermas's response, "Questions and Counterquestions," in *Habermas and Modernity*, ed. Richard J. Bernstein (Cambridge MA: MIT Press, 1985), 176–91 and 192–216.

[2] "und die gehemmte Neigung zur Mutter kehrt in der schwärmerischen, sentimentalen Empfänglichkeit für alle Symbole dunkler, mütterlicher, erhaltender Mächte wieder."

Cf. Andrew Hewitt's "A Feminine Dialectic of Enlightenment?" where he argues, not uncontroversially, that women are included in *Dialectics of Enlightenment* "— somewhat paradoxically — precisely *by* their exclusion" (*New German Critique* 56 [Spring-Summer 1992], 143–70, here 147, Hewitt's italics).

[3] "Daß der Begriff der Heimat dem Mythos entgegensteht, den die Faschisten zur Heimat umlügen möchten, darin ist die innerste Paradoxie der Epopöe beschlossen."

[4] "Ehemals weinte ich. Ich war so weit entfernt von meiner Heimat; es lagen so viele Berge, Seen, Wälder, Flüsse, Felder und Schluchten zwischen mir und ihr, der Geliebten, der Bewunderten, der Angebeteten. Heute morgen umarmt sie mich, und ich vergesse mich in ihrer üppigen Umarmung. Keine Frau hat so weiche, so gebieterische Arme, keine Frau, auch die schönste nicht, so gefühlvolle Lippen, keine Frau, auch die gefühlvollste nicht, küßt mit so unendlicher Inbrunst, wie meine Heimat mich küßt."

[5] See the chapter on beauty in my *Maria Beig und die Kunst der scheinbaren Kunstlosigkeit* (Eggingen: Edition Isele, 1997).

[6] "Vernunft und Nachdenken führen unsern Geist von den sinnlichen Eindrücken der Körperwelt zurück in seine Heimat, in das Reich der denkenden Wesen. . . ."

[7] "Das Weib als vorgebliches Naturwesen ist Produkt der Geschichte, die es [!] denaturiert." Interestingly, even though the Frankfurt School in general, and especially Horkheimer and Adorno in *Dialektik der Aufklärung*, were quite sensitive to the abuses of the feminine by the male world of philosophy, history, and psychology, the women's movement in Germany, when it began to gain momentum during the late 1970s and early 1980s, rejected to a large degree the male-dominated New Left, including the Frankfurt School. Cf. Peter Uwe Hohendahl, *Reappraisals: Shifting Alignments in Postwar Critical Theory* (Ithaca NY: Cornell UP, 1991), 196.

[8] Cf. Karin Hausen, "Die Polarisierung der 'Geschlechtscharaktere' — eine Spiegelung der Dissoziation von Erwerbs- und Familienleben" in *Sozialgeschichte der Familie in der Neuzeit Europas: Neue Forschungen,* ed. W. Conze (Stuttgart: Klett, 1976), 367–93.

[9] "Das ist dein Bruder! — das ist verdollmetscht: Er ist aus eben dem Ofen geschossen worden, aus dem du geschossen bist — also sei er dir heilig! — Merkt doch einmal diese verzwickte Consequenz, diesen poßierlichen Schluß von der Nachbarschaft der Leiber auf die Harmonie der Geister; von eben derselben Heimat zu eben derselben Empfindung; von einerley Kost zu einerley Neigung."

[10] "Sey mir gegrüßt, Vaterlands-Erde! *Er küßt die Erde.* Vaterlands-Himmel! Vaterlands-Sonne! — und Fluren und Hügel und Ströme und Wälder! Seyd alle, alle mir herzlich gegrüßt! — wie so köstlich wehet die Luft von meinen Heimatgebürgen! wie strömt balsamische Wonne aus euch dem armen Flüchtling entgegen."

[11] "Ich will Messen lesen lassen, den irrenden Geist in seine Heimat zu senden."

[12] "Worauf weist das ungeheure historische Bedürfniss der unbefriedeten, modernen Cultur . . ., wenn nicht auf den Verlust des Mythus, auf den Verlust der mythischen Heimat, des mythischen Mutterschoosses?"

[13] Although first published in 1857 — and at once notorious — *Les Fleurs du Mal* did not start to be read widely in French until after Baudelaire's death in 1867; it did not reach a general European audience until the 1880s and did not reach a general German audience until Stefan George's first translation into German in 1891.

[14] Schnitzler wrote *Reigen* in 1896–97 and published it first privately in 1900. The first book publication appeared in 1903, the year some of the scenes were first performed.

[15] No. 2 (1887–94), with soprano, alto, and choir; no. 3 (1895–96), with alto and choir of women and boys; no. 4 (1899–1900), with soprano solo; and no. 8 (1906–7), with three sopranos, two altos, one tenor, one baritone, one bass, boys' choir, and two mixed choirs.

[16] "Dem Bergsteiger ist die weisse Spitze eine stolze Jungfrau, die man durch Aufopferung und grenzenlose Liebe allmählich erobert, und die für das ganze Leben auf die Seele erhebend wirkt — dem Drahtseilbahnhelden ist sie eine Kellnerin, mit der man eine halbe Stunde schäkert."

[17] Interpretation is implicitly personified here: not the interpreter but the *Deutung* [interpretation] itself may ("*darf*") draw this conclusion.

[18] "Es kommt vor, daß neurotische Männer erklären, das weibliche Genitale sei ihnen etwas Unheimliches. Dieses Unheimliche ist aber der Eingang zur alten Heimat des Menschenkindes, zur Örtlichkeit, in der jeder einmal und zuerst geweilt hat. 'Liebe ist Heimweh,' behauptet ein Scherzwort, und wenn der Träumer von einer Örtlichkeit oder Landschaft noch im Traume denkt: Das ist mir bekannt, da war ich schon einmal, so darf die Deutung dafür das Genitale oder den Leib der Mutter einsetzen. Das Unheimliche ist also auch in diesem Falle das ehemals Heimische, Altvertraute. Die Vorsilbe '*un*' an diesem Worte ist aber die Marke der Verdrängung."

[19] *Austria as It Is* was originally published in English (London) in 1827; the first German publication appeared in 1919.

[20] "Gelände anschmiegen" and "gebettet."

[21] The Hegelian term *aufgehoben* could, of course, also be translated as "sublated," "canceled," or "preserved."

[22] "Wir wollen vor allem, scheint mir, deshalb so wenig Genaues über das Land wissen, damit es eine unbeschriebene Fläche bleibt, auf die wir ungehindert unsere Wunsch- und Wahnbilder projizieren können."

[23] "Ein Haremshimmel hatte fast über der ganzen Zimmereinrichtung des neunzehnten Jahrhunderts gestanden. . . ." The English translation cannot render the allusion to religion. The German word *Himmel* ["sky," but also "heaven"] has, of course, many religious associations.

[24] The two are Minnie Bruce Pratt, "Identity: Skin Blood Heart," in *Yours in Struggle: Three Feminist Perspectives on Anti-Semitism and Racism*, eds. Elly Bulkin, Pratt, and Barbara Smith (Brooklyn: Long Haul Press, 1984), 11–63; and Michelle Cliff, *Claiming an Identity They Taught Me to Despise* (Watertown: Persephone Press, 1980).

[25] Despite making the connection to the idea of Heimat explicit, Pelz's contribution "Europa in die Karten geschaut: Bilder und Figuren europäischer Herkunft" to *Kein Land in Sicht: Heimat — weiblich?*, ed. Gisela Ecker (Munich: Fink, 1997, 169–85), is less informative in regard to a general feminization of space — or a spatialization of the feminine — than her 1995 article, discussed here, which draws to some extent on the same evidence.

[26] In the context of gender and notions of space, see also Sigrid Weigel, *Topographien der Geschlechter: Kulturgeschichtliche Studien zur Literatur* [Topog-

raphies of Gender: Cultural Historical Studies for Literature] (Reinbek bei Hamburg: Rowohlt, 1990).

[27] Pelz refers here to her own more extensive study, *Reisen durch die eigene Fremde: Reiseliteratur von Frauen als autogeographische Schriften* [Travels Through One's Own Strange Lands: Travel Literature by Women as Autogeographical Writing] (Cologne: Böhlau, 1993).

[28] Telephone interview with Elisabeth Bütfering, January 14, 1998.

[29] "ihrer Heimat zur Leiche gehen"

[30] Telephone interview with Elisabeth Bütfering, January 14, 1998.

[31] In her contributions to the volume Ecker consistently places Heimat in quotation marks. She does not explain why she does so, but one can assume that the quotation marks stand for a certain distance she wants to maintain in order to discuss Heimat critically.

[32] Cf. Sander Gilman's *Freud, Race, and Gender* (Princeton: Princeton UP, 1993) and Eric Santner's *My Own Private Germany: Daniel Paul Schreber's Secret History of Modernity* (Princeton: Princeton UP, 1996), especially chapter 3, "Schreber's Jewish Question." Both discuss the effeminization anxieties of the male Jew. Their discussions repeatedly refer back to the book that Santner calls "the locus classicus of the fin-de-siècle obsession with Jewish effeminacy" (108), Otto Weininger's *Geschlecht und Charakter,* first published in 1903. In 1986, in his *Jewish Self-Hatred: Anti-Semitism and the Hidden Language of the Jews,* Gilman had already noted in *Die Fackel im Ohr,* the second part of Canetti's autobiographical trilogy, the portrayal of a male Eastern European Jew whose characteristics were those of a "feminized pet" (330).

5: Heimat, Nature, Landscape, and Ground

IN HIS ESSAY "HEIMAT, NATION, UNIVERSALITÄT" Gert Mattenklott argues that "through the enjoyment of landscapes . . .
one can acquire and possess a German identity without having
one" (49). In other words, Germans, according to Mattenklott, are
eager to appropriate an identity from their sense of the beauty of
nature — German nature — because they start out with none.
Mattenklott bases this observation on connections he perceives
between German Idealism and concepts of nature, of nation, and
of that pervasive nineteenth-century boredom that early in the
history of German bourgeois culture betrayed an inner sense of
emptiness and despair in the face of an increasing material comfort.
Mattenklott's arguments rely on a remarkable 1927[1] anthology of
landscape writing, *Der Deutsche in der Landschaft* [The Germans in
the Landscape], edited by the expressionist writer Rudolf Borchardt (1877–1945). Borchardt conceived this collection, says
Mattenklott, to support his conviction that "there is a specifically
German way of seeing when it comes to Heimat." For Borchardt,
in particular, German landscapes in writing are, as Mattenklott eloquently puts it, "not prose about the German's or any other Heimat; but it is a specifically German way of making oneself feel at
home in the world" (44).[2]

Simon Schama in his *Landscape and Memory* (1995) observes
that Anselm Kiefer's representation of the German myths surrounding woods in his famous painting *Varus* "is a consummation
of slaughter, followed by a momentous birth: the historical beginning of *Deutschtum,* of Germanness" (127).

Schama goes on to justify admirably the scholarly inquiry into
myth that brings him thus uncomfortably close to a source of cultural nationalism, the kind of nationalism that is driven less by
geographical boundaries than by the myth of national identities.
(There are, to be sure, good reasons for considering Heimat —

among other things — a modern national myth that carries within itself the ancient myth of paradise.) After reminding us of the "alarming cautionary tales" of the careers of Mircea Eliade and Joseph Campbell, after pointing to a "long line of devotees of archetypes, from Carl Jung to Friedrich Nietzsche" (133), all of whose lives in some way illustrate the uneasy relationship between myth and democratic politics, Schama asks:

> So how much myth is good for us? And how can we measure the dosage? Should we avoid the stuff altogether for fear of contamination or dismiss it out of hand as sinister and irrational esoterica that belong only in the unsavory market of "real" (to wit, our own) history? Or do we have to ensure that a *cordon sanitaire* of protective irony is always securely in place when discussing such matters? Should certifications of ideological purity be published attesting under oath that we are not doing dirty business with the Devil under the pretense of learned work . . .? (134)

From the tone of these rhetorical questions we already know what Schama's answer will be; nonetheless, I want to quote it in his own well-chosen words:

> Of one thing at least I am certain: that not to take myth seriously in the life of an ostensibly "disenchanted" culture like our own is actually to impoverish our understanding of our shared world. And it is also to concede the subject by default to those who have no critical distance from it at all, who apprehend myth not as a historical phenomenon but as an unchallengeable perennial mystery. As the great Talmudist Saul Lieberman said when he introduced Gershom Scholem's lectures on the Kabbalah that became *Major Trends in Jewish Mysticism:* "Nonsense (when all is said and done) is still nonsense. But the study of nonsense, that is science." (134)

In short, to study an irrational — or, rather, a counterrational — idea may be a profoundly rational undertaking.

In this chapter I will look at the intellectual movements toward the mythification of nature that are part of the modern idea of Heimat. We will see that when thoroughly modern uses of the term Heimat begin to be heard and read during the last decades of the eighteenth century, a crucial simultaneity occurs in German philosophy: the I, having acquired the subject's Kantian capacity for both experience and reason, feels separated from nature but does not stop there; instead, it attempts a return to nature. In, for instance, Fichte's and Schelling's philosophies, and in the poetry of Hölderlin, the I returns to an idealized nature again and again. This philosophical journey of the I toward its perceived potential for union with nature — often thought of as reunion — is also implicit (and often explicit) in the modern usage of the word Heimat as it appears in the German language since the last third of the eighteenth century. This chapter asserts that the interactions of German-speaking cultures with nature and landscape are remarkable, not to say peculiar, in that their concepts of nature and identity are curiously interdependent. In Schelling and Hölderlin, for instance, we find early expressions of that mythification of nature as the outward expression of the enigmas of an inner self that is a central theme in German Romanticism. The modern idea of Heimat is another way in which this mythification of nature expresses itself.

I observe in this period, also, a striking convergence in the way the ideas of Heimat and *das Naturschöne* [the beauty of nature] begin to be understood, for from this point on the idea of nature, on which both Heimat and *das Naturschöne* rest, is invested with the luminous innerness of a secularized divinity.

I examine in some detail that aspect of Schelling's philosophy of identity that is conceived, in common with much of his work, in an analogy to the fall from paradise and the struggle for a reunion. He finds the beginning of man's struggle in the *Entzweiung* [the split, the becoming two] (vol. 7, 425) that takes different forms in different places in his philosophy: the split into I and Not-I, or (in his earliest years — the Fichte years) into empirical I and absolute I; into spirit (or history) and nature (in his *Naturphilosophie*); or the split into consciousness [*Bewußtsein*] and being [*Wesen*] (425). In no case, however, does the split for Schelling simply end in alienation. Rather, division leads to sublation, to "eine Steigerung der Einheit" [a heightening of unity] (425). The eventual destination of this heightened form of unity is what Schelling calls "absolute identity" or a state of "intellectual intuition" (vol. 1, 207, 325–27). For Schelling, absolute identity resolves *Entzweiung*, because therein is no separation between self and self-consciousness, between subject and subject-as-object-to-itself. It is my contention that what is absolute identity for Schelling (a division sublated to heightened unity) finds its more popular, less abstract expression in the unifying notion of Heimat.

Regardless of where one locates the original *Entzweiung* that so many thinkers since Schelling have recognized as a central condition of modernity, during the last decades of the eighteenth century the divided, suffering subject begins to find consolation in hope of a reconciliation. In a subliminal way, buried in idiomatic language, landscape creeps into this proposition: in German literature and philosophy of the period, reconciliation finds both metaphysical and literal underpinnings in the term *Grund,* which in German signifies "earth" as well as "reason" and which occurs so frequently in German thought from Eckhart to Böhme and from Hegel to Heidegger. In German philosophy the word *Grund,* no matter how abstract its application, never seems to come away entirely from its concrete and literal root in "ground" or "earth." (Another example is Leibniz's Principle of Sufficient Reason, *nihil sine ratione* [nothing happens without a reason], which in German reads *Nichts ist ohne Grund* [Nothing is without ground].)

Schelling speaks of a *Grund der gemeinschaftlichen Realität* [ground of common reality], where absolute identity and undifferentiated nature flow together. This suggestive phrase illustrates a way of thinking about identity and nature that leads directly back to Heimat: the modern idea of Heimat, beginning in the same period, is a ground whereon *Entzweiung* is reconciled, a mental place in which landscape and identity, nature and self, reason and space become fused. Heimat, I conclude, offers a sense of originary unity to the divided, suffering subject. Heimat is a subjectivized aestheticization of nature inside of which the subject is capable of reaching a larger, communal self.

Fichte, Schelling, and Heimat: Reenchanting a Disenchanted World

Both Johann Gottlieb Fichte (1762–1814) and Friedrich Wilhelm Joseph Schelling (1775–1854) need to be seen — as they saw themselves — as heirs and reshapers of Kant's critical idealism, where the subject and its capacity for reason in experience turn into the center of the universe. This is what Kant had called the "Copernican turn" in his philosophy. Subjectivity here becomes constitutive of objectivity. For Kant — to put it in the simplest terms — nature was everything that could be experienced;[3] but Kant's philosophy left a crucial area beyond what can be experienced, beyond what can be expressed and perceived by the subject. Kant referred to this beyond as *das Ding an sich* [the thing in itself]. (While it is often correctly observed that Kant tried to overcome what he perceived as the limitations of the eighteenth-century British empiricist philosophers, much less note is taken, especially in English-language sources, of the pietistic religious tradition of eighteenth-century Germany, whose privileged notion of experience shines through Kant's philosophy. At times the pietistic elements seem so strongly present in Kant that one wants to claim his philosophy to be the secularized version of pietistic admonitions on how to experience God in the present world.[4]) Both Fichte and Schelling accept Kant's concept of an experiencing I at the center of the universe. They turn this I, however, into an active, productive, creative one, which seeks to establish its freedom in reality by looking at reality as formed by this I. Fichte took this notion to an extreme. In his early philosophy the I was the beginning and the end — or, at least, one could easily understand him that way. This claim made Fichte an easy target for criticism. He later updated his philosophy to include boundaries on the freedom of the absolute I, boundaries that lie where the I encounters other I's and where all I's are grounded [*begründet*] in the freedom of God. But the early Fichte did not include these qualifications, so his critics were able to ask: Where is God if the I forms everything? Fichte was unable to defend himself effectively against accusations of atheism during the so-called *Atheismusstreit* [atheism controversy] and, as a result, was forced to leave the University of Jena in 1799. Things had, in fact, been festering for some years before this scandal, with Fichte being the target of violence and the butt of jokes. In 1795 students had thrown rocks through his windows, and Goethe, amused, had commented on the events in a letter to C. G. Voigt: "You saw the absolute I [Fichte] in great embarrassment; and indeed it is quite impolite of the not-I's [the cobblestones] that had just been laid down to fly that way through the window panes" (195 [Jena, April 10, 1795]).[5]

Fichte's philosophy nevertheless had a profound impact on theories of the subject. It was not so much the notion of the I as creator of everything that endured — Schelling and, as mentioned, Fichte himself revised this aspect of his philosophy — but the notion of the I as creatively shaping the Other became basic. (We need to remember that the I of Fichte and of Schelling is not only the individualistic I — or self — we tend to think of in the post-Second World War Western world but also an absolute I. Indeed, a certain tension between an individualistic I and an absolute I runs through their philosophies. At the risk of overstating this point, one could argue that the I of German Idealism was a class-, group-, and gender-specific signifier for the shifting philosophical perceptions of the 1780s and 1790s. The I became a cipher for the educated bourgeois male's ability to self-reflexively negotiate God and the world.) This active imaginative I yielded Fichte's all-important concept of *intellektuelle Anschauung* [intellectual conception or intellectual intuition], which became a central principal of German Romanticism. Intellectual intuition is seen as the divine, the innermost unifying principle of life.

For instance, in his *Philosophische Briefe über Dogmatismus und Kritizismus* [Philosophical Letters on Dogmatism and Criticism, 1795] Schelling writes: "This intellectual intuition occurs where we stop being an object to ourselves, where — withdrawn into itself — the perceiving self is identical with the perceived" (vol. 1, 319).[6] A few pages later Schelling shows another dimension of the intellectual intuition. In its pure state it entails so much awareness that an ominous paradox results — it ceases to be aware of itself as awareness: "We awake out of the intellectual intuition as out of a condition of death. We awake through reflection, that is, through a forceful return to ourselves" (vol. 1, 325).[7]

We can detect here echoes of the seventeenth-century mystic Jakob Böhme, as well as influences from the speculative wing of Württemberg pietism — Friedrich Christoph Oetinger (1702–1782) and, to a lesser degree, Philipp Matthäus Hahn (1739–1790).[8] (That Hahn was a presence at least in the young Schelling's life can be seen from Schelling's first published text, "Elegie bei Hahn's Grabe gesungen" [Elegy Sung at Hahn's Grave, May 11, 1790]. The adult Schelling also writes in a letter that as a boy he had seen this great man and had had an "uncanny, incomprehensible awe" [geheime, unverstandene Ehrfurcht] of him.[9]) In Jakob Böhme man, after his fall from paradise, struggles to reunite with God. In Schelling's philosophy the beginning of man's struggle lies in what Schelling calls *Entzweiung* (vol. 7, 425), a split, a becoming two. But *Entzweiung* and its consequent alienation do not leave man in despair; they stimulate him to arrive at "eine Steigerung der Einheit" [a heightening of the unity] [425]) through which he may in due course reach absolute identity or a state of intellectual intuition (vol. 1, 207, 325–27).

I think it is fair to say that the main movements in philosophy between Kant and Hegel are all attempts of one kind or another to understand the experience of separation between nature and I, between subject and object; and, further, that they almost invariably lead to attempts to reconcile the separated entities, to return them — since unity was supposedly once there — to their original union (for instance, through an intellectual or an aesthetic intuition).

Kant's "Copernican turn" toward a subjective, experiencing I at the center of all we know began to unsettle the world of religion, just as his simile of Copernicus suggested. Fichte, not two decades after Kant had published his *Kritik der reinen Vernunft* [Critique of Pure Reason] in 1781, could no longer, despite earnest attempts, justify himself convincingly against accusations of atheism. By the end of the eighteenth century God in German-language philosophy had become an ill-fitting piece in a human puzzle, replacing the puzzled human trying to find his place in God's world.

The biographies of Fichte, Schelling, and Friedrich Schlegel give an interesting and, finally, less revolutionary twist to these developments. Kant had still perceived himself, despite his revolutionary philosophical insights, as living in a Christian world. The young Fichte, Schelling, and Schlegel all made forays away from this Ptolemaic world but soon reversed their steps. Even though they were philosophically well equipped to go forward, they all share a return to religion or to a religious worldview in their mature years. It is Hegel who — pulled inexorably into the future by the continuously contradictory spirit of his dialectics — continues to move forward uneasily (even if the *Rechtshegelianer* [Right Hegelians] of the nineteenth century, who used Hegel to support a Christian, absolutistic worldview, did not see it this way). Hegel, in contrast to German Idealism, with which he shares many concepts, does not look for reconciliation in a return to a unified sense of origin. This nostalgia for a lost union between I and nature has disappeared from Hegel's philosophy. (The young Hegel shared the longing for a lost unity with his fellow students Schelling and Hölderlin while at the *Stift* [seminary] in Tübingen. After the *Stift* years, however, Hegel began to move away from this position. And by the time he published his *Differenzschrift* in 1801 he certainly had matured beyond that youthful longing. As the thirty-year-old Hegel writes in a letter to Schelling dated November 2, 1800: "In my scholarly education, which began with the commoner desires of men, I had to be driven forward to scholarship; and the ideal notions of youth had to change into the form of reflection, and at the same time into a system" [qtd. in Brockard and Buchner, viii].[10]) For Hegel in his twenties, the 1790s indeed begin with an experience of alienation, which causes a longing for reconciliation or for a regaining of a sense of totality. In 1799 he depicts his age as full of inner tensions, as well as of striving for a closing of the gap between wish, hope, and ideal, on the one hand, and life on the other. He writes of the "ever increasing contradiction between the unknown which people unconsciously look for and the life which is offered to them and which they are permitted to lead."[11]

All of these late eighteenth- and early nineteenth-century developments in German philosophy are implicit in the contemporaneous emergence of the modern idea of Heimat; or, rather, both the developments and the idea reflect a general secularization of religious concepts in German-speaking cultures. German Idealism and Heimat come out of the same need for reenchantment of a disenchanted world. Fichte's I as beginning and end; his notion of the I as a creative force that actively shapes the Other; Schelling's version of the fall from paradise as *Entzweiung*, followed by the struggle for "a heightening of unity" in absolute identity: all of these concerns are resolved not only in Schelling's divine, originary principle of intellectual intuition but also in that more commonly expressed, less philosophically refined notion of Heimat. It is no coincidence that the modern idea of Heimat appears for the first time parallel to the longings expressed in philosophy and poetry for reunion with that nature from which the I feels it has become distant. If God in German-language philosophy had become an ill-fitting part in a human puzzle, then Heimat brought the idea of heaven, a unifying and sheltering space hitherto associated with the heavenly spheres, into more-human realms.

Heimat, Adorno, and the Subject's Imagined Reunion with Nature

Adorno's discussions of nature (that is, the Western bourgeois construct called "nature") are easily recognizable as being deeply indebted to Kant and Hegel. They also offer us a way of understanding the historical interrelations between conceptualizations of nature and conceptualizations of Heimat. Adorno, at a distance of more than a century and a half from Schelling and Fichte, alludes knowingly in his *Ästhetische Theorie* [Aesthetic Theory, 1970] to their notions of return and of becoming one again with an idealized nature — notions that by the 1960s had become part of the common, daily, unanalyzed social fabric. Here Adorno discusses that longing for a return to nature that from the beginning linked the admiration of natural beauty to the appreciation of art:

> Happiness in nature was tied to the conceptualization of the subject as being-in-itself and as existing within itself in virtual infinity; thus the subject projects itself onto nature and feels itself, while being separated from her, close to her; the subject's impotence in society, which calcified into a second nature, becomes the engine for the flight into the presumed first nature. (1970, 103)[12]

Happiness in nature was closely linked to nature's positive qualities. Hobbes's famous statement that in a state of nature human life is "nasty, brutish, and short" had, as we all know, no profound impact on the bourgeois taste for the beauty of nature after the late eighteenth century.[13]

Important for the subject's imagined reunion with nature is the German concept of an aestheticized nature, *das Naturschöne*, which is variably translated into English as "the beautiful in nature" (for instance — somewhat inconsistently — in Christian Lenhardt's first translation of Adorno's *Ästhetische Theorie* into English [1984]), or, more often, as "natural beauty" (for instance, sometimes in Lenhardt, but consistently in Robert Hullot-Kentor's second translation of *Ästhetische Theorie* [1997]), or (and I will resort to this use, as well) as "the beauty of nature" — as several Hegel translators and Michael Inwood, the author of *A Hegel Dictionary* (1992), have done.

A valuable insight we can gain from discussions of the *Naturschöne* is the ever-present assumption of a "heightening of unity" as occurring through a (re)unification of seemingly disparate elements — of, for instance, nature, gender, landscape, beauty, and the subject. By way of leading into our discussion of Heimat, let us be reminded of the limitations of this beauty of nature, which Adorno points out in his *Ästhetische Theorie:*

> In times when nature stands up to man and overpowers him there remains little space for the beauty of nature. Agrarian professions, to whom visible nature is an immediate object of action, have, as we know, little sense for landscape. The ostensibly eternal beauty of nature has its core in history. This legitimizes it as much as it relativizes its concept. Where nature was not really controllable the picture of her lack of control was frightening. From this comes the preference for symmetrical arrangements of nature — a preference that has seemed strange for quite a while. (102–3)[14]

Nature, "visible nature," is — as Adorno writes in his section on the interconnectedness of the beauty of nature and the beauty of art — both basis and reference for *das Naturschöne*. The beauty of art refers to nature "only as appearance" (103). This nature has lost its smell, its inner dimensions, its moments of dread and grotesque relief. Art's essential separation from any purpose of self-preservation confers the form of an aesthetic experience of nature: "Nature when it is visible beauty is not perceived as an object of action. The break with purposes of self-preservation — which is emphatic in art — is equally carried out in the aesthetic experience of nature" (103).[15] In Adorno's eyes, self-preservation is part neither of the beauty of nature nor of the beauty of art. Moreover, art is selective in what it chooses aesthetically to experience in nature.

The concepts of the beauty of nature and of Heimat are closely related. They both invest an inanimate Other with shining subjective qualities that reflect themselves back as identity. One could speak of the halo with which the subject invests both *Naturschönheit* and Heimat, giving them the misty glow of an originary space.

It is the imagined experience of a return to a unified sense of origin after the *Entzweiung*, the split between nature and the experience of nature. *Naturschöne* and Heimat are both routes back to the natural after the *Entzweiung* — though in Germany they are more likely to contain nicely groomed hiking trails than any trace of nature in the raw.

Looking at the *Naturschöne* and Heimat in relation to each other, however, we realize that the beauty of nature is not only closely related to the idea of Heimat but is an integral aspect of it. Heimat has absorbed the beauty of nature and given it a geographical grounding. The beauty of nature, invested with idealized qualities of the subject, is a formative part of conceptualizations of Heimat and, furthermore, is often perceived in opposition to culture, to a society shaped by humans.

In German, where the concepts of nature and the subject come together, both the beauty of nature and Heimat are likely to appear. That they rarely, if ever (I have been unable to find any instances of it), manifest themselves together can probably be attributed to the pure existence of *Naturschöne* as an aesthetico-philosophical concept. (Unlike "the beauty of nature" in English, the German concept of *das Naturschöne* has not become a commonplace of everyday language.) The beauty of nature is, as Adorno suggests above, neither inhabitable nor tangible. Heimat is both inhabitable and tangible. It is, in every sense of the word, more common.

The German Affinity for Grounding

From the beginning, this reconciliation after *Entzweiung* in German-speaking contexts is accompanied by literal, as well as metaphorical, grounding. In Schelling's *Darstellung meines Systems der Philosophie* [Presentation of My System of Philosophy, 1801], "absolute identity" is the "*Grund der gemeinschaftlichen Realität*" [ground of common reality] (vol. 4, 204). This grounding metaphor in Schelling, like the modern idea of Heimat, turns an imagined unity between subject and object — that is, "the organism's capacity for lack-of-difference [Indifferenzvermögen]" (204) — into an absolute identity that is based on this "ground of common reality."

It is worth remembering that the word *Grund* has a long history in German philosophy before Schelling. Meister Eckhart (1260–1327), the Dominican priest who speaks for an immediate interaction between God and man without the forceful mediation of priests, writes in one of his sermons:

> As truly as the Father brings forth from his unique God-nature the Son, so truly does he bring him forth in the innermost part of the spirit! And that is the inner world. Here God's ground is my ground and my ground God's ground; here I live out of my own, as God lives out of His own! . . . Out of this innermost ground you will accomplish all your works, without asking why! (qtd. in Waldemar 26)[16]

The German mystic Jakob Böhme (1575–1624) makes *Grund* one of the central elements in his system. To paraphrase Charles Waldemar's summary of Böhme's writings: Böhme explains the creation of the macro- and microcosms as coming out of God's *Urgrund* [primal ground] or, as he writes more often, out of God's unrevealed, most inner and untouchable *Ungrund* [unground] (qtd. in Waldemar 26).

In Schelling's philosophy the concept of *Grund* is used with a clear awareness of the tradition from Eckhart to Böhme. Hegel, in his turn, as he so often does, takes up this vocabulary from his forebears (for instance, in his long discussions of the "absolute ground," "the definite ground," and "the ground" in his *Wissenschaft der Logik* [Science of Logic, 1812–15] and his *Enzyklopädie der philosophischen Wissenschaften* [Encyclopedia of the Philosophical Sciences, 1817; revised, 1830]) but shifts the valence to a more secular and insistently rational one.

It is, in general, a significant aspect of German philosophical thought that ground and grounding are present when causal connections are being made. Other major thinkers who made *Grund* part of their philosophical treatises around the time when the modern idea of Heimat began to appear in the German language are Kant in his 1763 *Der einzig mögliche Beweisgrund zu einer Demonstrations des Daseyns Gottes* [The Only Possible Ground for a Demonstration of the Existence of God], Moses Mendelssohn in his 1785 *Morgenstunden oder Vorlesungen über das Daseyn Gottes* [Morning Hours; or, Lectures Concerning the Existence of God], Fichte in his 1794–95 *Grundlage der gesammten Wissenschaftslehre oder der sogenannten Philosophie* [Foundations of the Entire Science of Knowledge or the So-Called Philosophy], and Schopenhauer in his 1813 *Über die vierfache Wurzel des Satzes vom zureichenden Grunde* [On the Quadruple Root of the Sentence of Sufficient Ground/Reason].

If we look at the word field surrounding the German noun *Grund* [ground, base, reason], we find that quite a number of such compounds with *Grund* lose their literal grounding when they are translated into English. We find (translations are from *Langenscheidts Handwörterbuch* [1988]) *die Grundbedeutung* [primary or basic meaning], *die Grundbedingung* [basic condition, prerequisite], *das Grundgesetz* [fundamental law, Basic (Constitutional) Law], *der Grundgedanke* [basic (or fundamental) idea], *die Grundlage* [base, foundation, basis], *grundlos* [bottomless, groundless, for no reason], *der Grundsatz* [principle, maxim, axiom, theorem], *die Grundtugend* [cardinal virtue], *der Grundton* [keynote], *die Grundzahl* [cardinal number], *gründlich* [thorough, careful, painstaking, solid], *die Begründung* [foundation, establishment; argument(s), reason(s), grounds; substantiation], and *ergründen* [to fathom, to discover].

After the Second World War Martin Heidegger delivered several times a highly thought-provoking series of lectures titled *Der Satz vom Grund*.[17] The title, familiar to every German student of philosophy, translates as "The Principle of Causality" but on a literal level can also mean not only "the sentence of the ground" and "the sentence of the reason" but also, like philosophy in general, "the leap off the ground" (*Satz* = sentence and leap). In his lecture series Heidegger playfully takes this sentence and looks at it from all angles, weaving in and out of the literal and the metaphorical, reviewing in the process the history of philosophy from Leibniz to Existentialism. In German the principle of causality itself reads "Nichts ist ohne Grund" [literally, "Nothing is without ground"], or in Latin, *Nihil sine ratione* [nothing without reason]. Heidegger shows it to contain not only ground and reason but also the abyss. Relevant for the twentieth-century philosopher is not only the observation that nothing is without reason (that is, there is a reason for everything) but also the observation that Nothing is without ground (that is, as a statement about Nothingness that first of all reveals that *Nothing is* and, furthermore, that Nothingness has neither ground nor reason).

To sum up this chapter, we may say that in both a literal and a metaphorical sense there is no unifying ground of common reality like Heimat in its poetic and popular usages since the late eighteenth century. Across the bridge of spiritualized nature that is Heimat we reach a "heightening of unity" and our "ground of common reality."

(Heimat's "ground of common reality" may be related to, but is certainly not the same as, Foucault's concept of heterotopia, in which heterochronic spaces — such as cemeteries, movie theaters, gardens, libraries, museums, brothels, or colonies — juxtapose "in a single real space several spaces, several sites that are in themselves incompatible" [25]. Heterotopias are either "not freely accessible" to everyone, or, if they seem to be, they still have curious, hidden exclusions [26]. One could see Heimat as a heterotopic space with all the just-listed qualities — heterochronic, several spaces in one site, curious exclusions. But the crucial element absent from the concept of heterotopia — and fundamental in Heimat — is the quality of a humanized, spiritualized nature, and with it a sense of eternity and endlessness. The individualized and secular *Seele* [soul] and *Geist* [spirit] of German Idealism allow Heimat to not have any clear boundaries. These emotional correspondences make one feel part of Heimat, give to Heimat an internalized, individualized definition — which shares with pietistic revival the experiencing of God. In that crucial quality Heimat is very much unlike Foucault's heterotopias that have clear boundaries — often walls — and "always presuppose a system of opening and closing that both isolates them and makes them penetrable" [26].)

In Heimat, this "ground of common reality," nature is idyllic, and until the 1970s there is no such thing as an ugly Heimat. The examples for an idyllic nature in Heimat are so many that any list is a mere random sampling: The "Wanderer" in Hölderlin's poem of that title returns home and rejoices at the sight of his childhood garden: "Nature of my Heimat! how faithful to me you remained! / Tenderly caring, just as before, you still allow the refugee in."[18] Heine in the opening chapter of *Der Rabbi von Bacherach* [The Rabbi of Bacherach, 1840] tells of the rabbi's flight from his home after he has discovered the body of a dead child planted there to incriminate him. The rabbi and his wife, Sara, take a boat down the "dear, clear Rhine River," "the old, good-hearted Father Rhine," who consoles Sara: "And the tears of the beautiful Sara ran milder and milder; the whispering waves washed away her most violent pains; the night lost its dark horror; and the hills of the Heimat bade her the most tender good-bye" (622–23).[19] And Rilke in the fifteenth of his *Die Sonette an Orpheus* [Sonnets to Orpheus, 1928] presents us with a rather unusual exhortation for combining nature, landscape, rhythm, and dance. He asks "you warm girls, quiet ones" to "dance the flavor of the experienced fruit! // . . . Dance the orange. The warmer landscape, / cast it out of you so that the ripe one can shine / in airs of the Heimat! Glowing, disrobe // Scent upon scent" (740).[20] We see how, in Heimat, nature, ground, landscape, and identity melt into one.

Gisela Ecker observes: "It seems as if the identity of Germans is so labile and fleeting . . . that it has to be anchored in the earth, tied to a territory" (19). Not that constitutions of identity in other cultures exist completely independent of territorial aspects. But Ecker — without linking it to the German philosophical tradition inherent in the term *ground* — is drawing attention here to National Socialist invocations of German ground (*Volk ohne Raum* [people without space] and the *Blut-und-Boden* [blood-and-soil] ideology). And it is easy to see how cultural nationalism; concepts of space, ground, and identity; and the idea of Heimat can intermingle in a German tradition and provide support for expansionist desires. The German idea of Heimat is in that sense, as well, a ground of common reality and a ground of heightened unity. And the capacity to appreciate the beauty of nature is an all-important element of this ground of common reality.

Notes

[1] Mattenklott gives the year of the first publication of Borchardt's anthology and his afterword as 1925 ("Heimat, Nation, Universalität" in *Heimat im Wort: Die Problematik eines Begriffs im 19. und 20. Jahrhundert,* ed. Rüdiger Gröner [Munich: Iudicium, 1992], 36–49, here 45). The bibliographical credits in Rudolf Borchardt, *Gesammelte Werke in Einzelbänden, Prosa III,* ed. Marie Luise Borchardt with Ernst Zinn (Stuttgart: Klett, 1960) give the year as 1927 (476).

[2] Cf. also Friedmar Apel's strong reliance on Rudolf Borchardt in *Deutscher Geist und deutsche Landschaft: Eine Topographie* [German Mind and German Landscape: A Topography].

[3] Kant writes about nature, for instance: "Nature considered *materialiter* is the *sum of all objects of experience*. We are concerned here only with this, since otherwise things, which could never become objects of an experience if they had to be cognized according to their nature, would force us to concepts whose meaning could never be given *in concreto* (in any example of a possible experience), and we would therefore have to make for ourselves mere concepts of the nature of those things, the reality of which concepts, that is, whether they actually relate to objects or are mere beings of thought, could not be decided at all" (*Prolegomena to Any Future Metaphysics That Will Be Able to Come Forward as Science*, trans. Gary Hatfield [Cambridge: Cambridge UP, 1997], 49).

"Natur also, *materialiter* betrachtet, ist der *Inbegriff aller Gegenstände der Erfahrung*. Mit dieser haben wir es hier nur zu thun, da ohnedem Dinge, die niemals Gegenstände einer Erfahrung werden können, wenn sie nach ihrer Natur erkannt werden sollten, uns zu Begriffen nöthigen würden, deren Bedeutung niemals *in concreto* (in irgendeinem Beispiele einer möglichen Erfahrung) gegeben werden könnte, und von deren Natur wir uns also lauter Begriffe machen müßten, deren Realität, d. i. ob sie wirklich sich auf Gegenstände beziehen, oder bloße Gedankendinge sind, gar nicht entschieden werden könnte" (*Kants gesammelte Schriften* [Berlin: Reimer, 1902], vol. 4, 295–96).

[4] For an informative summary of eighteenth-century pietism, as well as its strong influence on German thought and literature, see chapter 3, "Klopstock und der Pietismus," in Gerhard Kaiser's *Klopstock: Religion und Dichtung* (Gütersloh: Gütersloher Verlagshaus Gerd Mohn, 1963), 123–203.

[5] "Sie haben also das absolute Ich in großer Verlegenheit gesehen und freilich ist es von den Nicht-Ichs, die man doch gesetzt hat, sehr unhöflich durch die Scheiben zu fliegen."

[6] "Diese intellektuale Anschauung tritt dann ein, wo [note the temporal-spatial mixing of *dann* — then — which is the antecedent for the spatial relative pronoun *wo* — where] wir für uns selbst aufhören Objekt zu seyn, wo, in sich selbst zurückgezogen, das anschauende Selbst mit dem angeschauten identisch ist."

[7] "Wir erwachen aus der intellektualen Anschauung wie aus dem Zustande des Todes. Wir erwachen durch Reflexion, d.h. durch abgenöthigte Rückkehr zu uns selbst."

[8] Cf. Ernst Benz's convincing arguments on pietistic influences on Schelling, especially Oetinger, in "Schellings schwäbische Geistesahnen" (*Schellings Philosophie der Freiheit* [Stuttgart: Kohlhammer, 1977], 75–138); see also

Priscilla Hayden-Roy's extensive and informative overview of Württemberg Pietism in her *"A Foretaste of Heaven": Friedrich Hölderlin in the Context of Württemberg Pietism* (Amsterdam: Rodopi, 1994), 19–87.

[9] Cited here after Friedrich Wilhelm Joseph Schelling, *Historisch-kritische Werke,* vol. 1, eds. Jacobs, Jantzen, Schieche (Stuttgart: Frommann-Holzboog, 1976) 31–45, here 35. Neither elegy nor letter are included in the Beck edition of *Schellings Werke.*

Cf. also Jürgen Habermas, who writes in his dissertation in a metaphorical vocabulary he later, I am sure, regretted: "Der junge Schelling philosophiert in Fichteschen Kategorien. Aber die Erfahrungen, die er mit solchen Kategorien rationalisiert, wurzeln tief in seiner schwäbischen Heimat. Wir wollen deshalb . . . den systematischen Ort im Denken des Fichteschülers suchen, an dem die 'heimliche' Tradition Oetingers einfließt" [The young Schelling philosophizes in Fichtean categories. But the experiences with which he rationalizes such categories are rooted deeply in his Swabian Heimat. We therefore . . . want to look for the place in the system where in the thinking of this Fichte student the *heimliche* (homey, but also secret) tradition of (the speculative pietist) Oetinger is flowing in] (*Das Absolute und die Geschichte. Von der Zwiespältigkeit in Schellings Denken* [Bonn: Bouvier, 1954], 122).

[10] "In meiner wissenschaftlichen Bildung, die von untergeordnetern Bedürfnissen der Menschen anfing, mußte ich zur Wissenschaft vorgetrieben werden, und das Ideal des Jünglingsalters mußte sich zur Reflexionsform, in ein System zugleich verwandeln."

[11] "Der immer sich vergrössernde Widerspruch zwischen dem unbekannten, das die Menschen bewußtlos suchen, und dem Leben, das ihnen angeboten, und erlaubt wird . . ." (*Schriften und Entwürfe [1799–1808],* in *Gesammelte Werke,* vol. 5 [Hamburg: Felix Meiner, 1998], 16 [this letter is not included in the Suhrkamp edition of the *Werke*]).

[12] "Das Glück an der Natur war verflochten mit der Konzeption des Subjektes als eines Fürsichseienden und virtuell in sich Unendlichen; so projiziert es sich auf die Natur und fühlt als Abgespaltenes ihr sich nahe; seine Ohnmacht in der zur zweiten Natur versteinerten Gesellschaft wird zum Motor der Flucht in die vermeintlich erste."

[13] Martin Seel's discussion of different forms of representations of nature in Western history in his *Eine Ästhetik der Natur* (Frankfurt am Main: Suhrkamp, 1991) is a helpful guide here. Cf. also the two short essays on the history of the concept of nature by Maurice Merleau-Ponty ("Der Naturbegriff") and by Ernst Bloch ("Natur als organisierendes Prinzip — Materialismus beim frühen Schelling"), both published (Merleau-Ponty's essay was assembled by the editors) in *Materialien zu Schellings philosophischen Anfängen,* eds. Manfred Frank and Gerhard Kurz (Frankfurt am Main: Suhrkamp, 1975), 280–91 (Merleau-Ponty) and 292–304 (Bloch). For helpful summaries of the (almost countless) theories on the concepts of nature and human

nature, see Karen Gloy, *Das Verständnis der Natur* (2 vols., Munich: Beck, 1995, 1996). Cf. also Leon Pompa's *Human Nature and Historical Knowledge: Hume, Hegel and Vico* (Cambridge: Cambridge UP, 1990); Martin Jay's *The Dialectical Imagination* (Boston: Little, Brown, 1973), 253–69, for a summary of the concept of nature in the Frankfurt School in general; and Joel Whitebook, *Perversion and Utopia* (Cambridge MA: MIT Press, 1995), 144–52, for a discussion of *Dialectics of Enlightenment* as it relates to a mastery of nature and self.

[14] "In Zeitläuften, in denen Natur den Menschen übermächtig gegenübertritt, ist fürs Naturschöne kein Raum; agrarische Berufe, denen die erscheinende Natur unmittelbar Aktionsobjekt ist, haben, wie man weiß, wenig Gefühl für die Landschaft. Das vorgeblich geschichtslos Naturschöne hat seinen geschichtlichen Kern; das legitimiert es ebenso, wie es seinen Begriff relativiert. Wo Natur real nicht beherrscht war, schreckte das Bild ihres Unbeherrschtseins. Daher die längst befremdende Vorliebe für symmetrische Ordnungen der Natur."

[15] "Natur als erscheinendes Schönes wird nicht als Aktionsobjekt wahrgenommen. Die Lossage von den Zwecken der Selbsterhaltung, emphatisch in der Kunst, ist gleichermaßen in der ästhetischen Naturerfahrung vollzogen."

[16] "So wahr der Vater aus seiner einzigen Gottnatur heraus den Sohn gebiert, so wahr gebiert er ihn in des Geistes Innerstes! Und das ist die innere Welt. Hier ist Gottes Grund mein Grund, und mein Grund Gottes Grund, hier lebe ich aus meinem Eigenen, wie Gott aus Seinem Eigenen lebt! . . . Aus diesem innersten Grunde heraus sollst du alle deine Werke wirken, ohne ein Warum!"

[17] Martin Heidegger, *Gesamtausgabe,* vol. 10 (Frankfurt am Main: Klostermann, 1997).

[18] "Heimatliche Natur! wie bist du treu mir geblieben! / Zärtlichpflegend, wie einst, nimmst du den Flüchtling noch auf."

[19] "Auch die Tränen der schönen Sara flossen immer milder und milder, ihre gewaltigsten Schmerzen wurden fortgespült von den flüsternden Wellen, die Nacht verlor ihr finstres Grauen, und die heimatlichen Berge grüßten wie zum zärtlichsten Lebewohl."

[20] "Mädchen, ihr warmen, Mädchen, ihr stummen, / tanzt den Geschmack der erfahrenen Frucht! // . . . Tanzt die Orange. Die wärmere Landschaft, / werft sich aus euch, daß die reife erstrahle / in Lüften der Heimat! Erglühte, enthüllt // Düfte um Düfte."

6: Heimat and Innocence (in Childhood, in Religion, in Language, and in *Antiheimat*)

THE IDEA OF Heimat is based on an imaginary space of innocence projected onto real geographical sites. Whether this innocence is religious (paradise), sexual (childhood), sociological (premodern, preindustrial), psychological (preconscious), philosophical (prerational, predialectical), or historical (pre-Holocaust) in character, in every case we find imageries of innocence laid over geographies of Heimat. The many *pre-* prefixes in the foregoing list point to a temporal dimension, a longing for an imaginary past, which affirms Heimat's regressive tendencies. But Heimat is more than memory, for it is here and now, as well as there and then. The temporal separation is canceled in a continuous actualization of a spatial and cognitive union. Therefore, Heimat is not like art that can be framed and presented to an audience at an opening. Nor is it an object that presents itself in a manner that can be easily analyzed by one who feels its powers. In fact, through analysis the analyzer necessarily excludes himself or herself from the shared preconsciousness, the common reassurance of which represents one of the constitutive rituals of innocence in Heimat.

As we saw in the chapter "Heimat and the Feminine," conceptualizations of Heimat are intimately related to each period's notions of womanhood, motherhood, and femininity. The masculine desire to reenter the feminine space of Heimat is also a desire to escape self-conscious, alienated adulthood. In this chapter we will investigate the puzzling turn where the feminized space called Heimat becomes, as well, the unsexualized (or presexualized) haven of a basic and unquestionable innocence.

Heimat and Morality

It is not hard to see how a day-to-day existence of concealed un-easiness — a state that describes adulthood in most civilized people — can quickly turn into an idealization of the innocent, sexually unaware, unself-conscious state of childhood. The space of childhood is another location where Heimat is powerfully present. As Ernst Bloch notes in a much-quoted statement from his 1959 *Das Prinzip Hoffnung,* "Heimat is that which shines everyone into his or her childhood, but it is a place where no one has ever been" (vol. 5, 1628).

Bloch's statement makes a point that is often neglected in discussions of Heimat and childhood. Heimat shines into childhood. But to do so it has to exist outside of it. Heimat is not childhood itself. It is that which is seen to lie in childhood from an adult point of view. Also important, for Bloch, is that Heimat is both a place and a source of gentle light, light that shines everyone into his or her childhood. Heimat, as we saw in chapter 2, frequently has this shining quality: "... *das allen in die Kindheit scheint und worin noch niemand war.*" A softly glowing, intermingled aura of innocence and authenticity is often curiously superimposed on the idea of Heimat.

The nostalgia associated with the idea of Heimat has its source in every adult's awareness of change and of the losses that accompany the loss of youth. As the adult Jean Améry says, "The young person gives credit to himself. He isn't only who he is, but also the one who he will be" (33). The adult, in contrast, is reduced to the one he or she is. In fact, it is the nostalgia of adulthood that allows for a look into Heimat in the first place. (Therefore, polls that test what Heimat means to young people can be of only limited relevance. Such a poll certainly can not be used as an argument to show that the idea of Heimat is in the process of disappearing.) In Heimat there is consolation for this reduction to adulthood. "All the losing transactions, never to be balanced again, which life consists of" (Sebald 104) are forgotten — because they have not happened yet — in Heimat.

Heimat is, in part, a deeply sentimental nostalgia for one's own personal childhood; and the attachment to one's childhood shows itself in many ways, one of them being that the personal Heimat is often irrationally defended. Gisela Ecker had to realize this fact while researching the idea of Heimat. As has been mentioned, people recoiled in suspicion from such an analytical approach to Heimat: "People smelled behind every critical statement about 'Heimat' the intention to destroy their individual sentiments about the place of their childhood" (12).

Not only through childhood, however, do Heimat and innocence share one meaning. In *Eine Ästhetik der Natur* Martin Seel describes the "corresponsive" relationship that individuals believe they can have with nature. In this relationship the beauty of nature obtains an ethical quality: the capacity to recognize the beauty of nature characterizes a person as a "good" person. This notion explains the rather self-insistent air of virtue that surrounds such different social entities as health-food stores, food co-ops in North American university cities, the Green Party in Germany, open-air kindergartens in Norway, free-roaming chicken farms, Greenpeace, and the *Naturschutzbund* [Nature Conservation League]. Seel states correctly (at least for the German-speaking context) that the perception of the beauty of nature is assumed to be "a reflection of a good life" (90). Thus, recognizing the beauty of nature not only provides an escapist idyll that protects one from the modern, disenchanted world but also serves as an antidote against moral discomfort. The communal celebration of the beauty of nature (for instance, during a *Heimatfest*) can provide participants with a subtle reassurance of their moral integrity.

The German everyday is rife with customs that deliver this ethical reassurance: walking your dachshund on Sunday afternoons through the local woods; membership in the *Heimatvereine* or in the *Wandervereine* [hiking clubs] or in the *Alpenvereine* [Austrian (ÖAV), German (DAV), Swiss (SAC), or Southern Tyrolian (AVS) associations organizing and preserving everything that relates to hiking in the Alps]; or taking walks after a celebratory meal (only to go right back to eat more cake and drink more coffee). An interesting development occurred recently with downhill skiing, which has long been associated with an appreciation of nature. In part because nature preservationists condemned the "violent" cutting of slopes and lifts into the land and the resulting erosion of "good soil," winter tourism, despite a youth boom of snowboarding, has lost celebrants; and the Alpine winter tourism industry is fighting to stem an overall decline in numbers of visitors.[1] (To attribute the declining number of skiers entirely to this shift in the ethics of appreciating nature would, however, be incorrect. Also contributing is the increasing affordability of airplane travel, combined with relatively inexpensive vacation packages in sunny climates. It now is often cheaper to fly for a week to Majorca than to drive your own car and ski for a week in Austria.) For many now, *not* skiing is an act of appreciating nature. But in general, looking at nature and seeing its beauty represents more than simple aesthetic pleasure; it is an act of reassuring oneself of one's beautiful, innocent inner self.

Despite only subconscious awareness of this function of Heimat among most people who either celebrate or discuss Heimat, it is a basic element of Heimat — at times even the main element. Along with this assumption of innocence goes a simple equation with a long tradition: it is widely believed that what is beautiful cannot be evil. We see this idea, for instance, in a 1933 document written for the Austrian *Heimatschutz* movement by one of its leaders, Karl Giannoni. (During Austria's border disputes after the end of the First World War nationalistic militia groups, collectively called *Heimatschutz* or *Heimatwehr,* sprang up not so much along official political borders as along German versus non-German language boundaries. The *Heimatschutz* groups "protected" the interests of the German territories. They became part of the Austrian government in 1930 and in 1933 joined forces with Dollfuss's nationalistic Austrian *Vaterländische Front* [Front of the Fatherland]. After the *Anschluss* in 1938 the *Vaterländische Front* was dissolved, and its *Heimatschutz* units, which had remained semiseparate entities, were often incorporated first into the SA and later into the SS.) In this essay, "Heimatschutz: Rückschau und Ausblick" [Heimatschutz: Looking Back and Ahead], Giannoni writes:

> "The beautiful is the symbol for the good," said Kant; this holds true in the negative as well, and we can say: The ugly is the symbol of the evil. Therefore the thinking observer can see the outward traits of his Heimat as clear signs of the world he lives in; both are inseparable. And getting used to bad appearances, and thus to their continual repetition, only produces more bad conditions, just as the forming of good ones creates good ones. (qtd. in Nikitsch 288)

Thus, there is an obligation to produce that which is considered beautiful. But it is a consoling obligation, because to create something beautiful automatically relieves the producer of worry about potentially less comforting moral questions.

This moral reassurance that supports the assumption of innocence explains, in part, how the idea of Heimat, and along with it the entire *Heimatfilm* genre from the mid-thirties to the early sixties, could persist in many minds untainted by the experience of National Socialism and its aftermath, despite being heavily used by the NS propaganda machinery. (The term *Heimatfilm* was first used in 1933–34 for the film *Die blonde Christel* [Blond Christine], based on Ludwig Ganghofer's novel *Der Geigenmacher von Mittenwald* [The Violin Builder from Mittenwald] [Höfig, 143]. By the beginning of the 1960s the *Heimatfilm* had started to fall out of favor. *Heimatfilme* and their images have, however, a continued impact on German culture that is hard to overestimate.) Heimat — so goes the underlying conviction — is naturally grown, organic, and larger and older than any political, public entity and its powers; and it (she) is beautiful and, therefore, good. Thus, for instance, the popularity of Luis Trenker, Heinz Rühmann, and Hans Albers was not hurt by the political shifts between 1940 and 1960. All three actors have an ambiance of Heimat about them, even if they are by no means exclusively actors in Heimat movies.

Heimat, in its regressive tendencies, is closely related to memory and tradition and, as such, to the notion of what Claude Lévi-Strauss calls "reversible time." A selective memory is at work in shaping representations of Heimat, so that even a reeking sewage canal receives a glossy sheen. Near the beginning of his 1974 Swiss Schiller-Prize acceptance speech, "Die Schweiz als Heimat?" [Switzerland as Heimat?] Max Frisch, after greeting the president and the gathered ladies and gentlemen, described the beloved play places of his childhood: "Here I stand, bowing, a midget, barefoot in stinking sewage water" (365–66). The proximity between his address to the audience and his immediate "Here I stand" allows for much speculation about Frisch's attitude toward Switzerland and about the Schiller-Prize, which he nevertheless accepted. In his speech Frisch goes on to conjure a nonpolitical kind of personalized Heimat, a Heimat with which he could identify. Frisch's Heimat is not uncritical of Switzerland as a political entity. What is unusual about this post-1968 view of Heimat is not so much that it is critical of the political entity sometimes also called Heimat — earlier Heimat conceptualizations had made that point, as well (although usually implicitly rather than explicitly). But this post-1968 Heimat is unusual because it goes on to use Heimat to become politically engaged. First, Frisch tells us what a nonpolitical Heimat consists of for him: the block of houses where he grew up, the homeland, the native landscape, and the local dialect. He does not specifically list childhood as belonging to Heimat. But all the images he conjures up as examples of a sense of Heimat are from his childhood. Then, in contrast, his adult awareness produces discomforting rhetorical questions such as, "Can ideology be Heimat?" Or it states acerbically:

> Heimat seems to be sensitive. She doesn't like it, the Heimat, when one looks too closely at what the people who own most Heimat — in acres or in a safe — do; or who else, if not these people and their revered spokespeople, could have the simple right to deny that we love our Heimat? (367)[2]

This 1974 Heimat challenges the old idea of Heimat (and the old establishment). The new Heimat is no longer innocent. Or is it? We will come back to the notion of a new and critical Heimat after the mid-1960s. Before doing so, however, I would like to look at a few more instances of how Heimat can provide a sense of innocence to those sharing in it.

Horkheimer observes that the individual's adolescence "repeats the ontogenetic passage of society into a rational age" (292). Bourgeois society created childhood[3] in order to get out of the aporia between rational perception and ideology (292). In this type of longing for innocence and childhood, which includes Heimat longings, comments Mecklenburg, "lives the Old Testament myth which surrounded paradise" (1987, 40). We remember that in 1494 Johannes Geiler von Keisersberg wrote, "Death guides you to the Heimat of your fatherland, to eternal salvation" (qtd. in Grimm 864); we recall that Paul Gerhardt wrote in 1666, "My Heimat is up there" (147); and that in Schiller's *Die Räuber*, written in 1779/1780, Karl Moor says, "I will have masses read so that this lost spirit may be sent into his Heimat" (112).

The many attributes that, from the adult point of view, Heimat and childhood have in common include the fact that they can both become instruments of repairing cracks in one's feeling of identity. Both are part of an adult regressive strategy for negotiating the dissolution of what is seen in retrospect as a lost, originary unity. Not surprisingly, Horkheimer also sees the sentimental glorification of the child in its innocence as a means and an expression of the internalization of instinctual drives [*Triebregungen*]. One projects onto the child a freedom from the desires one has trouble renouncing oneself (94).

If we see participation in mass culture and its utopias as a form of self-infantilization, we realize that in the idea of Heimat cure and symptom have become one. Heimat, especially in its more stereotypical manifestations after about 1880, is at once a sign of malaise and the ideal medicine for it, that is, for the sense of emptiness of both the private and the social self, among the petty and the propertied bourgeoisie [*Klein-* and *Besitzbürgertum*] and at times also for the educated middle classes [*Bildungsbürgertum*]. (For the late nineteenth century, when the *Honoratioren* — local notables such as teachers, parsons, doctors, lawyers, *Beamten* [civil servants], engineers, mayors, military officers, professors at universities and *Gymnasien* — were often founding, but always influential, members in the Heimat associations, this inclusion of the educated bourgeoisie is, as Celia Applegate's and Alon Confino's research shows, certainly warranted.) By making much of the Heimat, the bourgeoisie can have its sense of ontological security through a sense of belonging (embeddedness); and it can remain loyal to a sense of innocence in childhood, as well as to an underlying feeling of powerlessness that is, paradoxically, a comfort to it. Martin Jay, in his discussion of Adorno's notion of the bourgeois *intérieur,* calls this feeling "the typical petit-bourgeois sense of impotence" (67–68). In Heimat a naïve state of mind is not only promoted: it is a precondition. Through Heimat the fear and uncertainty of self-definition and the fear of responsibility for one's own decisions and, ultimately, for one's own happiness are laid to rest. Heimat, through a shared tradition that, like childhood, extends back beyond the roots of memory, provides an unquestionable sense of self — and not only of self but also of a morally good self.

"Why did the oppressed classes carry their yoke for so long?" (134) wonders Horkheimer in his 1936 essay "Autorität und Familie." ("Oppressed" here stands, in the early Frankfurt School manner, for the oppressed in the Marxist sense, and never overtly for the Jews.) Horkheimer answers his own question, citing Nietzsche and pointing at religion and the dynamics within religion: a "psychic processing of earthly situations" (134–35) occurs, which in the end accepts a status at the bottom of a hierarchy supposedly predetermined by nature (142).

Heimat constructs fulfill the same function: they dutifully process earthly situations, and the one doing the processing comes to the conclusion that his or her situation is not that bad. After all, is one not assured of being someone (that is, of having a self) and of innocence and goodness as long as one celebrates one's Heimat and only one's Heimat?

Heimat: Growing Up without Growing Up

Voltaire comments in a letter to d'Alembert (September 2, 1768) on the limited target group for the idea of enlightened reason: "But we never intended to enlighten shoemakers and maids; that's a task for apostles" (qtd. in Horkheimer 281). It was the middle classes whom the Enlightenment philosophers most enlightened. During the nineteenth century, while in German-speaking countries bourgeois ideals became more dominant and, at the same time, less clear about their justifications, Heimat moved into the position of religion — or, at least, began to share its berth — in many middle-class families and thus furnished a sense of the divine in the lifeless (and deathless[4]) rooms of their new houses. Through the idea of Heimat a new petty bourgeoisie could grow up and yet not grow up. Where previously the crucifix hung above the kitchen table, now German interiors showed (and still show) comfortable representations of nature that every good person must admire. We know them well: the popular motifs of Alpine landscapes, Black Forest scenes, and cheerfully sunny hometowns nestled into bright green valleys. Such iconography of mass culture is yet another area in which Heimat colludes in offering free innocence to all.

Mass culture, as Leo Löwenthal points out in his much-quoted dictum, is "psychoanalysis in reverse." Löwenthal does not mean to suggest, in Orwellian fashion, that the mass producers and marketers first shrewdly psychoanalyze the masses and then provide them with wish-fulfillments in some displaced and sublimated form. (Even though they have, in fact, by now learned to do so with an astonishing degree of sophistication.) Instead, what interested Löwenthal was the directions into which mass culture gravitated. (Mass culture, for Löwenthal, usually meant the cultures first of Nazi Germany and then of the United States of the 1950s.) He saw that the symbols, figures, and products mass culture soaked up were indirect reflections of subconscious desires, desires not fully, if at all, understood by the masses themselves. To study Heimat is to look searchingly at a persistent element in German mass culture in an attempt to understand what moves Germans — intellectuals and masses alike. But mass culture should not be perceived all negatively.

In a discussion of Benjamin's essay "Das Kunstwerk im Zeitalter seiner technischen Reproduzierbarkeit" [The Work of Art in the Age of Mechanical Reproduction], Russell Berman notes that "in contrast to Adorno, Benjamin draws attention to putatively emancipatory tendencies in mass culture" (20). The crucial term in this Benjamin essay is "aura," the aura that surrounds an authentic work of art. At first sight Benjamin seems to be mourning the disappearance of this "aura" in the age of mechanical reproduction. But Berman, a more thorough reader of Benjamin, notes correctly that "there is an ambivalence in the essay" (20) about the loss of this "aura." The mass-production of images requires that the "work of art becomes less like an idol" (20), and, therefore, we also find potential here for a democratizing of culture. The democratizing of art can, however, become part of an aestheticization of politics that is associated with a different kind of mass adoration, one in which Germany is most deeply implicated.

The relevance of an aestheticization of politics is immediately evident to critical reflection on the idea of Heimat. Not by coincidence, the idea of Heimat is an important element in both German fascism and German mass culture. In Heimat, politics is aestheticized and aesthetics is politicized. But in Heimat the effect is softened by the sense of an inherited tradition whose origins are blurry, or out of sight. ("One doesn't chose one's Heimat; one just has it.") In fact, some people thought during the National Socialist period (and some people still think) that the supposedly apolitical Heimat celebrations were and are a bulwark against fascism. Such overpoliticization from the outside seemed invasive to the local notables who tolerated — and sometimes even welcomed — the new regime. But they wanted their local customs left just as they were.[5] Nevertheless, in Heimat we recognize the counteremancipatory efforts of mass culture at work: We see a small town on a Sunday morning. From the soccer field we hear the oom-pah-pah of the *Musikverein*. There are sunny beer benches, already full of guests who drink their *Frühschoppen* [morning beer]. Today is *Gerümpelturnier*, a soccer tournament for everyone — the seven-year-old, the butcher, the mailman, the grocer, and the fifty-five-year-old elementary-school teacher. And at night the big bass drum beats hard and clear: march and polka and waltz. The tuba plays the quarter notes. And in the end everyone and everything clings together again, all united in harmless fun; everyone feels good about having contributed.

Language as Heimat

Heimat is a word in the German language. Heimat is a well of innocence for its users and, as a word, always hovers at a boundary between the sayable and the unsayable. Heimat, a favored word among German writers, conveys a metaphysical dimension in the everyday: it struggles to bring language to a nonspeaking external world, a geography, a landscape, with which identification needs to be perfect; and it does so through an imagistic and, thus, regressive representation of an ideal life, or at least of a lost ideal stage in life.

Language is, nevertheless, an essential element of a German Heimat. Heimat is, in fact, so intimately connected to its language that when all its property claims are stripped away, one may say — as, for instance, Peter Handke, Christa Wolf, Martin Heidegger, and Heinrich Heine have said — that language is Heimat.

Since the early 1950s the so-called linguistic turn in intellectual thought has begun to place language for some in the ever problematic and, in the end, comfortingly undefinable space that nature had occupied in eighteenth- and nineteenth-century scholarship. Not surprisingly, Heimat for some writers has changed parallel to developments toward a more linguistified self. Heimat, like nature, like language, is accepted as a given. Thus, language, like nature, like Heimat, is looked at as basically innocent. Not everyone expresses this Heimat-language relation as explicitly as Wolfgang Frühwald, who writes in his contribution to Horst Bienek's 1985 collection of essays *Heimat: Neue Erkundungen eines alten Themas* [Heimat: New Inquiries Into an Old Topic] that "language has become — from Thomas Mann to Elias Canetti, Christa Wolf, Horst Bienek, and other contemporary authors — the quintessence of belonging in a world which looks for justice, freedom, and consciousness" (40). Language as Heimat, as innocence, exists through both "Mother Language" ("*Mutter Sprache*" [41]; Frühwald divides the usually compound *Muttersprache* [mother tongue] to emphasize its literal meaning, "Mother Language") — that is, language's motherly qualities — and through language's promiscuous, ownerless, politically innocent qualities. As Thomas Mann notes in his "Ansprache im Goethejahr 1949" [Address During the Goethe Year 1949]: "Who should look out for, and present to others, the unity of Germany if not an independent writer whose true Heimat, as I have already said, is the free German language untouched by occupation forces" (qtd. in Frühwald 40). Rainer Nägele comments similarly in his 1986 essay on temporal spaces of Heimat in Peter Handke: "Writing [*Schrift*] is the only remaining Heimat" (130).

Jean Améry, as well, connects language and Heimat, and, like Frühwald, he does it through the link of the mother. As the mother-language is without grammar, writes Améry, so the world in which we feel Heimat is without grammar: "Mother-language and the world of our Heimat grow with us, grow into us and become in this way a trustedness which guarantees us [*verbürgt uns*] a sense of security" (24).

Born in 1912 and raised in a small town in Vorarlberg by a Jewish mother and a Catholic father, Améry tries desperately in his essay "Wieviel Heimat braucht der Mensch?" [How Much Heimat Does a Human Need?] to come to an understanding of the changes and losses that overtook him with the annexation of Austria when the Nuremberg Laws suddenly turned him from a citizen into a Jew. He tries to grasp his imprisonment and torture in a concentration camp; his changing of his original name, Hans Mayer, to Jean Améry; and his quarter-century of exile. Certainly there is as much wishfulness as resignation in his reflection that future generations would have to make do without the kind of set-tled Heimat from which he had barely escaped with his life.

Améry's most extreme moment of identification with a Heimat set in language that was no longer his, a Heimat that was, in fact, trying to kill him, occurred in Brussels during the war. Heimat had become central to the way his NS pursuers understood the world. Any identification with it on his part meant an extreme case of emotional self-betrayal, his own collaboration against himself. In Brussels in 1943 an SS officer who lived in the same house was disturbed during his afternoon nap by the noise of the printing press that Améry and his friends used to print resistance pamphlets. He suddenly knocked hard on their apartment door and stepped angrily across the threshold. The printing press, fortunately, stood in the next room. But the intruding officer spoke Améry's native Vorarlberg dialect. Améry writes:

> For quite a while I hadn't heard this tone of voice; therefore I sensed in me the mad wish to answer him in his own dialect. I found myself in a paradoxical, almost perverse emotional state of trembling fear and at the same time of exuberant family-like warmth, because this guy . . . whose joyfully gratifying task it was to bring as many of my kind as possible on their way to a death camp, seemed to me suddenly a potential friend. Wouldn't it be enough to address him in my language in order then to drink wine and celebrate a Heimat- and reconciliation *Fest*? As luck would have it, fear and rational control were strong enough to keep me from my absurd plan. I stammered a few exculpatory phrases in French, which obviously calmed him. (25)

Important in Améry is that in Heimat, language, the mother language, usually means for German-speaking people some form of dialect. Dialect is the quickest way — even functioning on the distance-bridging telephone — to create a sense of Heimat or to exclude those who do not speak quite the same way. Frisch's provocative new ideal of Heimat in 1974, "Die Schweiz als Heimat?" makes sure, therefore to assert that language should no longer serve to create insiders and outsiders: "Those who don't speak our language are part of it as well" (367).

Antiheimat as **Heimat**

With the late 1960s and early 1970s a more self-conscious, self-analytical inquiry into one's own personal make-up prepared the way for an intensification of a politically disillusioned celebration of individuality. (The terms for this period in German letters are New Subjectivity, New Inwardness, or, less respectfully, Navel Gazing [*Neue Subjektivität, Neue Innerlichkeit, Nabelschau*].) But those products of the time most often perceived as critical of Heimat — the anti-Heimat films, plays, and literature — proved to be the beginning, as we will see, of a revival of innocence through the idea of Heimat chastened into anti-Heimat for a new era.

As part of this newly critical interest in the idea of Heimat the traditional *Volksstück*, theatrical precursor to the *Heimatfilm*, reappeared, first on the experimental stage, then in mainstream theaters, as well, turning, however, the traditional values of the *Volksstück* upside down. In the *Neue Volksstück* [New People's Play] idyll became anti-idyll. The old comedies of love in the countryside with their village heiresses, loyal and clever farmhands, and inevitable happy endings became, in the plays of Franz Xaver Kroetz, Rainer Werner Fassbinder, Martin Sperr, and Peter Turrini, cruel stories of abuse, adultery, crude sex, and mental limitations of the country folk. Kroetz, who by 1973 was the most-performed living playwright in the German language (Downey xi), made a name for himself through provocatively anti-idyllic representations of rural life. Defecation, masturbation, and the rape of a mentally retarded girl were features of his *Stallerhof* (1972), and the defecation and masturbation were actually portrayed on stage. In Sperr's *Jagdszenen aus Niederbayern* [Hunting Scenes from Lower Bavaria, 1966 (in the 1968 movie by Peter Fleischmann, Sperr plays the protagonist)], a village, in a campaign inflamed by suicide, murder, and other brutalities, hunts down a bisexual man and gets rid of him. In Fassbinder's *Katzelmacher* (which premiered in 1968 and was made into a movie in 1969) a Greek guest worker who has love relationships with local women is brutalized by the village community. His woman employer stands up for him and talks him into staying. Fassbinder adds, however, one of his typical turns, which complicates an otherwise easy ethical message. The Greek, despite the support he has received, nevertheless leaves at the end because his employer, happy with her high profits from one guest worker, hires another one of a nationality — Turkish — with which the Greek refuses to work.

By the late 1970s and early 1980s one could hear observing minds talk about a "Renaissance of the Heimat sentiment" (for instance, Kelter [1978] and Bredow and Foltin [1981] in the titles of their studies; while Solms comments on the phenomenon in 1989 in retrospect [173]). Young Germans sang, in philo-Semitic pride, songs composed by early concentration-camp inmates (probably not Jewish): "We are the peat bog soldiers. . . . One day we'll joyfully sing: Heimat, you're mine again."[6] Peter Handke finished his tetralogy, which appeared under the title *Langsame Heimkehr* [A Slow Return Home], with a long dramatic poem, "Über die Dörfer" [On Villages]. The Left in Germany, as elsewhere in Western intellectual circles — under the influence of Foucault's highlighting of spatial concepts during the 1970s — charged ahead in a "reassertion of space" (Soja 5) and even in a "spatial hermeneutic" (Soja 1).

All in all, the German idea of Heimat received much creative and scholarly attention during the 1970s and 1980s. In fact, the 1980s are the decade when renegotiations of the idea of Heimat became an important way through which Germany was attempting not only to escape from its political history but also to understand itself — until the reunification tremors began. Edgar Reitz's 924-minute television monumentary *Heimat* — conceived in opposition to what Reitz saw as an Americanization of German history in the NBC-TV series *Holocaust* (Reitz called it German history "made in Hollywood") — is such an attempt at self-understanding. It became, as already mentioned, the most watched film in the history of German television.

Twenty-five million Germans (or 54 percent of the total West German viewing public [Geisler 25]) watched part or all of this monumental film about a provincial village and house and family in the stony hills of the *Hunsrück* region west of the Rhine. Reitz's *Heimat* allowed a large number of Germans to find themselves and their anxieties in a changing time mirrored in film. Above all, Maria, the main character, born in 1900, embodies German history in the twentieth century. Her life is a chronicle in which all of German history since the First World War reflects itself: rural youth, awakening enthusiasm, the loss of provincial innocence, the post-Second World War disillusionment, the generous and condescending American influence and Maria's competent insistence on maintaining her own identity, her sons' self-absorption and driven materialism, and, finally, her sad loneliness and death in the early 1980s.

The scandals surrounding U.S. President Ronald Reagan's visit to the Second World War veterans' cemetery in Bitburg and the unearthing of the unsavory wartime record of former UN Secretary General Kurt Waldheim after he was nominated for the Austrian presidency; the *Sonderweg* debates, and the growing perception of the ever-dwindling significance of localities (for example, farmers under pressure from the Common Market began to feel that their production had no perceptible relation to their immediate surroundings, and the threat of NATO Pershing II nuclear-missile installations made Germans see their country less as a collection of sheltering localities than as a possible pawn in a global chess game) — taken together, these events have to be seen as contexts for a renewed interest in Heimat and its unlikely appearance in settings as various as the hundreds of *Heimatmuseen* [Heimat museums] that sprang up in towns and regions, the fast flourishing of the Green Party, the temporary rise of the extremist right Republican party, and, more recently, the surprising popularity of the PDS [Partei des demokratischen Sozialismus — Party for Democratic Socialism], the successor to the Communist Party of the former East Germany that is often referred to by analysts as a "*Regionalpartei*" [regional party].

Michael Geisler writes in 1985 that the term Heimat as a New Regionalism "with its grass-roots alliances and its counterhegemonic orientation" provided in the 1980s a political focus for the hitherto depoliticized notions of the Left's desires "for some form of national identification" (29). He also shows how by the mid-1970s "regionalism had established itself as a political, social and cultural factor to be reckoned with" (39).

During the 1970s, and especially during the 1980s, there occurred in detail yet again what had happened several times before: the most crucial concerns of an era found their reflections in Heimat. Questions of language, gender, identity, experience, and the body became part of recharged, often new conceptualizations of

Heimat. Max Frisch wrote: "Disgrace is part of my Heimat as well. Heimat is not defined by comfort. Whoever says HEIMAT takes on a lot more than that" (373).[7] Anna Wimschneider and Maria Beig described a Heimat that is cruel, does not give options, and hurts — hurts especially women who dare to love. And according to the plays of Kroetz, Heimat produces only cripples, insane people, and sexually depraved monsters. At first these ugly images of Heimat seem the farthest thing from positive expressions, but they are, in fact, exactly that. Frisch makes sure that orderly, neutral, cow-dotted Switzerland gets its full cut of the German cultural torments; Wimschneider and Beig write their own perspective — that of underprivileged rural women — into Heimat; and Kroetz has the satisfaction of representing a Heimat that to his mind was more authentic than any Heimat that had come before. His anti-Heimat Heimat was part of what has been described as an *Erfahrungsästhetik* [aesthetics of experience] new to the 1970s and 1980s, a "philosophy of consciousness with skin and hair (and teeth)" (Sloterdijk 16).[8]

These developments went hand-in-hand with a turn toward more localized concepts of identity. In the 1970s social philosophers such as Anthony Giddens and Nikos Poulantzas began to call for a significant retheoretization of the "spatiality of social life" (Soja 119). Giddens writes that the suppression of space in social theory derives "probably in some part from the anxiety of sociological authors to remove from their works any hint of geographical determinism" (1979, 202). And he observes that the term "ecology" did not help, because it made "spatial characteristics part of 'environment'" (202).

Immediately after 1945 time had been largely privileged, in part because time was (and often still is) associated with rationality and progressiveness, while space was (and often still is) generally associated with propertied interests, hierarchy, regression, and the irrational. Foucault, for instance, observed in an interview with the editors of the Marxist geographers' journal *Hérodote* published in 1976: "Did it start with Bergson, or before? Space was treated as the dead, the fixed, the undialectical, the immobile. Time, on the contrary, was richness, fecundity, life, dialectic" (70). In 1984 Foucault can tell an anecdote that lets us know how much the situation has changed in respect to the concept of space since

1966. He remembers that, at a congress of architects in 1966 a "Sartrean psychologist" had attacked him with the claim: "Space is reactionary and capitalist, but history and becoming are revolutionary" (qtd. in Soja 19). Today, says Foucault in 1984, "everyone would be convulsed with laughter at such a pronouncement, but not then" (qtd. in Soja 19).

Also interesting in this shift of emphasis is which arguments are being employed by each side. The ethical resonances in the terms *reactionary, capitalist,* and *revolutionary* date the first statement from the mid-1960s. But Foucault's invocation of public laughter in 1984 makes an argument by public ridicule. This price — a methodology of laughter — for the rehabilitation of the dimension of space in social theory was a steep one. And this laughter about those who consider space regressive has certainly quieted down since the undemocratic territoriality of geographies became a political liability again in the former Yugoslavia and the former USSR. The breakups and civil strifes of these nations quickly reminded everyone, at least for a few years, that space — if not inherently reactionary and capitalist — is still, even in Europe, a metaphor for collective identity, with all its exclusionary jealousies: a politically potentially deadly tool for rationalizations of power, authority, violence, and murder.

The new negotiations of the idea of Heimat — we can see it in retrospect more clearly — too confidently perceived the reassertion of space as part of a new enlightenment. Hans-Georg Wehling writes in his introduction to the 1983 collection of essays *Heimat heute* [Heimat Today]: "We are attempting here a *Heimatkunde* . . . which wants to open eyes — an 'enlightened *Heimatkunde*'" (9). And the oppositional position of such a newly enlightened Heimat is clear when he writes: "Old Left and old Right meet here [where the word Heimat is used] against the progressive-dynamic movers [*Macher*]" (7).[9]

The promotion of the new idea of Heimat takes place in opposition to what the old Heimat stood for. This Heimat of the New Left, this anti-Heimat, is conscious, oppositional, and democratic, or, at least, has the courage for conflict. Jürgen Liebing asserts in 1982 — maybe claiming a little too much — that "today, not all citizen interest groups [*Bürgerinitiativen*], not all those who protect the environment, nor all anti-nuclear-power movements, nor all squatters use the word Heimat, but they all do take care of their Heimat" (10).

In general, one can see the 1970s and 1980s as decades that turned increasingly toward a rehabilitation, with differences, of what had been, for a time, excluded from serious attention because of its supposed dangerous "irrationality": space, Heimat, experience, paradox, women. A skeptical self-awareness of one's symptoms occurred; recovering from what they now understood as a naïve belief in utopias, people struck an anti-utopian stance (anti-Heimat, antireason, anti-industry) that was uncritically accepted as an answer. Oskar Negt's essay "Wissenschaft in der Kulturkrise und das Problem der Heimat" [Academics in the Cultural Crisis and the Problem of the Heimat] is a telling example of how the Left and the Right could meet in the idea of Heimat during the 1980s. Negt presents Heimat as an "idea for the future" [Zukunftsbegriff] that "has removed from itself all traces of the reactionary irrationalism to which blood and soil are clinging" (191).

But in the anti-Heimat movement of the 1970s and 1980s the new idea of anti-Heimat was like the old idea of Heimat in that it still provided a spatially conceived identity based on mental boundaries and exclusions. But it was the old idea of Heimat gutted of everything the male, bourgeois subject had packed into it until then, all the automatic assumptions about gender, identity, and culture. The anti-Heimat of fiction writers such as Franz Innerhofer, Josef Winkler, Maria Beig, Gerhard Roth, and, with some qualifications, Thomas Bernhard provided identity through suffering and unsweetened depictions of many a painful, marginal life.[10]

By providing a spatially defined constitutive part of one's identity — this time a space where true experience was offered — the purveyors of the anti-Heimat movement fought an old utopian conception of nature and the countryside with a realism that was, however, but a new utopian conception, this one corresponding to a new generation's needs.

Now innocence was associated with the ability to take a hard, even merciless, look at things the way they really were. The corrupt bourgeois qualities of Heimat were purged. But a spatially conceived chance for identity was preserved; and this time it came — typically for the 1980s — in the form of the body, of true experience, and of the willingness to engage in life's cruelties and paradoxes. It was the time of the aesthetics of experience that promoted pain and paradox as signs of authenticity. Habermas summarizes these developments, based on extensive paraphrasing of H. Böhme and G. Böhme's *Das Andere der Vernunft* [The Other of Reason] as follows: "Now it is the unmediated, vital powers of a separated and suppressed subjective nature; . . . it is the aesthetic, body-centered experiences of a decentered subjectivity which functions as a stand-in for the Other of reason" (1985, 357–58).[11]

The paradox functioned as a signal of authenticity because it represented an acceptance of the contradictions confronting us. Embracing the paradox was perceived as a sign for allowing life (experienced life) to determine understanding, rather than explaining away contradictions by forcing them into preconceived higher forms of cognition.[12]

Through authenticity's defining moment — a nonseparation of self and nature — nature regained its ethical qualities: The positive (and innocent) "goodness" that the 1950s still ascribed to the recognition of the beauty of nature became the positive (and innocent) "truth" that the 1980s credited to the recognition of the cruelty of nature.

Through the Heimat movies of the 1950s Germans could have a sense of their own innocence and identity, of the continuity of their own lives, and they could have it without having to question the politics of the recent past. Eric Rentschler in a 1993 essay on Luis Trenker's *Der verlorene Sohn* [The Prodigal Son, 1934] writes about Heimat; and his observations hold true for the 1940s, for the authenticity dominated anti-Heimat of the 1970s and 1980s, and for today. In a short space Rentschler sums up the ways that German culture has preserved, and continues to preserve, a willful innocence through the idea of Heimat: "Heimat is an intoxicant, a medium of transport; it makes people feel giddy and spirits them to pleasant places. To contemplate Heimat means to imagine an uncontaminated space, a realm of innocence and immediacy" (1993, 37).

The element of innocence in Heimat is not secondary but is one of its basic qualities. Heimat's innocence comes from being uncontaminated, from being pleasantly inebriated, perhaps even abstractly sexual (people feel giddy), from feeling vaguely religious but guilt-free (people are spirited to pleasant or authentic places), and from being immersed in, that is, undistanced from, true experience. Heimat, like nature, religion, language, and the mother, is for German-speaking middle-class citizens something larger than oneself, something worth caring for, but also something in the face of which one feels essentially innocent and taken care of.

Notes

[1] For more information on this phenomenon, see Bernd Loppow, "Der Ritt auf der Trendkante" (*Die Zeit* 51 [12 December 1997]: 61) and data from the Internet site of the Wirtschaftsuniversität Wien: <http://www.wu-wien.ac.at/inst/tourism/tourdat/local.html>.

[2] "Sie scheint empfindlich zu sein; sie mag es nicht, die Heimat, wenn man den Leuten, die am meisten Heimat besitzen in Hektaren oder im Tresor, gelegentlich auf die Finger schaut, oder wer sonst, wenn nicht diese Leute und ihre honorierten Wortführer, hätte denn das schlichte Recht, uns die Heimatliebe abzusprechen?"

[3] About the bourgeois creation of the concept of childhood, see Philippe Ariès, *Centuries of Childhood: A Social History of Family Life,* trans. Robert Baldick (New York: Knopf, 1962).

[4] Benjamin writes in his famous essay "Der Erzähler" [The Storyteller] (in *Illuminationen* [Frankfurt am Main: Suhrkamp, 1977], 385–410) that "Today, *Bürger* [= citizens = city-dwellers = the bourgeoisie] are, in rooms that have remained pure of death, dry-dwellers of eternity" (395). ("Heute sind die Bürger in Räumen, welche rein vom Sterben geblieben sind, Trockenwohner der Ewigkeit.") The term *Trockenwohner* [dry-dweller] does not, as far as I know, exist in English. It used to refer to occupants of a newly built apartment house whose walls, mortar, and plaster were still filled with moisture, which was thought to be unhealthy. Occupants who rented (or had to rent, because of the cheaper prices) such an apartment were called *Trockenwohner.*

[5] Cf., for instance, Alfred Lutz's article "Das Rutenfest während des Dritten Reiches (1933–39): Zwischen Beharrung und Anpassung" in *Ravensburg im Dritten Reich,* ed. Peter Eitel (Ravensburg: Oberschwäbische Verlagsanstalt, 1998), 295–303.

[6] "Wir sind die Moorsoldaten. . . . Einmal werden froh wir sagen: / Heimat, du bist wieder mein."

[7] "Zu meiner Heimat [gehört] auch die Schande. Heimat ist nicht durch Behaglichkeit definiert. Wer HEIMAT sagt, nimmt mehr auf sich."

[8] Sloterdijk does not talk specifically about the idea of Heimat (or *Antiheimat*) when he discusses a "Bewußtheitslehre mit Haut und Haaren (und Zähnen)."

[9] It is probably not coincidental that the renewed interest in the concept of Heimat happened — and both Bolten and Enzensberger allude to this — directly after the oil crisis of the early 1970s (especially in 1973), when unemployment figures started to climb steadily (Jürgen Bolten, "Heimat im Aufwind: Anmerkungen zur Sozialgeschichte eines Bedeutungswandels," in *Literatur und Provinz: Das Konzept "Heimat" in der neueren Literatur*, ed. Hans-Georg Pott [Paderborn: Schöningh, 1986], 23–38, here 31). Hans Magnus Enzensberger observes that the negative attitude toward immigrants only started with the appearance of a growing German structural unemployment (Enzensberger, *Die große Wanderung: Dreiunddreißig Markierungen* [Frankfurt am Main: Suhrkamp, 1992], 56).

[10] Cf. Simon Schama's term: the contemporary "anti-landscape" (*Landscape and Memory* [New York: Knopf, 1995], 12).

[11] "Nun also sind es unmittelbar die vitalen Kräfte einer abgespaltenen und unterdrückten subjektiven Natur; . . . sind es die ästhetischen, leibzentrierten Erfahrungen einer dezentrierten Subjektivität, die als Statthalter für das Andere der Vernunft fungieren."

[12] Cf. the contributions — most of them going back to a 1987 symposium — to *Paradoxien, Dissonanzen, Zusammenbrüche: Situationen offener Epistemologie* [Paradoxes, Dissonances, Collapses: Situations of an Open Epistemology], eds. Hans Ulrich Gumbrecht and K. Ludwig Pfeiffer (Frankfurt am Main: Suhrkamp, 1991).

7: Conclusion

ALTHOUGH STILL AS INFREQUENTLY NOTICED by ordinary people as the color of the grass or the sky, the notion of Heimat is as formative an element in German culture today as it ever was. It is an important reference point for questions of identity, history, gender, and nature. The highly spatialized sensitivity on which the idea of Heimat depends expresses itself in a wide variety of forms, as, for example, in *Heimatkunde,* which is still a mandatory subject in many states for third and fourth graders; as in daily references to Heimat in titles and photo captions in almost any German newspaper or political weekly; as in *Heimatsport* pages in regional newspapers, newspapers that, according to a 1997 article in the weekly *Die Zeit,* are generally on a *Heimatkurs* [trajectory toward an increased promotion of Heimat] anyway (Kruse 9). And Heimat is seen, as ever, in the *Heimatromane* for sale at every train station and newsstand and in *Heimatfilm* reruns on television, but also in Jens Sparschuh's *Der Zimmerspringbrunnen* [The Living Room Fountain, 1995], a so-called *deutsch-deutscher Heimat-Roman* that pokes comforting fun at idiosyncrasies shared by Germans in the new and old states. One's pride in one's living room, the adoration of tame nature, the middle class's weakness for buying what is "in": all the ways of the German middle classes come together in this novel in which an unemployed former East German trusts his horoscope, invents a living-room fountain, and strikes it rich despite his own charming self-subversions — a happy ending for a new age in a new parodic strain of Heimat literature.

There is also exquisite parody in Swiss playwright Thomas Hürlimann's unsentimental drama *Das Lied der Heimat* [The Song of Heimat, 1998], which is a fascinating mix of contemporary Swiss farce and literary allusion. The Turk Ali is trying to return home to his apartment building in Switzerland, where his wife, his Swiss "Mutti," awaits him. Accidentally, since all these apartment houses look alike, Ali goes into the wrong one and ends up with Lola, who dances for him in a Swiss miniskirt while her drunken

Swiss lover lies on the sofa and watches voyeuristically. The writer
Gottfried Keller [*Keller* = basement] is alluded to in a scene in
which safes full of Nazi gold in Swiss basements are repeatedly
mentioned; in another scene a Swiss sergeant in a prison camp orders a Polish composer to write a beautiful and elevating *Heimat-
lied:* "You'll drink this tea now and compose the song, otherwise
you'll crawl outside in the snow. Have I made myself clear?" (463)[1]

To German minds, even trains need a Heimat. Two newspaper
articles show that this is true not only of real trains but also of
model ones. The travel section of *Die Zeit* carries an article about
the National Tramway Museum in the English town of Crich under the headline "Neue Heimat für alte Bahnen" [New Heimat for
Old Streetcars] (Glauert). And the daily newspaper *Schwäbische
Zeitung*, a little more tongue in cheek, reports on the town of
Oberteuringen's clearing out of its historical model train from one
of the town's buildings. The vice mayor, Werner Knisel, gives the
assurance that the town "is currently doing everything to give the
friends of the historical model train a new Heimat [for the train]"
("Schultes").

Since German reunification in 1989 and 1990 many shifts and
splinterings have occurred in the uses of Heimat. The range extends from an extremist Right's perception of itself as Heimat loy-
alist (versus those who would allow too many foreigners into the
country) to the Left's continued thinking about Heimat in anti-
Heimat terms. But as left and right became less clearly defined
during the 1980s and 1990s, and as women's and other previously
marginalized voices joined the discussion, Heimat began to be pluralized. Now it was not only one's own Heimat but also that which
an Other, in contradistinction to oneself, might call Heimat.

Elisabeth Bütfering's 1990 article "Frauenheimat Männerwelt:
Die Heimatlosigkeit ist weiblich," discussed earlier, which shows
that Heimat often signifies different things for women than for
men and then suggests ways to research the idea of Heimat with a
heightened sensitivity to questions of gender, is a perfect instance
of how Heimat offered inclusiveness, as well as fragmentation,
during the 1990s. Still, the emphases on identity, space, the feminine, nature, and innocence remain.

More than a sensitivity to gender is needed for new under-
standings of the idea of Heimat. Second- and third-generation

guest workers in Germany have their multiple notions of Heimat, as do younger and older homosexuals and lesbians,[2] as do third- and fourth-generation *Heimatvertriebene* [the German term for those who had to leave the central European lands that after the Second World War were returned from German into Polish, Czech, and Romanian hands], as do Tyrolian farmers, unemployed twenty- and fifty-year-old women and men in Rostock, and unemployed fishermen in Husum. The fragmentation and pluralization of identities and Heimaten goes hand in hand with a self-reflexive sense of dislocation and crisis in temporal, social, and spatial spheres. And, as every modern turn of a century seems to have done, the 1990s were greatly shaped by this painful, yet intellectually profitable, jostling proximity of the regressive and the avant-garde, of the intellectual and the popular, of the exotic and the self.

Still, Heimat during the 1990s and the first decade of the 2000s remains, as ever, an important reference point for questions of identity, history, gender, and nature. For instance, the theme of Barbara Honigmann's *Eine Liebe aus nichts* [A Love Out of Nothing, 1991] is Heimat — or, rather, the negativity of an absent and impossible Heimat (encoded as masculine and fatherly in her case). The narrator of this novel, a young German-Jewish woman who has left East Germany for Paris, finds consolation in reviewing in her memory her inability to be at home anywhere, an inability that she shared with her recently dead father and that allows her to feel close to him. Her statement that "Ellis Island is my Heimat" (57) is mirrored in her memory of her father's last line in an important letter: "Anyway, I was — however you look at it — Heimatless; and I always felt that way" (65).

Jurek Becker, the East German author who moved to the West in 1977, said in an interview in Dublin in 1993 that he considered himself to be "well integrated" in his life in the old (that is, former West German) states. Still, he noted, all his works continued to be set in the GDR, a country that did not even exist any longer. "A case for the psychiatrist," he joked, but continued seriously that all attempts to write a book about the "new, strange [*fremde*] Heimat" made him feel like a liar or like someone who mingles in the affairs of other people, affairs he thinks are none of his business (Wallmann). Becker's use of the term Heimat here is just as ambiguous as it was in his work and life in general. Did he wish to contrast the old familiar Heimat of the GDR with the new and strange one of the Federal Republic? Or did he think that the West in general provided only a strange Heimat? Becker never answered that question. Instead, he made the question one of the focal points of his oeuvre.

In April and May 1993 Edgar Reitz's twenty-six-hour-long (!) *Die zweite Heimat* [The Second Heimat] aired in thirteen segments on the ARD channel. This time the number of viewers was somewhat lower than for the airing of the first *Heimat* in 1984.

Since 1995 over 400 books bearing Heimat in their titles have been published by German firms. The *Verzeichnis lieferbarer Bücher* (the German *Books in Print*) shows a steady increase in the amount of attention that the idea of Heimat is receiving in the book-publishing world: the number of books with Heimat in their titles increased each year, from 37 in 1991 to 92 in 1999, the last year for which complete data is available. Even if we allow for books that have gone out of print, these numbers are evidence of the intense currency of Heimat and the positive signal that the word Heimat in a title is sending.[3]

Since we live in a period in which states and regions in Europe are moving toward a postnational nationalism where national identity is defined less every year by passports and political borders and more by a shared language and a shared sense of history, the idea of Heimat is moving into ever greater prominence. Celebrations of the Tyrolian Heimat, co-organized by Italians and Austrians across the old Austro-Italian border, are but one instance. Germany's boundaries are becoming more open, and at the same time, for better or worse, the question of what it means to be German is becoming less determined by the period between 1933 and 1945. The idea of Heimat — deeply embedded in language, deeply involved in German self-identity and regional self-understanding beyond the political domain — is one of the main elements in contemporary German renegotiations of what it means to be German and to live in a German-speaking environment.

In the summer of 2000 the Berlin daily *Der Tagesspiegel* ran on page 2 an interview with Cem Özdemir, a German-Turkish member of parliament for the Green Party. The page bears the headline "Die Macht der Begriffe" [The Power of Words]; below it runs the subtitle "Heimat, Nation, Identität, Volk, Patriotismus, Bevölkerungspolitik — Wörter, die Rechtsextreme besetzen und Konservative verteidigen wollen" [Heimat, Nation, Identity, Volk, Patriotism, Population Politics — Terms, Which the Right Wants to Occupy and the Conservatives Want to Defend].

And, indeed, the greater part of the page, next to the one-column interview, is devoted to a lexicon of long quotations from reference books on political history and political science dealing with the terms *Heimat, Nation, Identität, Volk,* and *Patriotismus.* These quotations are introduced by an editorial warning that "whoever occupies [*besetzt*] these terms, wins the political power to interpret them."

The interview with Özdemir was part of the debate over the inscription above the entrance to the German Reichstag, which, since the construction of the building outside the old city limits in the late nineteenth century (the Kaiser did not want the building close to his residence), has read *Dem deutschen Volke* [To the German People]. The controversy was — and still is — that *Volk,* like *Heimat* and *Nation,* is a term strongly implicated in Germany's National Socialist past. Now, in the summer of 2000, the Right is trying, so we read, to "occupy" these terms again.

In the interview Özdemir is first asked about *Nation:* whether Germans need a positive sense of a national identity. As far as identity is concerned, he replies, there are certain issues with which one would rather deal on the level of Europe as a whole. And he is outspoken against the Christian Democratic Party's efforts to instill fear into the common people by telling them that a positive sense of Germanness depends on a strong German nation-state and not on an openness toward new Germans, including first- and second-generation immigrants.

The interviewer, Armin Lehmann, then asks Özdemir about Heimat. "The Left," says Lehmann, "is always ready to speak [pejoratively] of *Deutschtümelei* [a folksy sense of Germanness with an undertone of German superiority], when such terms as identity, Heimat, and nation come up. Why is that?" In other words, the interviewer assumes — incorrectly — that the Left (including Özdemir) will always associate the term Heimat with an arrogantly positive sense of Germanness and, implicitly, with animosity toward foreigners, and that Özdemir will, therefore, resist the term.

But Özdemir does not agree. "I don't count myself among those people," he says, and continues:

> I don't do that; and I don't have any problem with it. I find terms such as Heimat not at all negatively occupied. I don't think one should leave the term Heimat to the Right. On the contrary: Heimat is where one grew up, where one knows everything, where one has one's friends. That in itself is not a negative thing — and it shouldn't become one either. It is understandable that in an age of globalization people want to rely on certain traditions and find a sense of security in them. But politics ought not to fuel fears. ("Macht")

In other words, for Özdemir Heimat is a positive and innocent term. It should not be confused with nationalism; it should not be seen as necessarily going hand-in-hand with a German sense of superiority and, therefore, with the negative history of the German Reich.

The deep innocence inherent in the idea of Heimat is also demonstrated in the *Leben* [Living] supplement to *Die Zeit*, in what it considered its last issue of the old millennium. In the six months leading up to this December 29, 1999, issue *Die Zeit* had asked the Allensbach polling institute to inquire how Germans felt about 128 key words from their everyday lives. The survey starts with *Alkohol*, goes on to *Amerika, Arbeit, Auto, Autorität,* and *Berlin*, and ends with *Wissenschaft* [Science], *Zeit* [Time], and *Zukunft* [Future]. Only eight key words received more positive reactions than did *Heimat: nature* was the most positively regarded term, with 98 percent favorable responses, followed by *freedom* (96 percent), *loyalty* (96 percent), *family* (95 percent), *justice* (94 percent), *knowledge* (93 percent), *security* (93 percent), and *property* (92 percent). Tied at 90 percent were *Heimat, wood* [not forest, but the building material], and *responsibility*.

Terms that had only slightly fewer positive responses than *Heimat* were *ich* [I] (89 percent positive), *book* (88 percent), *law and order* (88 percent), *reason* (88 percent), *Germany* (85 percent), *youth* (85 percent), *auto* (83 percent), and *order* (83 percent). Surprisingly far behind were *the past* (43 percent positive), *stock market* (35 percent), *intellectual* (33 percent), *alcohol* (30 percent), *psychoanalysis* (25 percent), and *Russia* (25 percent).[4]

That Heimat should appear in this list of 128 German key words underscores one of the claims of this study: Heimat is a crucial idea with which German speakers negotiate their understanding of the world in which they live. That Heimat is understood so much more positively than, for instance, *politics* (35 percent positive), *the past* (as mentioned, 43 percent), *Christian* (60 percent in the former West Germany, 38 percent in the former East Germany), *prayer* (60 percent in the former West Germany, 29 percent in the former East Germany), *national sentiment* (61 percent), *tradition* (72 percent), *sexuality* (78 percent), *soul* (78 percent), or even *future* (82 percent) reaffirms the special place that the idea of Heimat holds in minds that look at the world with values arising out of a German language tradition ("Entscheiden").

This highly positive and innocent relation to a spatially conceived notion of identity, one that is taken as standing outside of politics and only vaguely related to any past other than the shiningly innocent past of nature and childhood, needs to be better understood both by its users and by those who study German language, culture, history, and literature.

It has been the goal of this study to provide tools for such an understanding. As I have said several times, however, its foci — beginning with modernity, nation, identity, childhood, nature, innocence, and the feminine — should not be taken as an exhaustive list but, rather, looked at as a grid, a pattern of coordinates through which the idea of Heimat can be located and scrutinized in its complexities. Even though these coordinates are not the only possible ones, I would maintain that where Heimat is, they, too, are always there, as a basic configuration with which we must start if we want to come to a complete understanding of the German idea of Heimat.

As I have shown, the idea of Heimat interpenetrates German notions of modernity, identity, the feminine, nature, nation, landscape, ground (as both a physical and an intellectual concept), and innocence (in childhood, in religion, in language). And vice versa. To neglect such interlinkages when working with the idea of Heimat means to let a partial picture stand for the whole.

This study asks us to reflect on that persistent German longing for a mythical space of innocence that Heimat always implies. It points out that the invocation of an idea that is associated with innocence is not the same as innocence. And it shows how the idealization of a home ground in Heimat has led again and again to borders of exclusion. Therefore, it is my hope that this study widens and deepens our understanding of the ubiquitous Heimat idea in its historical uses. Clearly, for instance, the term Heimat was already in place and highly charged when Hitler's propaganda machine made use of it in its blood-and-soil campaign to support territorial claims based in German cultural superiority.

A better understanding of the German idea of Heimat should also provide us with new insights into otherwise puzzling phenomena in German-speaking contexts: consider, for instance, the emphatic German pride in the local. (Expressing this notion more provocatively, one could speak of a German pride in provinciality, a pride that Thomas Mann, as mentioned in the introduction to this book, calls "German world-seclusiveness," "melancholy world-unfitness," and a German "cosmopolitanism in a night-cap" [1963, 49]).

We continue to think about the exclusionary potential that lies behind the seemingly so innocent idea of Heimat, behind those insistently idyllic representations of Alpine scenes and German forests that decorate the walls of many a German household. The innocence that shines out of Heimat is more enduring than the memory of any speech by Adolf Hitler. Nevertheless, Hitler celebrated the *Anschluss* of Austria to Germany in his address at the Vienna *Nordbahnhof* [North Train Station] on April 9, 1938, with the words: "Can anyone wonder, then, that there remained in me that longing to enclose my own Heimat [that is, Austria] into this dearest *Reich*?" (1965, 849). In one of Hitler's early speeches (1920) we already find the stance that would permeate his thinking: "But it is impossible that those who are at home everywhere [that is, mobile populations, but here, especially, Jews and Sinti and Roma] can know what Heimat is, because they do not have one [strong applause]" (1980, 151–52).

Finally, we must take heed of the grounding and spatial metaphors that are so important in German philosophy in general and, in particular, in the German philosophy of the subject. We must consider the proof of private virtue that an appreciation of nature guarantees in German contexts, side by side with the longing for a *Biergarten* and a *gemütliches Beisammensein* that in Germany transcends class, educational, and geographic divisions to a surprising degree.

Not sharing in this sense of Heimat, on the other hand, excludes a person — and I am sure Cem Özdemir understands that quite well — from claims to Germanness, excludes him or her from being able even to participate in discussions about Germany's future. The idea of Heimat may be suspect to some. But those who deny its relevance for their understanding of themselves in the world turn themselves into outsiders when it comes to discussions of Germany and German culture.

The German idea of Heimat continues to be a trope for many purposes. In it we find reflected the despicable, as well as the positive, elements of the last 200 years in German history. And there is no reason to think that this will stop any time soon.

The writer Herta Müller contributes a personal statement, "Heimat oder Der Betrug der Dinge," to the 1997 volume *Kein Land in Sicht: Heimat — weiblich?* (ed. Gisela Ecker). Her final sentences read:

> Since the reunification intellectuals want to redefine the word "Heimat." They talk about making it accessible to young people. They say, young people become skinheads or neo-Nazis because they miss "Heimat." I don't believe that, and I don't participate in revitalizing the word "Heimat." When I feel at home, I don't need "Heimat." And when I don't feel at home, then I don't need "Heimat" either. It happens sometimes that in the morning when I wake up, the wall in my room appears stranger to me than the train station on the day before. That is "Heimat." (219)[5]

The notion that one can stay aloof from the bad old word Heimat by finding new spaces for Heimat is shared by many intellectuals.

For many, the idea of Heimat in the 1990s and the early 2000s has something resigned about it. It is not a Heimat of glamor and ideal. It is a Heimat that we find ourselves unable to let go of entirely, but that we also do not wholly trust. Reflecting on Heimat now is clearly an attempt to make sense of one's own situation in a world in which anyone "could be a stranger in one's own nest" (Frisch 371) one day, and the wise try to live calmly, but attentively, with that fact.

Notes

[1] "Sie trinken jetzt den Tee und komponieren das Lied, oder Sie kriechen da draußen im Schnee, ist das klar?"

[2] Cf., for instance, Jens Weizer's *Vom anderen Ufer: Schwule fordern Heimat in der Kirche* (Düsseldorf: Patmos, 1995).

[3] On 6 December 2000 the *Verzeichnis lieferbarer Bücher* (www.buchhandel.de) listed 819 entries under the *Titelstichwort* [title keyword] Heimat. The numbers for each year since 1991 are: 37 in 1991, 42 in 1992, 44 in 1993, 50 in 1994, 57 in 1995, 65 in 1996, 74 in 1997, 86 in 1998, and 92 in 1999.

[4] *America* and *Asia* were recorded at 68 percent and 50 percent positive responses, respectively.

[5] "Seit der Wiedervereinigung wollen Intellektuelle das Wort 'Heimat' neu besetzen. Sie versprechen sich davon, es jungen Menschen zugänglich zu machen. Die werden Skins oder Neonazis, heißt es, weil sie 'Heimat' vermissen. Ich glaube das nicht und mache an der Neubelebung des Wortes 'Heimat' nicht mit. Wenn ich mich zu Hause fühle, brauche ich keine 'Heimat.' Und wenn ich mich nicht zu Hause fühle, auch nicht. Es kommt vor, daß mir morgens beim Aufwachen die Zimmerwand fremder vorkommt als am Tag davor der Bahnhof.

Das ist 'Heimat.'"

Works Cited

Adorno, Theodor W. *Ästhetische Theorie* (1970). 13th ed. Frankfurt am Main: Suhrkamp, 1993. Translated by Christian Lenhardt as *Aesthetic Theory*. London: Routledge & K. Paul, 1984. Translated by Robert Hullot-Kentor as *Aesthetic Theory*. Minneapolis: U of Minnesota P, 1997.

———. *Negative Dialektik* (1966). 8th ed. Frankfurt am Main: Suhrkamp, 1994. Translated by E. B. Ashton as *Negative Dialectics* (1973). New York: Continuum, 1995.

Alacacioglu, Hasan. *Deutsche Heimat Islam*. Münster: Waxmann, 2000.

Améry, Jean. *Unmeisterliche Wanderjahre*. Stuttgart: Klett, 1971.

———. "Wieviel Heimat braucht der Mensch?" In his *Jenseits von Schuld und Sühne: Bewältigungsversuche eines Überwältigten*. Munich: Deutscher Taschenbuch Verlag, 1988, 59–80.

Amodeo, Immacolata. *Die Heimat heißt Babylon: Zur Literatur ausländischer Autoren in der Bundesrepublik Deutschland*. Opladen: Westdeutscher Verlag, 1996.

Apel, Friedmar. *Deutscher Geist und deutsche Landschaft: Eine Topographie*. Munich: Knaus, 1998.

Applegate, Celia. *A Nation of Provincials: The German Idea of Heimat*. Berkeley: U of California P, 1990.

Ariès, Philippe. *Centuries of Childhood: A Social History of Family Life*. Translated by Robert Baldick. New York: Knopf, 1962.

Bachofen, Johann Jakob. *Das Mutterrecht*. Stuttgart: Krais and Hoffmann, 1861.

Baier, Lothar. "Der Bauer stund im Kopfe auf." *Freibeuter* 6 (1980): 43–49.

Bakhtin, Mikhail. *Formen der Zeit im Roman*. Frankfurt am Main: Suhrkamp, 1989.

Bastian, Andrea. *Der Heimat-Begriff: Eine begriffsgeschichtliche Untersuchung in verschiedenen Funktionsbereichen der deutschen Sprache*. Tübingen: Niemeyer, 1995.

Bausinger, Hermann. "Auf dem Wege zu einem neuen, aktiven Heimat-verständnis: Begriffgeschichte als Problemgeschichte." In *Heimat heute*. Edited by Hermann Bausinger and Hans-Georg Wehling. Stuttgart: Kohlhammer, 1984, 11–27.

———. *Typisch deutsch: Wie deutsch sind die Deutschen?* Munich: Beck, 2000.

Belschner, Wilfried, ed. *Wem gehört die Heimat? Beiträge der politischen Psychologie zu einem umstrittenen Phänomen.* Opladen: Leske+Budrich, 1995.

Benjamin, Walter. *Illuminationen: Ausgewählte Schriften 1.* Frankfurt am Main: Suhrkamp, 1977.

Benz, Ernst. "Schellings schwäbische Geistesahnen." In his *Schellings Philosophie der Freiheit*. Stuttgart: Kohlhammer, 1977, 75–138.

Berlin, Isaiah. *Vico and Herder: Two Studies in the History of Ideas.* New York: Viking Press, 1976.

Berman, Russell. *Cultural Studies of Modern Germany: History, Representation, and Nationhood.* Madison: U of Wisconsin P, 1993.

Bettelheim, Bruno. *Die Geburt des Selbst: The Empty Fortress. Erfolgreiche Therapie autistischer Kinder.* Translated by Edwin Ortmann. Frankfurt am Main: Fischer, 1983.

Blessing, Werner. "Heimat im Horizont der Konfession: Bemerkungen zu ihrer kulturellen und politischen Dimension am Beispiel Frankens." In *Heimat: Konstanten und Wandel im 19./20. Jahrhundert. Vorstellungen und Wirklichkeit.* Edited by Katharina Weigand. Munich: Deutscher Alpenverein, 1997, 179–208.

Blickle, Peter. "Comparing Longings for a Sense of Belonging: German *Heimat*, Czech *Domov*, Russian *Rodina*," in *Germano-Slavica: A Canadian Journal of Germanic and Slavic Comparative and Interdisciplinary Studies* 11 (1999): 39–46.

———. *Maria Beig und die Kunst der scheinbaren Kunstlosigkeit.* Eggingen: Edition Isele, 1997.

Bloch, Ernst. *Gesamtausgabe.* Frankfurt am Main: Suhrkamp, 1965.

———. "Natur als organisierendes Prinzip — Materialismus beim frühen Schelling." In *Materialien zu Schellings philosophischen Anfängen.* Edited by Manfred Frank and Gerhard Kurz. Frankfurt am Main: Suhrkamp, 1975, 292–304.

Boa, Elizabeth, and Rachel Palfreyman. *Heimat: A German Dream. Regional Loyalties and National Identity in German Culture, 1890–1990.* Oxford: Oxford UP, 2000.

Bolten, Jürgen. "Heimat im Aufwind: Anmerkungen zur Sozialgeschichte eines Bedeutungswandels." In *Literatur und Provinz: Das Konzept "Heimat" in der neueren Literatur.* Edited by Hans-Georg Pott. Paderborn: Schöningh, 1986, 23–38.

Borchardt, Rudolf. "Nachwort." In *Der Deutsche in der Landschaft.* Edited by Rudolf Borchardt. Munich: Verlag der Bremer Presse, 1927, 483–501. Rpt. in *Gesammelte Werke in Einzelbänden: Prosa III.* Edited by Marie Luise Borchardt with Ernst Zinn. Stuttgart: Klett, 1960, 23–37.

Bourdieu, Pierre. "Structures, Habitus, Power: Basis for a Theory of Symbolic Power." In his *Outline of a Theory of Practice.* Cambridge: Cambridge UP, 1977, 159–97. Rpt. in *Culture / Power / History: A Reader in Contemporary Social Theory.* Edited by Nicholas B. Dirks, Geoff Eley, and Sherry B. Ortner. Princeton: Princeton UP, 1994, 155–99.

Bredow, Winfried von, and Hans-Friedrich Foltin. *Zwiespältige Zufluchten: Zur Renaissance des Heimatgefühls.* Berlin: Dietz, 1981.

Brockard, Hans, and Hartmut Buchner. Einleitung to Georg Wilhelm Friedrich Hegel, *Jenaer Kritische Schriften (I).* Hamburg: Felix Meiner, 1979, vii-xx.

Burckhardt-Seebass, Christine. "'Schützenswert': Anmerkungen zur Frühzeit des Schweizer Heimatschutzes." In *Heimat: Konstanten und Wandel im 19./20. Jahrhundert. Vorstellungen und Wirklichkeit.* Edited by Katharina Weigand. Munich: Deutscher Alpenverein, 1997, 307–18.

Bütfering, Elisabeth. "Frauenheimat Männerwelt: Die Heimatlosigkeit ist weiblich." In *Heimat,* vol. 1. Edited by Will Cremer and Ansgar Klein. Bielefeld: Westfalen Verlag, 1990, 416–36.

Camenzind, Elisabeth, and Kathrin Knüsel, eds. *Frauen schaffen sich Heimat in männlicher Welt.* Zurich: Kreuz, 1995.

Cassell, Philip. Introduction to *The Giddens Reader.* Edited by Philip Cassell. Stanford CA: Stanford UP, 1993, 1–37.

Castoriadis, Cornelius. *The Imaginary Institution of Society.* Translated by Kathleen Blamey. Cambridge MA: MIT Press, 1987.

Confino, Alon. *The Nation as a Local Metaphor: Württemberg, Imperial Germany, and National Memory, 1871–1918.* Chapel Hill: U of North Carolina P, 1997.

Cremer, Will, and Ansgar Klein. *Heimat.* Bielefeld: Westfalen Verlag, 1990.

Deleuze, Gilles, and Felix Guattari. *Kafka: Toward a Minor Literature.* Translated by Dana Polan. Minneapolis: U of Minnesota P, 1986.

Dirks, Nicholas B., Geoff Eley, and Sherry B. Ortner. Introduction to *Culture / Power / History: A Reader in Contemporary Social Theory*. Edited by Dirks, Eley, and Ortner. Princeton: Princeton UP, 1994, 3–45.

Dörner, Andreas. "Die Inszenierung politischer Mythen: Ein Beitrag zur Funktion symbolischer Formen in der Politik am Beispiel des Hermannsmythos in Deutschland," in *Politische Vierteljahreszeitschrift* 34 (1993): 199–218.

Downey, Roger. Introduction to Franz Xaver Kroetz, *Through the Leaves and Other Plays*. Translated by Roger Downey. New York: TCG Translations, 1992, vii–xv.

Ecker, Gisela. "'Heimat': Das Elend der unterschlagenen Differenz (Einleitung)." In *Kein Land in Sicht: Heimat — weiblich?* Edited by Gisela Ecker. Munich: Fink, 1997, 7–32.

Eley, Geoff. "Nations, Publics, and Political Cultures: Placing Habermas in the Nineteenth Century." In *Habermas and the Public Sphere*. Edited by Craig Calhoun. Cambridge MA: MIT Press, 1992, 289–339.

Elias, Norbert. *Studien über die Deutschen: Machtkämpfe und Habitusentwicklung im 19. und 20. Jahrhundert*. Frankfurt am Main: Suhrkamp, 1989.

Emonds, Friederike. "Contested Memories: *Heimat* and *Vaterland* in Ilse Langner's *Frau Emma kämpft im Hinterland*," in *Women in German Yearbook* 14. Edited by Sara Friedrichsmeyer and Patricia Herminghouse. Lincoln: U of Nebraska P, 1999, 163–82.

"Entscheiden, Nationalgefühl, Sexualität," in *Die Zeit: Leben* (supplement) 1/2000 (December 29, 1999): 8.

Enzensberger, Hans Magnus. *Die große Wanderung: Dreiunddreißig Markierungen*. Frankfurt am Main: Suhrkamp, 1992.

Erikson, Erik. *Identität und Lebenszyklus: Drei Aufsätze*. Frankfurt am Main: Suhrkamp, 1970.

Flusser, Vilém. "Wohnung beziehen in der Heimatlosigkeit." In his *Von der Freiheit des Migranten: Einsprüche gegen den Nationalismus*. Bensheim: Bollmann, 1994, 15–30.

Foucault, Michel. "Of Other Spaces." Translated by Jay Miskowiec, in *Diacritics* 16 (Spring 1986): 22–27.

———. "Questions on Geography" (1976). Translated by Colin Gordon. In *Power/Knowledge: Selected Interviews and Other Writings 1972–1977*. Edited by Colin Gordon. New York: Pantheon, 1980, 63–77.

Freud, Sigmund. *The Standard Edition of the Complete Psychological Works of Sigmund Freud*, 19 vols. Translated under the general editorship of James Strachey, in collaboration with Anna Freud, assisted by Alix Strachey and Alan Tyson. London: Hogarth Press, 1953.

———. "Das Unheimliche." In his *Gesammelte Werke, chronologisch geordnet*, vol. 12. Ed. Anna Freud et al. London: Imago, 1947, 229–68.

Frisch, Max. "Die Schweiz als Heimat?" In his *Die Schweiz als Heimat?* Frankfurt am Main: Suhrkamp, 1990, 365–73.

Frühwald, Wolfgang. "Deutschland, bleiche Mutter: Die Auseinandersetzung um Wort und Begriff der Heimat Deutschland zwischen dem Nationalsozialismus und der Literatur des Exils." In *Heimat: Neue Erkundungen eines alten Themas*. Edited by Horst Bienek. Munich: Hanser, 1985, 27–41.

Fuchs, Eduard. *Illustrierte Sittengeschichte vom Mittelalter bis zur Gegenwart*, vol. 2: *Die galante Zeit*. Munich: A. Lange, 1909.

Geisler, Michael. "'Heimat' and the German Left: The Anamnesis of a Trauma," in *New German Critique* 36 (Fall 1985): 25–66.

Gellner, Ernest. *Nations and Nationalism*. Ithaca NY: Cornell UP, 1983.

Gerhardt, Paul: *Lieder Paul Gerhardts: Mit Bildern von Rudolf Schäfer*. Hamburg: Schloeßmann, 1907.

Giddens, Anthony. *Central Problems in Social Theory: Action, Structure and Contradiction in Social Analysis*. Berkeley: U of California P, 1979.

———. *The Consequences of Modernity*. Stanford CA: Stanford UP, 1990.

———. *Modernity and Self-Identity: Self and Society in Late Modern Age*. Stanford CA: Stanford UP, 1991.

———. *The Nation-State and Violence*. Berkeley: U of California P, 1985.

Gilman, Sander. *Freud, Race, and Gender*. Princeton: Princeton UP, 1993.

———. *Jewish Self-Hatred: Anti-Semitism and the Hidden Language of the Jews*. Baltimore: Johns Hopkins UP, 1986.

Glauert, Martin. "Neue Heimat für alte Bahnen," in *Die Zeit* 47/1997 (November 14, 1997): 72.

Gloy, Karen. *Das Verständnis der Natur*, 2 vols. Munich: Beck, 1995, 1996.

Goethe, Johann Wolfgang von. *Goethes Briefe und Briefe an Goethe*, vol. 2. Hamburger Ausgabe in 6 Bänden. Edited by Karl Robert Mandelkow. Munich: Beck, 1988.

Gollwitzer, Helmut. "Gesprächsprotokoll." In *Heimat deine Heimat: Ein Lesebuch*. Ed. Jürgen Liebing. Darmstadt: Luchterhand, 1982, 124–27.

Greverus, Ina-Maria. "The 'Heimat' Problem." In *Der Begriff "Heimat" in der deutschen Gegenwartsliteratur = The Concept of "Heimat" in Contemporary German Literature*. Edited by Helfried W. Seliger. Munich: Iudicium, 1987, 9–28.

———. *Der territoriale Mensch: Ein literaturanthropologischer Versuch zum Heimatphänomen*. Frankfurt am Main: Athenäum, 1972.

Grimm, Jacob und Wilhelm. *Deutsches Wörterbuch*. Leipzig: S. Hirzel, 1877.

Gruber, Reinhard P. "Heimat ist, wo das Herz weh tut." In his *Heimwärts, einwärts*. Frankfurt am Main: Athenäum, 1980. Rpt. in *Heimat: Ein Lesebuch*. Edited by Manfred Kluge. Munich: Heyne, 1993, 322–27.

Gumbrecht, Hans Ulrich, and K. Ludwig Pfeiffer, eds. *Paradoxien, Dissonanzen, Zusammenbrüche: Situationen offener Epistemologie*. Frankfurt am Main: Suhrkamp, 1991.

Habermas, Jürgen. *Das Absolute und die Geschichte: Von der Zwiespältigkeit in Schellings Denken*. Bonn: Bouvier, 1954.

———. "Further Reflections on the Public Sphere" (translation of "Vorwort zur Neuauflage 1990"). Translated by Thomas Burger. In *Habermas and the Public Sphere*. Edited by Craig Calhoun. Cambridge MA: MIT Press, 1992, 421–61.

———. *Der philosophische Diskurs der Moderne: Zwölf Vorlesungen*. Frankfurt am Main: Suhrkamp, 1985.

———. "Questions and Counterquestions." In *Habermas and Modernity*. Edited by Richard J. Bernstein. Cambridge MA: MIT Press, 1985, 192–216.

———. "Vorwort zur Neuauflage 1990." In his *Strukturwandel der Öffentlichkeit: Unstersuchungen zu einer Kategorie der bürgerlichen Gesellschaft*. Frankfurt am Main: Suhrkamp, 1990, 11–50.

Hausen, Karin. "Die Polarisierung der 'Geschlechtscharaktere' — eine Spiegelung der Dissoziation von Erwerbs- und Familienleben." In *Sozialgeschichte der Familie in der Neuzeit Europas: Neue Forschungen*. Edited by W. Conze. Stuttgart: Klett, 1976, 367–93.

Hayden-Roy, Priscilla A. *"A Foretaste of Heaven": Friedrich Hölderlin in the Context of Württemberg Pietism*. Amsterdam: Rodopi, 1994.

Hegel, Georg Wilhelm Friedrich. *Werke,* 20 vols. Edited by Eva Moldenhauer and Karl Markus Michel. Frankfurt am Main: Suhrkamp, 1969–71.

Heidegger, Martin. *Gesamtausgabe*. Frankfurt am Main: Klostermann, 1975ff.

———. "Sprache und Heimat." In his *Über Johann Peter Hebel*. Tübingen: Wunderlich, 1964, 99–124.

———. *Vorträge und Aufsätze*. Pfullingen: Neske, 1954.

Heine, Heinrich. *Der Rabbi von Bacherach*. In his *Werke*, vol. 2. Edited by Wolfgang Preisendanz. Frankfurt am Main: Insel, 1968, 613–50.

Herder, Johann Gottfried. *Sämtliche Werke*. Edited by Bernhard Suphan. Hildesheim: Olms, 1967.

Hermand, Jost, and John Steakley, eds. *Heimat, Nation, Fatherland: The German Sense of Belonging*. New York: Peter Lang, 1996.

Herrmann, Hans Peter, Hans-Martin Blitz, and Susanna Moßmann, eds. *Machtphantasie Deutschland: Nationalismus, Männlichkeit und Fremdenhaß im Vaterlandsdiskurs deutscher Schriftsteller des 18. Jahrhunderts*. Frankfurt am Main: Suhrkamp, 1996.

Hewitt, Andrew: "A Feminine Dialectic of Enlightenment?" in *New German Critique* 56 (Spring-Summer 1992): 143–70.

Hitler, Adolf. *Reden 1932 bis 1945*. Edited by Max Domarus. Munich: Dr. Max Domarus Süddeutscher Verlag, 1965.

———. *Sämtliche Aufzeichnungen 1905–1924*. Edited by Eberhard Jäckel with Axel Kuhn. Stuttgart: Deutsche Verlagsanstalt, 1980.

Höfig, Willi. *Der deutsche Heimatfilm 1947–1960*. Stuttgart: Ferdinand Enke, 1973.

Hohendahl, Peter Uwe. *Reappraisals: Shifting Alignments in Postwar Critical Theory*. Ithaca NY: Cornell UP, 1991.

Hölderlin, Friedrich. *Gedichte. Hyperion*. Munich: Goldmann, 1979.

Honigmann, Barbara. *Eine Liebe aus nichts*. Reinbek: Rowohlt Taschenbuch, 1993.

Horkheimer, Max. *Traditionelle und kritische Theorie: Fünf Aufsätze*. Frankfurt am Main: Fischer, 1992.

Horkheimer, Max and Theodor W. Adorno. *Dialektik der Aufklärung: Philosophische Fragmente*. Frankfurt am Main: Fischer, 1988.

Hunt, Lynn. *The Family Romance of the French Revolution*. Berkeley: U of California P, 1992.

Hürlimann, Thomas. *Das Lied der Heimat*. In his *Das Lied der Heimat: Alle Stücke*. Frankfurt am Main: Fischer, 1998, 445–87.

Inwood, Michael. *A Hegel Dictionary*. Oxford: Blackwell, 1992.

Jay, Martin. *The Dialectical Imagination: A History of the Frankfurt School and the Institute of Social Research, 1923–1950.* Boston: Little, Brown, 1973.

Kaes, Anton, *Deutschlandbilder: Die Wiederkehr der Geschichte als Film.* Munich: edition text + kritik, 1987.

——, ed. *Weimarer Republik: Texte und Dokumente zur deutschen Literatur 1918–1933.* Stuttgart: Metzler, 1983.

Kaiser, Gerhard. *Klopstock: Religion und Dichtung.* Gütersloh: Gütersloher Verlagshaus Gerd Mohn, 1963.

Kant, Immanuel. *Kants gesammelte Schriften,* 23 vols. Edited by the Prussian Academy of Sciences and the Berlin Academy of Sciences. Berlin: Reimer, 1900–1955.

——. *Prolegomena to Any Future Metaphysics That Will Be Able to Come Forward as Science.* Translated by Gary Hatfield. Cambridge: Cambridge UP, 1997.

Kaplan, Caren. "Deterritorializations: The Rewriting of Home and Exile in Western Feminist Discourse," in *Cultural Critique* 6 (Spring 1987): 187–98.

——. *Questions of Travel. Postmodern Discourses of Displacement.* Durham NC: Duke UP, 1996.

Kelter, Jochen. "Provinz — Aufmarschbasis gegen die Metropolen? Zur Renaissance von Heimat und Dialekt in der westdeutschen Linken." In *Literatur im alemannischen Raum: Regionalismus und Dialekt.* Edited by Jochen Kelter and Peter Salomon. Freiburg: Dreisam, 1978, 97–102.

Kittler, Friedrich A. "De Nostalgia." In *Literatur und Provinz: Das Konzept 'Heimat' in der neueren Literatur.* Edited by Hans-Georg Pott. Paderborn: Schöningh, 1986, 153–68.

Königsdorf, Helga. "Dichtung und Heimat." In her *1989 oder Ein Moment Schönheit: Eine Collage aus Briefen, Gedichten, Texten.* Berlin: Aufbau, 1990, 15–22.

Krockow, Christian Graf von. *Heimat: Erfahrungen mit einem deutschen Thema.* Stuttgart: Deutsche Verlagsanstalt, 1989.

Kruse, Kuno, Horst Röper, and Dietrich Willier. "Zeitungen auf Heimatkurs: Gegen das Fernsehen setzt die Regionalpresse auf das Dorf als Mittelpunkt der Welt," in *Die Zeit* 29/1997 (July 11, 1997): 9–10.

Kunne, Andrea. *Heimat im Roman: Last oder Lust? Transformationen eines Genres in der österreichischen Nachkriegsliteratur.* Amsterdam: Rodopi, 1991.

Landes, Joan. *Women and the Public Sphere in the Age of the French Revolution.* Ithaca NY: Cornell UP, 1988.

Liebing, Jürgen. *Heimat deine Heimat: Ein Lesebuch.* Darmstadt: Luchterhand, 1982.

Lipp, Wolfgang. "Heimat in der Moderne: Quelle, Kampfplatz und Bühne von Identität." In *Heimat: Konstanten und Wandel im 19./20. Jahrhundert. Vorstellungen und Wirklichkeit.* Edited by Katharina Weigand. Munich: Deutscher Alpenverein, 1997, 51–72.

Loewald, Hans. *Sublimation. Inquiries into Theoretical Psychoanalysis.* New Haven: Yale UP, 1988.

———. "The Waning of the Oedipus Complex." In his *Papers on Psychoanalysis.* New Haven: Yale UP, 1980, 384–404.

Loppow, Bernd. "Der Ritt auf der Trendkante," in *Die Zeit* 51/1997 (December 12, 1997): 61.

Lukács, Georg. *Die Theorie des Romans: Ein geschichtsphilosophischer Versuch über die Formen der großen Epik.* Darmstadt: Hermann Luchterhand, 1971. Translated by Anna Bostock as *Theory of the Novel: A Historico-Philosophical Essay on the Forms of Great Epic Literature.* Cambridge MA: MIT Press, 1971.

Lutz, Alfred. "Das Rutenfest während des Dritten Reiches (1933–39): Zwischen Beharrung und Anpassung," in *Ravensburg im Dritten Reich.* Edited by Peter Eitel. Ravensburg: Oberschwäbische Verlagsanstalt, 1998, 295–303.

"Die Macht der Begriffe — aktuelles Lexikon. Heimat, Nation, Identität, Volk, Patriotismus, Bevölkerungspolitik — Wörter, die Rechtsextreme besetzen und Konservative verteidigen wollen," in *Der Tagesspiegel* (Berlin) no. 17138 (August 11, 2000): 2.

Mahler, Margaret, and Fred Pine. *The Psychological Birth of the Human Infant: Symbiosis and Individuation.* New York: Basic Books, 1975.

Mann, Thomas. "Deutschland und die Deutschen." In his *Gesammelte Werke in zwölf Bänden,* vol. 11. Frankfurt am Main: Fischer, 1960, 1126–48.

———. "Germany and the Germans." In *Thomas Mann's Addresses: Delivered at the Library of Congress 1942–1949.* Washington, DC: Library of Congress, 1963, 45–66.

Marcuse, Herbert. *Eros and Civilization: A Philosophical Inquiry into Freud.* Boston: Beacon Press, 1955.

Masterson, James. *Psychotherapy of the Borderline Adult: A Developmental Approach.* New York: Brunner/Mazel, 1976.

Matt, Beatrice von. "'Wer Heimat sagt, nimmt mehr auf sich': Max Frischs Auseinandersetzung mit der Schweiz." In *Heimat im Wort: Die Problematik eines Begriffs im 19. und 20. Jahrhundert.* Edited by Rüdiger Gröner. Munich: Iudicium, 1992, 140–54.

Mattenklott, Gert. "Heimat, Nation, Universalität." In *Heimat im Wort: Die Problematik eines Begriffs im 19. und 20. Jahrhundert.* Edited by Rüdiger Gröner. Munich: Iudicium, 1992, 36–49.

McCarthy, Thomas. "Reflections on Rationalization in the *Theory of Communicative Action.*" In *Habermas and Modernity.* Edited by Richard J. Bernstein. Cambridge MA: MIT Press, 1985, 176–91.

Mecklenburg, Norbert. *Erzählte Provinz: Regionalismus und Moderne im Roman.* Königstein/Taunus: Athenäum, 1982.

———. *Die grünen Inseln: Zur Kritik des literarischen Heimatkomplexes.* Munich: Iudicium, 1987.

Mendelssohn, Moses. *Phädon oder über die Unsterblichkeit der Seele: In drey Gesprächen.* In his *Gesammelte Schriften: Jubiläumsausgabe,* vol. 3.1. Edited by Fritz Bamberger and Leo Strauss. Berlin: Akademie, 1932, 5–128.

Merleau-Ponty, Maurice. "Der Naturbegriff." In *Materialien zu Schellings philosophischen Anfängen.* Edited by Manfred Frank and Gerhard Kurz. Frankfurt am Main: Suhrkamp, 1975, 280–91.

Müller, Herta. "Heimat oder Der Betrug der Dinge." In *Kein Land in Sicht: Heimat — weiblich?* Edited by Gisela Ecker. Munich: Fink, 1997, 213–19.

Nägele, Rainer. "Simili Modo: Zeiträume der Heimat. Zu Peter Handkes 'Langsame Heimkehr.'" In *Literatur und Provinz: Das Konzept "Heimat" in der neueren Literatur.* Edited by Hans-Georg Pott. Paderborn: Schöningh, 1986, 113–30.

Negt, Oskar. "Wissenschaft in der Kulturkrise und das Problem der Heimat." In *Heimat,* vol. 1. Edited by Will Cremer and Ansgar Klein. Bielefeld: Westfalen Verlag, 1990, 185–95.

Negt, Oskar and Alexander Kluge. *Geschichte und Eigensinn: Geschichtliche Organisation der Arbeitsvermögen, Deutschland als Produktionsöffentlichkeit, Gewalt des Zusammenhangs.* Frankfurt am Main: Zweitausendundeins, 1972.

Der Neue Herder von A bis Z. Freiburg im Breisgau: Herder, 1949.

Nietzsche, Friedrich. *Werke: Kritische Gesamtausgabe,* 30 vols. Edited by Giorgio Colli and Mazzino Montinari. Berlin: De Gruyter, 1967–78.

Nikitsch, Herbert. "Zur Organisation von Heimat: Die Heimatschutzbewegung in Österreich." In *Heimat: Konstanten und Wandel im 19./20. Jahrhundert. Vorstellungen und Wirklichkeit.* Edited by Katharina Weigand. Munich: Deutscher Alpenverein, 1997, 285–306.

Pateman, Carole. "The Fraternal Social Contract." In *Civil Society and the State.* Edited by John Keane. London: Verso, 1988, 101–28.

———. *The Sexual Contract.* Stanford CA: Stanford UP, 1988.

Pelz, Annegret. "Karten als Lesefiguren literarischer Räume," in *German Studies Review* 18 (February, 1995): 115–29.

———. *Reisen durch die eigene Fremde: Reiseliteratur von Frauen als autogeographische Schriften.* Cologne: Böhlau, 1993.

Phillips, Caryl. *The European Tribe.* New York: Farrar, Straus & Giroux, 1987.

Plener, Peter, and Péter Zalán. *"— Als hätte die Erde ein wenig die Lippen geöffnet —": Topoi der Heimat und Identität.* Budapest: Druckerei der Loránd-Eötvös-Universität, 1997.

Pompa, Leon. *Human Nature and Historical Knowledge: Hume, Hegel and Vico.* Cambridge: Cambridge UP, 1990.

Pott, Hans-Georg. "Der 'neue Heimatroman'? Zum Konzept 'Heimat' in der neueren Literatur." In *Literatur und Provinz: Das Konzept "Heimat" in der neueren Literatur.* Edited by Hans-Georg Pott. Paderborn: Schöningh, 1986, 7–22.

Rentschler, Eric. "There's No Place Like Home: Luis Trenker's *The Prodigal Son* (1934)," in *New German Critique* 60 (Fall 1993): 33–56.

Riedl, Joachim, ed. *Heimat: Auf der Suche nach der verlorenen Identität.* Vienna: Brandstätter, 1995.

Rilke, Rainer Maria. "Die Sonette an Orpheus." In his *Sämtliche Werke,* vol. 1. Edited by Ernst Zinn. Frankfurt am Main: Insel, 1955, 727–73.

Ritter, Joachim, and Karlfried Gründer. *Historisches Wörterbuch der Philosophie.* Darmstadt: Wissenschaftliche Buchgesellschaft, 1992.

Rollins, William. *A Greener Vision of Home: Cultural Politics and Environmental Reform in the German Heimatschutz Movement, 1904–1918.* Ann Arbor: U of Michigan P, 1997.

Rousseau, Jean-Jacques. *Aemil, oder Von der Erziehung.* Translated by Johann Jakob Schwabe. Berlin: n.p., 1762.

Santner, Eric. *My Own Private Germany: Daniel Paul Schreber's Secret History of Modernity.* Princeton: Princeton UP, 1996.

Schama, Simon. *Landscape and Memory.* New York: Knopf, 1995.

Schelling, Friedrich Wilhelm Joseph. *Schellings Werke, nach der Original-ausgabe in neuer Anordnung,* 6 vols. Edited by Manfred Schröter. Munich: Beck, 1968–72.

Schiller, Friedrich. *Die Räuber,* in *Schillers Werke: Nationalausgabe,* vol. 3. Edited by Herbert Stubenrauch. Weimar: Hermann Böhlaus Nachfolger, 1953.

———. *Wilhelm Tell.* In *Schillers Werke: Nationalausgabe,* vol. 10. Edited by Siegfried Seidel. Weimar: Hermann Böhlaus Nachfolger, 1980.

Schlegel, Friedrich. "Kritische Fragmente." In *Kritische Friedrich-Schlegel-Ausgabe,* vol. 2. Edited by E. Behler and others. Paderborn: Schöningh, 1967, 147–63.

Schmidt, Thomas E. *Heimat: Leichtigkeit und Last des Herkommens.* Berlin: Aufbau, 1999.

Schmitt, Carl. *Theorie des Partisanen: Zwischenbemerkung zum Begriff des Politischen.* Berlin: Duncker & Humblot, 1963.

Schmitt, Hans A. "From Sovereign States to Prussian Provinces: Hanover and Hesse-Nassau, 1866–1871," in *Journal of Modern History* 57 (March 1985): 24–56.

"Schultes dreht der Bahn den Dampf ab," in *Schwäbische Zeitung* 149/1998 (July 2, 1998): 6 (local, Ravensburg-Weingarten).

Sebald, W. G. *Unheimliche Heimat: Essays zur österreichischen Literatur.* Salzburg: Residenz, 1991.

Seel, Martin. *Eine Ästhetik der Natur.* Frankfurt am Main: Suhrkamp, 1991.

Shumannfang, Barbara Ann. "Envisioning Empire: Jewishness, Blackness and Gender in German Colonial Discourse from Frieda von Bülow to the Nazi Kolonie und Heimat." Diss., Duke U, 1998.

Sloterdijk, Peter. *Kritik der zynischen Vernunft.* Frankfurt am Main: Suhrkamp, 1983.

Soja, Edward W. *Postmodern Geographies: The Reassertion of Space in Critical Social Theory.* London: Verso, 1989.

Solms, Wilhelm. "Zum Wandel der 'Anti-Heimatliteratur.'" In *Wesen und Wandel der Heimatliteratur.* Edited by Karl Konrad Polheim. Bern: Peter Lang, 1989, 173–89.

Spranger, Eduard. *Der Bildungswert der Heimatkunde,* 2nd ed. Stuttgart: Reclam, 1949.

Strzelczyk, Florentine. *Un-heimliche Heimat: Reibungsflächen zwischen Kultur und Nation.* Munich: Iudicium, 1999.

Symington, Neville. *Narcissism: A New Theory*. London: Karnac, 1993.

Torgovnick, Marianna. *Gone Primitive: Savage Intellects, Modern Lives*. Chicago: U of Chicago P, 1990.

Vroon, Ronald. "Cycle and History: The Case of Aleksandr Blok's 'Rodina,'" in *Slavic and East European Journal* 28 (Fall 1984): 340–57.

Waldemar, Charles. "Leben und Werk." In *Jakob Böhme: Der schlesische Mystiker*. Edited by Charles Waldemar. Munich: Goldmann, 1959, 5–34.

Wallmann, Jürgen P. "Neue, fremde Heimat," in *Schwäbische Zeitung* 153/1996 (July 5, 1996): "Kultur": n.p.

Walser, Martin. *Ironie und Selbstbewußtsein: Frankfurter Vorlesungen*. Frankfurt am Main: Suhrkamp, 1981.

Walser, Robert. "An die Heimat," in *Der Samstag* (Basel) May, 1905. Rpt. in *Das Gesamtwerk*, vol. 1. Edited by Jochen Greven. Geneva: Helmut Kossodo, 1972, 233–34.

Weber, Samuel: *The Legend of Freud*. Minneapolis: U of Minnesota P, 1982.

Weber, Shierry M. "Aesthetic Experience and Self-Reflection as Emancipatory Processes: Two Complementary Aspects of Critical Theory." In *On Critical Theory*. Edited by John O'Neill. Lanham MD: UP of America, 1989, 78–103.

Wehling, Hans-Georg. Vorwort to *Heimat heute*. Edited by Hermann Bausinger and Wehling. Stuttgart: Kohlhammer, 1984, 7–9.

Weigel, Sigrid: *Topographien der Geschlechter: Kulturgeschichtliche Studien zur Literatur*. Reinbek bei Hamburg: Rowohlt, 1990.

Weizer, Jens. *Vom anderen Ufer: Schwule fordern Heimat in der Kirche*. Düsseldorf: Patmos, 1995.

Whitebook, Joel. *Perversion and Utopia: A Study in Psychoanalysis and Critical Theory*. Cambridge MA: MIT Press, 1995.

———. "Reason and Happiness: Some Psychoanalytic Themes in Critical Theory." In *Habermas and Modernity*. Edited by Richard J. Bernstein. Cambridge MA: MIT Press, 1985, 140–60.

Winnicott, D. W. "The Location of Cultural Experience" (1967). In his *Playing and Reality*. London: Tavistock, 1971, 95–103.

———. "Transitional Objects and Transitional Phenomena" (1953). In his *Through Paediatrics to Psycho-Analysis*. New York: Basic Books, 1975, 229–42.

Zebhauser, Helmuth, and Hans-Michael Körner. Vorwort to *Heimat: Konstanten und Wandel im 19./20. Jahrhundert. Vorstellungen und Wirklichkeit*. Edited by Katharina Weigand. Munich: Deutscher Alpenverein, 1997, 9–12.

Index